Russia

A concise but extraordinarily rich survey of Russian politics in the twentieth century focusing on the problem of state development in all its aspects – territorial, institutional, economic, cultural and geopolitical. An outstanding synoptic study and theoretically challenging analysis of the challenges facing Russia as it enters the twenty-first century: rich in detail and firmly located in the literature of comparative politics, the book is ideal both for newcomers to the field and for those looking for an orginal interpretation of Russia's evolution.

Professor Richard Sakwa, *The University of Kent at Canterbury*

A thoughtful analysis, and one that offers us a novel interpretation in terms of the 'problem of the Russian state'.

Professor Stephen White, *University of Glasgow*

A very useful analysis of the problems of the contemporary Russian state. In an age when globalisation is the main focus in academe, it is very useful to have a reminder of the continuing significance of the state, along with an assessment of the problems pertaining to the Russian case.

Associate Professor Peter Shearman, *University of Melbourne*

Over the last hundred years, Russia has undergone a succession of failed projects of state construction – from Tsarist modernization to Soviet state socialism to liberal democratic market capitalism. This new book introduces these vastly different projects, and explains their failure in order to illuminate the common problems of balancing social and economic transformation with political stability that Russia's rulers have faced during the twentieth century.

Russia: a state of uncertainty traces Russia's complex historical development in the last century, as well as its recent political troubles and economic misfortunes, and its place in the contemporary international system. Providing up-to-date information on Russian political developments, including the elections of 1999 and 2000, Neil Robinson assesses the chances of success of future projects of political and economic reconstruction. Written in a clear and accessible way, this book will be an invaluable text for students learning about Russia for the first time, as well as anyone interested in the state and history of Russia.

Neil Robinson is Lecturer in Politics at the University of Limerick. His writing includes: *Ideology and the Collapse of the Soviet System*; he is the co-author of *Post-Communist Politics: An introduction* and edited *Institutions and Change in Russian Politics*.

Postcommunist States and Nations

Books in the series

Russia

A state of uncertainty

Neil Robinson

London and New York

First published 2002 by Routledge
11 New Fetter Lane, London EC4P 4EE

Simultaneously published in the USA and Canada
by Routledge
29 West 35th Street, New York, NY 10001

Routledge is an imprint of the Taylor & Francis Group

© 2002 Neil Robinson

Typeset in Baskerville by Keyword Publishing Services Ltd
Printed and bound in Great Britain by MPG Books Ltd, Bodmin

British Library Cataloguing in Publication Data
A catalogue record for this book is available from the British Library

Library of Congress Cataloging in Publication Data
Robinson, Neil, 1964–
    Russia: a state of uncertainty/Neil Robinson.
        p.cm—(Postcommunist states and nations)
    Includes bibliographical references and index.
    1. Soviet Union—Politics and governing 2. Russia (Federation)—
    Politics and government—1991–3. Russia (Federation)—Economic
    conditions—1991– I. Title II. Series.
    DK266.R57 2002
    947–dc21

                                                    2001041989

ISBN 0-415-27113-4 (pbk)
ISBN 0-415-27112-6

For Maura

Contents

Tables

Chronology
Russia's twentieth century

1903	July:	Russian Social Democratic Labour Party splits and the Bolshevik faction under Lenin's leadership is created
1904	January:	Russo-Japanese war begins
1905	January:	Bloody Sunday massacre sparks revolution
	October:	General strike; Tsar issues October manifesto promising moderate political reform
	December:	Armed suppression of revolution in Moscow
1906	April:	First Duma opens
	July:	First Duma dissolved
	November:	Stolypin decree on agricultural reform issued
1907	February–June:	Second Duma convened
	November:	Third Duma convened
1911	September:	Stolypin assassinated
1914	August:	World War I begins
1915	September:	Nicholas II dissolves the Duma and takes over personal responsibility for Russia's war effort
1916	December:	Murder of Rasputin
1917	February:	Riots and rebellion in Petrograd; Soviets formed
	March:	Nicholas II abdicates; power is transferred to the Provisional Government; period of 'dual power' begins
	April:	Lenin returns to Russia and calls for the radicalization of the revolution
	May:	Provisional Government becomes a coalition of moderate socialists and conservatives
	July:	A failed Russian offensive against the Germans leads to the rebellion in Petrograd; Kerensky replaces Prince Lvov as Prime Minister; Bolsheviks are suppressed and Lenin goes into hiding
	September:	Kornilov uprising and fear of counter-revolution leads to the unbanning of the Bolsheviks;

		Bolsheviks win majorities in Moscow and Petrograd Soviets
	October:	(November by new calendar) Bolshevik uprising in Petrograd, declaration of Soviet power
	November:	Elections to Constituent Assembly
	December:	Negotiations begin between the Bolsheviks and Germany on armistice; Cheka (secret police) established; Civil war begins in earnest
1918	January:	Constituent Assembly dissolved by Bolsheviks; creation of Red Army
	March:	Treaty of Brest-Litovsk ends war with Germany; British troops land at Murmansk as part of a loose anti-Soviet coalition, to be followed by the French, the Japanese, and the Americans
	June:	Industry nationalized
	July:	Tsar and royal family murdered in Ekaterinburg; Social Revolutionaries try to overthrow Bolsheviks
	September:	Declaration of Red Terror
	November:	End of World War I
1919	January:	Comintern founded to promote international revolution
	March:	Kolchak offensive against Bolsheviks; creation of Politburo
	June:	Denikin offensive against Bolsheviks
	October:	White forces threaten Petrograd and Orel
1920	April:	Poland invades
	August:	Red Army defeated at Warsaw; peasant rebellion breaks out against Bolsheviks in Tambov
	November:	Red Army defeats Whites in the South to end the main campaigns of the Civil War
1921	March:	Revolt against Bolsheviks at Kronstadt; 10th Party Congress adopts New Economic Policy (NEP) and bans factional activity in the party
	Summer:	Famine begins
1922	April:	Stalin becomes General Secretary of the Communist Party
	May:	Lenin has a stroke
	December:	Declaration of the formation of the Union of Soviet Socialist Republics
1923	March:	Lenin incapacitated by another stroke; Trotsky fails to press Lenin's criticisms of Stalin at 12th Party Congress
	July:	First Soviet Constitution published

	Summer:	Economic crisis
1924	January:	Lenin dies; Petrograd renamed Leningrad
	November:	Trotsky publicly attacks Stalin's allies, Zinoviev and Kamenev
1925	January:	Trotsky dismissed from post as Commissar for War
	April:	14th Party Congress accepts Stalin's idea of building 'socialism in one country'
1926	October:	Trotsky dismissed from Politburo
1927	Autumn:	Start of grain procurement crisis as collection of grain from the peasantry falls
	December:	15th Party Congress resolves to collectivise agriculture
1928	January:	Stalin urges forced collection of grain from peasantry
	May:	Show trial of bourgeois specialists accused of Anti-Soviet activities
	August:	Announcement of first five-year plan for industrialization, initial growth targets are modest
	October:	Start of attacks on Bukharin and 'Right Opposition'; first five-year plan begins
1929	April:	Industrialization targets are raised dramatically
	July:	Compulsory grain delivery targets issued as a Prelude to collectivization
	Autumn:	Collectivization and dekulakization begin
	November:	Bukharin expelled from Politburo
1930	March:	Collectivization temporarily halted by Stalin
	November:	Second show trial of bourgeois specialists accused of anti-Soviet activities
1932		Famine begins and lasts until 1934
	December:	Introduction of internal passports and residency registration to control movement of population; completion of first five-year plan declared
1933		Nazis come to power in Germany
1934	January:	17th Party Congress, the 'Congress of Victors', declares that main battles in socialist construction have been won
	December:	Kirov assassinated in Leningrad
1935	January:	Zinoviev and Kamenev tried for complicity in Kirov assassination and sentenced to prison terms
	August:	Introduction of Stakhanovite movement to try to increase labour productivity

1936		Stalin sends aid to Republican forces in Spanish Civil War
	August:	Second trial of Zinoviev and Kamenev for Kirov murder; Trotsky, Bukharin and others are also implicated; Zinoviev and Kamenev are condemned to death
	September:	Yezhov becomes head of NKVD; purges pick up pace
	December:	'Stalin' Constitution introduced
1937	January:	Trial of Radek, Pyatakov and other former party leaders
	May–June:	Arrest and execution of Marshal Tukhachevsky and leaders of armed forces; purges reach their height
		Soviet–Japanese forces clash on Soviet–Chinese border
1938	March:	Trial of Bukharin and other leaders
	November:	Beria replaces Yezhov as head of NKVD
	December:	Introduction of 'labour books' to control industrial workers and their movements
1939	August:	Nazi-Soviet non-aggression pact
	September:	Germany invades Poland from the West, USSR invades Poland from the East; World War II begins
	December:	Soviet–Finnish war begins
1940	June:	USSR annexes Baltic states, Bessarabia and Bukovina
	August:	Criminalization of absenteeism from work; Trotsky murdered in Mexico
	November:	Relations with Germany begin to deteriorate
1941	June:	Germany invades USSR
	July:	Anglo-Soviet alliance against Germany and Italy proclaimed
	September:	Siege of Leningrad begins
	December:	German advance on Moscow halted
1942	January:	Soviet, British, American 'Grand Alliance' formed
	September:	Siege of Stalingrad begins
	November:	Soviet offensive encircles German army at Stalingrad
1943	January:	German army at Stalingrad surrenders
	July:	Soviet forces prevail at battle of Kursk; German retreat slowly begins
1944	January:	Siege of Leningrad ends

	June:	Allied invasion of France; Soviet forces begin to move into Eastern Europe
1945	February:	Yalta conference between Churchill, Stalin and Roosevelt
	May:	Germany surrenders
	December:	Potsdam conference begins and the wartime alliance begins to fragment
1946		Famine in Ukraine; 1946–1948 establishment of communist regimes in Eastern Europe under Soviet tutelage
1948	January:	Purge of Jewish intelligentsia begins
	June:	Break with Yugoslavia; USSR blockades Berlin as Cold War takes shape
	August:	Death of Leningrad party leader, Zhdanov, followed by purge of the Leningrad party
1949	September:	Soviet atom bomb tested
	December:	Communists take power in China
1950	January:	Sino-Soviet alliance
	June:	Start of Korean war
1953	January:	'Doctors' Plot' announced, a new wave of purges looms
	March:	Stalin dies; Malenkov becomes Prime Minister
	June:	Beria arrested
	July:	Armistice in Korean war; release of some Gulag prisoners
	September:	Khrushchev becomes General Secretary of the CPSU
1954		Khrushchev begins 'Virgin Lands' campaign
1955	February:	Bulganin replaces Malenkov as Prime Minister
	May:	Warsaw Pact established
1956	February:	Khrushchev makes 'Secret Speech' to the 20th CPSU Congress; destalinization begins
	November:	Soviet invasion of Hungary
1957	February:	Khrushchev announces formation of regional economic councils (*Sovnarkhozy*)
	June:	CPSU Central Committee supports Khrushchev against the 'Anti-Party Group'
	October:	Launch of *Sputnik*, the world's first space satellite
1958	February:	Khrushchev replaces Bulganin as Prime Minister Start of split with China
1959	September:	Khrushchev visits the USA
1960	May:	USSR shoots down US spy plane over its territory
1961	April:	Launch of first manned space flight

	June:	Crisis in Berlin leads to building of the Berlin Wall
	November:	22nd CPSU Congress introduces a new party programme and advances destalinization; Stalin's body is removed from the Lenin Mausoleum on Red Square
1962	June:	Riots in Novocherkassk over food price rises are violently suppressed
	October:	Cuban missile crisis
	November:	Khrushchev announces the bifurcation of the CPSU; Solzhenitsyn's *One Day in the Life of Ivan Denisovich* is published
1964	November:	Khrushchev removed from office; Leonid Brezhnev becomes General Secretary of the CPSU; reversal of many of Khrushchev's reforms begins and destalinization is halted
1965	September:	Kosygin economic reforms begins
	December:	Pushkin Square demonstration in Moscow calling for the observation of the Soviet Constitution marks the beginning of the dissident movement
1966	February:	Trial of Sinyavsky and Daniel begins as a warning to dissidents to curtail their activities
1967	May:	Yuri Andropov becomes head of the KGB
1968	January:	Dubček becomes head of the Czechoslovak communist party and the reforms of the 'Prague Spring' begin
	August:	Warsaw Pact countries invade Czechoslovakia; dissident movement in USSR grows
	September:	Promulgation of the 'Brezhnev Doctrine'
1970	October:	Solzhenitsyn wins Nobel Prize for Literature
1971	February:	Khrushchev dies
1972	May:	Brezhnev–Nixon summit in Moscow marks height of period of *détente*
1973	October:	Arab–Israeli war leads to confrontation with USA
1974	February:	Forced deportation of Solzhenitsyn from the USSR
	December:	Brezhnev has heart attack and begins slow physical and mental decline
1975	October:	Dissident physicist Andrei Sakharov wins Nobel Peace Prize
1977	June:	Brezhnev becomes President of the USSR
	November:	Introduction of a new Soviet Constitution

1978	November:	Gorbachev appointed Central Committee Secretary in charge of agriculture
1979	November:	Gorbachev becomes candidate member of the Politburo
	December:	USSR invades Afghanistan; second Cold War begins in earnest
1980	Summer:	US and other countries boycott of Moscow Olympics
	August:	Strikes begin in Poland leading to creation of the Solidarity trade union
	October:	Gorbachev becomes full member of the Politburo
1981	December:	martial law introduced in Poland
1982	November:	Leonid Brezhnev dies after 18 years as leader of the USSR. Yuri Andropov succeeds as General Secretary; Andropov launches anti-corruption campaign, tries to increase labour discipline and begins to assemble what will eventually be reform team under Gorbachev
1984	February:	Andropov dies. Konstantin Chernenko succeeds him. Chernenko temporarily stops reform
1985	March:	Chernenko dies. Gorbachev succeeds as General Secretary
	May:	Anti-alcohol campaign begins; Gorbachev calls for economic reform
	November:	First meeting between Gorbachev and Ronald Reagan in Geneva
1986	February–March:	27th CPSU Congress. Gorbachev begins to broaden and deepen reform and criticizes Brezhnev era as the 'period of stagnation'
	April:	disaster at Chernobyl increases financial crisis of Soviet state but allows Gorbachev to extend *glasnost'*
	October:	Reagan–Gorbachev summit in Reykjavik
	December:	Sakharov released from internal exile; riots in the capital of Kazakhstan are the first sign of nationalist unrest
1987	January and June:	Major CPSU Central Committee plenums; Gorbachev begins internal party reform and democratization, and presses for economic decentralization
	June:	Experiment with multi-candidate elections in 5 per cent of constituencies at local elections
	July:	Major law on industrial organization passed allowing limited autonomy for economic

		enterprises from central bureaucracy and planners
	August:	Rallies in Baltic republics against their forced inclusion in the USSR in 1940
	October:	Boris Yeltsin criticizes slow pace of reform at Central Committee meeting; Yeltsin is removed as head of Moscow City CPSU in November and begins drift into opposition
	November:	70th anniversary of October 1917 revolution; Gorbachev talks of different paths to socialism in different countries – a sign of weakening control over Eastern Europe
1988	June:	19th CPSU Conference; Gorbachev launches reform of state structures. Promises new parliaments and multi-candidate elections
	August:	Independent political activity grows throughout USSR in response to 19th CPSU Conference
	October:	Gorbachev becomes Chair of the Supreme Soviet
	December:	Constitutional amendments passed establishing Congress of Peoples Deputies and new electoral system
1989	March:	elections to Congress of People's Deputies
	April:	Army kills peaceful demonstrators in Tblisi, capital of Georgia
	May–June:	First Congress of People's Deputies sessions; election of Supreme Soviet; Gorbachev elected Chair of the Supreme Soviet
	July:	first outbreak of labour unrest in mining regions
	September:	CPSU Central Committee plenum on nationalities policy
	Autumn:	Collapse of communist regimes in Eastern Europe
	December:	Lithuanian Communist Party declares itself independent of the CPSU
1990	January:	CPSU begins to break up as radicals inside the CPSU set up the 'Democratic Platform'
	February:	CPSU Central Committee agrees to abolish Article Six of the Soviet constitution that gave the party the legal right to power and supports move towards a presidential system; Supreme Soviet passes bill on presidency at the end of the month
	March:	Local and republican elections; Russian radical movement 'Democratic Russia' wins large

		number of seats in Russian Congress of People's Deputies and takes over city government in Moscow and Leningrad; nationalists win in most of the republics; USSR Congress of People's Deputies elects Gorbachev President and changes the constitution to remove Article Six; Lithuania declares independence; Estonia suspends the Soviet Constitution
	May:	Latvia declares independence; Yeltsin elected head of Russian parliament by 'Democratic Russia' deputies; 'War of laws' begins between the republics and the central government over who controls what
	July:	28th CPSU Congress; Yeltsin and other radicals quit the CPSU; the Congress supports Gorbachev, but comes up with no new ideas about how to get out of crisis
	August–October:	Gorbachev attempts to find economic reform strategy; makes a brief alliance with Yeltsin to support the radical '500 Days' plan for economic reform, but caves in under conservative pressure and begins his 'drift to the right'
	September:	Gorbachev granted additional presidential powers by USSR Congress of People's Deputies
	December:	Shevardnadze resigns as Minister of Foreign Affairs and warns of the prospect of a right wing coup; Gorbachev forces the election of Gennady Yanayev as vice president and proposes referendum on the future of the Union; Yeltsin later adds a question on the establishment of a Russian presidency to the referendum.
1991	January:	Military intervention in Lithuania and Latvia as hardliners attempt to assert central control; Yeltsin pledges solidarity with the Baltic states
	February:	Majority vote for Union in ambiguously worded referendum; Russians vote for the establishment of a Russian presidency
	April:	'9 + 1' agreement signed by Gorbachev and the leaders of nine of the republics; agree a new Union treaty to be signed in August that will substantially revise the balance of power in favour of republics
	June:	Conservatives attempt a constitutional coup by asking for more powers for the Prime Minister

August:	Hardliners led by Yanayev launch coup attempt on the eve of the signing of the new Union Treaty; coup fails after three days
September–November:	Yeltsin accumulates power to begin economic Reform; is granted additional powers for a year by the Russian parliament and appoints his own government, making himself Prime Minister and Yegor Gaidar Minister of Finance; negotiations for a new Union treaty fail; Chair of Russian parliament and Russian vice president begin to oppose government economic policies; coup in Chechnya, Dzhokar Dudayev becomes leader
October:	Dudayev elected President of Chechnya and Chechen declaration of independence
November:	Yeltsin declares state of emergency in Chechnya, but attempted Russian intervention fails; state of emergency is revoked and troops withdraw
December:	Ukraine votes for independence in referendum and all hope of new Union treaty dies; Belarus and Russia persuade Ukraine to join in Commonwealth of Independent States; Central Asian states, Azerbaijan and Armenia join a week later; Gorbachev resigns as President on 25 December; USSR officially ceases to exist on 31 December
1992 January:	Prices liberalized in Russia in attempt to control inflation, create basis of market economy and break up the power of industrial managers
March:	Federation treaty signed by all of Russia's republics except Tatarstan and Chechnya
April:	Russian Parliament backs government economic policy but with reservations and Yeltsin is forced to compromise on the composition of the government; Russia receives a $24billion aid package from the West
June:	Privatization legislation passed; Yeltsin appoints Gaidar acting Prime Minister
October:	voucher privatization begins
December:	Russian parliaments oppose government. Gaidar removed as Prime Minister by Viktor Chernomyrdin; Yeltsin does deal with the parliaments and gets the promise of a referendum on the constitution
1993 March:	Parliament reneges on deal on referendum and attempts to strip Yeltsin of his powers; Yeltsin

		decrees emergency rule and referendum; parliament responds by trying to impeach him, but fails; eventually a deal is done on the referendum
	April:	Referendum on economic reform, prospect of new elections for the presidency and the parliaments and confidence in Yeltsin; Yeltsin wins on all questions.
	June:	Yeltsin calls Constitutional Conference to try to get an agreement on a presidential system from major political actors. Fails
	September:	Yeltsin brings Gaidar back into the government and then suspends the parliaments and decrees emergency rule; parliament meets in emergency session and makes Rutskoi president
	October:	Pro-parliament demonstrators clash with riot police; Yeltsin calls in the army to restore order; over 100 people killed (at least); elections for new parliaments and a referendum on the constitution called for December
	November:	Campaigning begins. Some parties fail to get sufficient signatures to stand for PR seats; state controlled television throws weight behind Gaidar and the Russia's Choice party
	December:	Victory for Yeltsin on new constitution gives him extra powers as President, but Russia's Choice does poorly at the polls; surprise success for Zhirinovsky's extremist Liberal Democratic Party
1994	January:	Economic reformers quit the government in response to the December 1993 Duma elections.
	February:	Treaty signed between federal government and Tatarstan; Duma pardons the 1991 coup leaders and the parliamentary leaders imprisoned in 1993
	October:	Rouble crisis
	November:	Russian Security Council votes to send troops to Chechnya
	December:	Russian troops invade Chechnya and advance on the capital, Grozny
1995	January:	Grozny is brought under Russian control; many Russian troops and civilians are killed in the fighting
	May:	Yeltsin vetoes law passed by both the Duma and the Council of Federation calling for

		unconditional talks with the Chechens; Our Home is Russia party set up by Chernomyrdin
	June:	General Alexander Lebed resigns as commander of 14th Army in Moldova to go into Russian politics; Chechens take hostages at Budennovsk and provoke a government crisis
	July:	Yeltsin hospitalized with heart complaint
	October:	Yeltsin hospitalized for second time
	December:	Duma elections; CPRF heads the party list voting
1996	January:	Kozyrev resigns as foreign minister and is replaced by Primakov; Russia admitted to Council of Europe
	March:	Duma vote condemns the agreements that founded the CIS; Yeltsin unveils peace plans as a part of his electoral campaign
	April:	Treaty with Belarus establishing Community of Sovereign States
	May:	Korzhakov calls for the election to be postponed; bulk of democratic forces declare their support for Yeltsin
	June:	First round of voting in the presidential elections sees Yeltsin and CPRF leader Zyuganov through to a second round run-off; Yeltsin makes Alexander Lebed (third in the voting) Secretary of the Security Council; Defence Minister Grachev is removed from office; Korzhakov and other hardliners in the government are removed for plotting to upset the second round of voting
	July:	Yeltsin disappears from public view on eve of second round of the presidential elections; rumours circulate about his ill-health, but he beats Zyuganov convincingly in the second round of voting; Chechens protest that the terms of the peace deal are being broken by Russia; Lebed charged with securing peace in Chechnya by Yeltsin; fighting restarts in Chechnya; Chubais appointed head of the presidential administration
	August:	Yeltsin hospitalized; power struggle between Lebed and other members of government develops; Lebed brokers a peace deal in Chechnya that promises troop withdrawals and autonomy for the area

	October:	Yeltsin fires Lebed from post as Secretary of the Security Council
	November:	Yeltsin has quintuple heart bypass operation
	December:	Russian troops begin to withdraw from Chechnya
1997	February:	Government reshuffle introduces new wave of economic reform headed by Chubais and Boris Nemtsov
	Summer:	'Bank wars' begin over privatization
	November:	Yeltsin removes Boris Berezovsky from the Security Council; Chubais is accused of corruption by media owned by Berezovsky; Chubais just holds on to office
1998	January:	Chernomyrdin's powers as Prime Minister are expanded
	March:	Yeltsin fires Chernomyrdin and reorganizes cabinet; battle starts with Duma on approval of Sergei Kiriyenko as Prime Minister
	April:	Kiriyenko approved as Prime Minister on third Duma vote
	August:	Rouble devalued, Russia defaults on debts and entire government is sacked by Yeltsin; Chernomyrdin appointed as interim Prime Minister
	September:	Duma refuses to approve Chernomyrdin's appointment as Prime Minister twice and Yeltsin nominates Primakov for the post
1999	May:	Yeltsin fires the entire government; impeachment proceedings begin in the Duma but vote fails; Duma approves Sergei Stepashin as Prime Minister
	Summer:	Chechen incursions into neighbouring territories and bombings in Moscow and other towns lead to calls for a new invasion of Chechnya; support for Primakov as Yeltsin's successor grows
	August:	Yeltsin fires Stepashin; Duma approves nomination of Vladimir Putin as Prime Minister; military action begins in Chechnya
	December:	Duma elections; CPRF tops the poll, but Putin's favoured party, Unity, features strongly in the voting; Yeltsin resigns on New Year's Eve and Putin becomes acting President
2000	March:	Putin elected President in first round of elections; attacks on 'oligarchs' begin

May: Putin begins to attack media and commercial interests of the 'oligarchs'; seven new Federal districts created as part of reform of federal system and centre-regional relations

August: The submarine *Kursk* sinks whilst on exercises

Preface and acknowledgements

The title of this book is not accidental: this is a book about the Russian state and its uncertain future. Consequently, it is also a book about the uncertainty of life in Russia – and *with* Russia for those of us who do not live there – created by the Russian state's instability. The Russian state, its dysfunctions, and the efforts that have been made to resolve them over the course of the twentieth century, are the book's main object of enquiry. Russia has been plagued throughout its recent history by the inability of its political leaders to create a strong state. The dimensions of this failure are multiple: Russia is, and has been, uncertain about its geographical boundaries as a state, first because of its existence within empire, and subsequently because of the collapse of empire. Russian politicians are, and have been, uncertain about what the institutions that they inhabit, control and contest are capable of, of the purpose of state power and its use. At many points in Russia's recent history there has even been a great deal of uncertainty about what constitutes the Russian state. Under the Tsars, the private concerns and fate of one family, the imperial dynasty of the Romanovs, overlapped with the state and the struggle of parts of it to become more representative of Russian society and to modernize it. It almost makes no sense to talk of the 'state' as an autonomous set of institutions during the Soviet period since state structures were permeated and controlled at all levels by the Communist Party of the Soviet Union (CPSU). As a result, where authority and responsibility lay became confused and personal relationships substituted for clear lines of authority and effective governance. This situation has not notably improved since the collapse of the Soviet 'party-state'. Russia's weak state is a barrier to the consolidation of democracy and the stabilization of the Russian economy (let alone the procurement of economic growth), and makes Russia a fickle and variable partner in the reconstruction of post-Cold War international relations.

We need to remember, however, that Russia's 'state of uncertainty' is more than a problem of politicians' defining and using political institutions, and of establishing and maintaining the borders of the state. There is another 'state' of uncertainty that is both a product and a cause of the failure of Russian political leaders to create a strong state. This is the state of uncertainty experienced by Russians about how life is to be lived in desperate times.

The failure of Russian politicians to build an effective state is responsible in large measure for this other 'state of uncertainty'. Social life all over the globe was subject to dramatic change in the twentieth century, but in twentieth century Russia change was more traumatic, violent, rapid and fundamental than the norm. Russia underwent three fundamental shifts in social organization in the twentieth century – from agrarian society to state socialism and to a hybrid form of capitalism – and each of these changes caused massive social disruptions and privations. Each shift in social organization began with the failure of the Russian state and the collapse of the ruling political order or regime. Each new form of social organization was constructed by a new political regime to consolidate state power and was carried out by state officials.

This process has not reached an end. Russians today look to Vladimir Putin to create a political system that can guarantee a more peaceful and prosperous way of life. Whether or not he will succeed cannot be stated with certainty, especially since his political programme remains unclear in many important aspects. This book does not aim to second-guess the success of Putin, but to examine the problems of state building in twentieth century Russia to see what the general problems are that have faced Russian leaders, and what the legacies of the recent past are for Vladimir Putin. The book is not about Putin, although it does make some reference to his policies at the end. Rather, it is an attempt to talk about the problems of the Russian state. This is as necessary as any discussion of Putin because at present the Russian state is too often talked about as a synonym of democracy: democratization has failed, so the argument runs, because the Russian state has failed and vice versa. Whilst this is not untrue in that state failure is antithetical with democratic consolidation, we should, through the study of the state, recognize that state building is not the same as building democracy, and that Russia's current state formation is as likely to throw up a strong state that is not democratic as it is to evolve into a strong democratic state. To recognize this, however, means that we have to have some idea about the variety of forms that a state can take and the different things that rulers can do with them. Consequently, this book starts and ends with a discussion of the state and tries to analyse state building failures and problems in light of this discussion in an effort to highlight the wide range of possibilities that lie before Russia and that make it so uncertain.

This book was mostly written in rural Ireland in a house that has seen better days (and will one day see them again). That I was able to spend so much time writing rather than carving out a habitable niche is due to the hard work and cheerful tolerance of filth of John Adshead, Theresa Adshead, Jim Cahill, Helen Cahill, Sara Ryklif, Luke Ashworth and Elizabeth de Baor-Ashworth. Many of the ideas in the book were developed whilst I was working at the University of Essex and I am very grateful to my former colleagues at Essex for their advice, help and encouragement. I would particularly like to thank Peter Frank, Alastair McAuley, Frances Millard, Tony Swift, David

Howarth, Todd Landman and Aletta Norval. Parts of the book's arguments have appeared in conference papers and seminar presentations and many people have made suggestions or raised questions that have helped me clarify my thought. Particularly important to me were two ECPR workshops organized by Hugh Ward and Colin Hay on 'The evolution of the state' at Warwick in 1998, and by Phil Cerny on 'National models and transnational structures' at Mannheim in 1999, and a panel on 'Regime and political actors in post-communist Russia' organized by Richard Sakwa at the ICCEES World Congress in Tampere in 2000. I am grateful to all of them and to the other participants in these events for their comments, and am particularly grateful to Richard Sakwa for his encouragement and thoughts over the last few years. Finally, but not last and never, ever least, one person above all is responsible for anything that is good about this book and for all that has been good about the time that I have spent on it, Maura Adshead. Words and the dedication of the book to you cannot repay the debts that I owe, but I'll try and repay you with the same love and patience that you give to me.

Neil Robinson
Baile Hoibeaird
October 2000

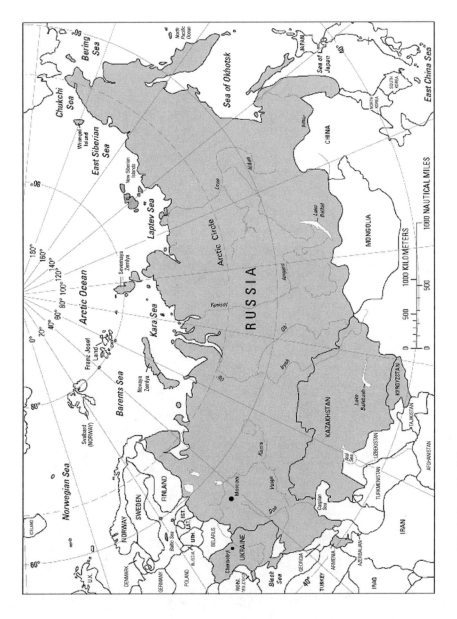

Source: US Geographical Survey

1 Introduction

Strong states, weak states and the Russian problem

The cycles of state failure and reconstruction that make up Russian history in the twentieth century have created a paradox. The failure of the state and the brutality with which the state has tried to reconstruct Russia in the past has lead many Russians to distrust the state, to see it as something alien and predatory that has imposed new ways of life on them against their will. The very idea of state power was not legitimate in the eyes of many Russians for much of the twentieth century and as Russia enters the twenty-first century, popular esteem for political institutions is at what might be its lowest ever ebb. Many Russians prefer private life to the vicissitudes of public life and are loyal to family and networks of friends and kin rather than to the state. However, despite this, and as Vladimir Putin, Russia's new President, has noted, Russians expect the state to play a larger role in public life than might be common in established liberal democracies and expect it to take the lead in solving Russia's political, economic and social crises.[1] This is not as surprising as it might seem at first glance. The brutality of Russia's rulers has destroyed public institutions and eroded faith in public life to the point where the only body left that might act for the collective good is the state, or some part of it. Moreover, Russians are right to want action from the state since only a reconstructed state in Russia can provide the public goods (goods that all citizens share equally, that no one in a society can be excluded from enjoying) necessary for a decent, peaceful and prosperous life. Only the state can provide for the rule of law across Russia, for a relatively stable currency that is honoured throughout the country, for security of property rights, and the enforcement of contracts whether they are between businessmen, banks and their clients, employers and employees, or welfare recipients such as pensioners and those agencies responsible for paying them.

If the state's role is desired and also necessary to the reconstruction of public life in Russia, how can we explain the failure of the Russian state in the past and its current weakness? There are two common explanations for Russia's problems that appear in the media when Russia has a crisis, or that are often to be found in the academic literature on Russia: the argument that Russia's problems are historically inevitable, and the argument that

Russia's problems are culturally determined and hence unavoidable. Neither of these arguments is very good. The causes of state failure in Russia have been different at different times. It is not simply a matter of state weakness and failure explaining state weakness and failure *ad infinitum*. Variously, different combinations of personality, ideology, the pressures of modernization and international forces have caused state failure in Russia. A history of state failure does make constructing a stable polity and economy more difficult. Each failure means that a state and nation lags behind its competitors and is overtaken by emerging powers. Consequently, there is further to go to deliver comparable standards of living and security, to produce goods of a comparable technological level and quality, etc., and it is harder to attract investment, capture markets, or command respect and project influence in international politics. Nevertheless, failure, whilst it may get harder to avoid, is not inevitable. Structural factors (which states cannot easily change or avoid because they are beyond their individual control) such as international competition, the health of the global economy and one's position in it, or the fact that society and economy are agrarian rather than industrial, or industrial rather than post-industrial, are important influences on the outcome of state building projects, but they are not necessarily decisive. Success and failure are contingent on many things and the influence of structural factors can be mediated by how politicians approach them. Nor is failure to be surprised at or despised. State failure is more common than success; very few states had stable political systems over the course of the twentieth century and the majority of states that appear to be most stable and most successful have only recently so become.[2] The lessons of history are the same for Russia as for any other state: failure is not surprising, nor is it inescapable.

Arguments that assert that the failure of the Russian state over the last century is explicable by reference to culture are not much better. The Russian state does not fail because it is Russian; past and present crises of political authority and state failure have not been caused by something intrinsic to 'Russianness' or the Russians. Certain common Russian traditions and attitudes have not helped state building in Russia. However, these traditions and attitudes are often themselves the result of state failure and can be amended by fresh state building projects, or serve as their basis or inspiration. It is therefore inappropriate to blame culture for all of the failings of the Russian state, especially if this means that factors specific to a particular moment at which the Russian state failed are not given their proper due and explanatory weight.[3] To put it another way, why say a crisis is due to some vague quality of 'Russianness' if it is better blamed on some clearly visible combination of poor leadership, economic crisis, international apathy or hostility and inadequate institutions, each of which has a form unique to its own time of crisis? The cultural argument is also contradictory; it blames state collapse and failure of 'Russianness', but also argues that Russians have a cultural affinity for order and discipline, two features of any well-ordered state.

If we cannot blame Russia's problems on historical inevitability or on some innate cultural tendency, we must seek answers to state failure that are more specific. We must explain how the forms taken by the Russian state in the twentieth century proved inadequate and how contemporary politicians have made decisions that have produced a particular form of state to the detriment of democratization and economic transformation. This requires us to understand something about states in general. The fact that the state has been the problem in Russia and yet is necessary if the resolution of Russia's current problems is to be a happy one demonstrates something about states in general: they are not easy to define and it is not easy to distinguish what affect, positive or negative, that they have on societies and their fate. Nevertheless, it is to these questions that we must now turn. If we are to argue that a failure to build a strong state is at the heart of Russia's historical and contemporary problems, we must have some notion of what constitutes a strong state so that we can measure Russia's historical and contemporary state weakness against it.

Defining the state is difficult since they are 'not the sort of abstract, formal object which readily lend themselves to a clear-cut, unambiguous definition'.[4] This is because states are defined by political factors and phenomena that are often unstable and contested. Essentially and basically, we can say that states have three main features.[5] The state is, first, 'a set of institutions ... manned by the state's own personnel'. This means that the state is not a unitary actor, a single organism that always acts according to a common purpose. It cannot 'decide' to do something and do it even when great power is vested in a single ruler like a Tsar, a General Secretary of the Communist Party of the Soviet Union (CPSU), or a president. A state is a composite of different institutions, leaders and interests, and even when one institution is more powerful than the rest it relies on other institutions to implement its orders and they may often subvert its will. Second, the state has a dual character because the institutions that comprise it 'are at the centre of a geographically-bounded territory, usually referred to as a society'. As a result, the state both looks inwards to the society that it manages and 'outwards to larger societies [the international system of states] in which it must make its way'. Thus, the domestic policies of the state are often the product of its international concerns and vice versa. Finally, the state 'monopolizes rule making within its territory', to 'define and enforce collectively binding decisions on the members of a society in the name of their common interest or general will'.

The basic features of a state – the fact that it comprises institutions, has tasks of social management and an international role, and that it seeks to monopolize rule making in a specific territory – all demand that the state strive to create three things: capacity, autonomy and organizational integrity. A state has capacity where it has the ability to get things done: rules are made, policies are formulated and the machinery (institutions) exists to ensure that policy is implemented and rules are kept. A state is autonomous when it is able to define policy independently of social groups and act independently of their

interests, when private interests do not 'capture' it. Finally, a state has organizational integrity when its machinery and the officials who serve in it
(bureaucrats, civil servants) are unified by a clear set of norms and goals,
and where officials do not subvert state policy for private ends. States strive
to create some measure of capacity, autonomy and organizational integrity
because creating autonomy, capacity and organizational integrity enables
them to better respond to international events and to the changing demands
of social management. The manner in which they achieve capacity, autonomy
and organizational integrity depends on two things: the type of political
regime that exists in a state and the character of administrative organization.
For simplicity's sake, we can reduce both types of regime and of administrative
organization to two basic forms and from this derive four basic types of state
formation that can be used to describe modern states in general, the Russian
state in its Tsarist, Soviet and contemporary forms in particular, and the form
of state that it has been struggling to develop over the last decade.

Regimes, the systems of rule that endure beyond the life span of any
particular politician's government, can be classified as either absolutist or
constitutional, the character of administrative organization can be classified
as either patrimonial or bureaucratic.[6] A regime is absolutist where both
executive and legislative power is combined in the person of a ruler or a set
of institutions, and constitutional where legislative powers are divided
between the executive branch of government and a representative assembly.
Administrative organization is patrimonial where office holders are selected
through patronage as clients of a ruler, or as clients of one of the ruler's
clients, and possess the ability (and sometimes the right) to use state resources
for personal ends. This is called 'proprietary officeholding'. Bureaucratic
organization, in contrast, exists where the appointment of officials is impersonal and formal regulations govern administration so that there is no 'proprietary officeholding'.

Combining these ideas about regime and state organization we can produce four classifications of state formation: constitutional-bureaucratic, absolutist-patrimonial, absolutist-bureaucratic and constitutional-patrimonial.
The basic characteristics of these four forms of state are laid out in Table
1.1. Constitutional-bureaucratic, absolutist-patrimonial and absolutist-
bureaucratic state forms correspond respectively to modern consolidated
democracies such as exist in countries such as the USA and Western
Europe, Tsarist Russia (and other states where monarchs have ruled in con-
junction with aristocratic elites), and the Soviet Union (and other twentieth
century dictatorships such as Democratic Kampuchea under Pol Pot and
communist China). Describing the generic types of constitutional-bureaucratic, absolutist-patrimonial and absolutist-bureaucratic state will enable
us to see how stable modern political systems work, the strains that development puts on absolutist-patrimonial states, and the inherent problems of
absolutist-bureaucratic states. This is important first, because Russia has
gone from absolutist-patrimonialism, through an absolutist-bureaucratic

Table 1.1 State formations and their characteristics

	Constitutional-bureaucratic	Absolutist-patrimonial	Absolutist-bureaucratic	Constitutional-patrimonial
Most prevalent form of state power	Infrastructural	Despotic	Despotic	None: the possibility of infrastructural power developing is blocked by patronage, but constitutional considerations limit despotic power
State autonomy	Relative	High but not embedded	High but not embedded; constrained by ideological imperatives governing bureaucratic behaviour	Relative but not embedded because of patronage
State capacity	High and sustained	High for simple tasks, but declines if tasks conflict with elite interests.	High for a small number of simple tasks, otherwise low and declines as complexity of social management increases	Low
State organizational integrity	High as integrity is ensured by shared bureaucratic norms	Low and diminishes further if state tasks become more complex	High where compliance with and state orders is enforced by coercion, declining as propensity to use violence declines	Low, with tension between constitutional norms and the practice of patronage
Reliance on coercion	Low	Frequent	High for social and political control	Variable and inconsistent use of coercion; coercion is often used for personal, rather than state, goals
Ability to gather resources from society over time for redistribution and provision of public goods	High and constant over time because extraction is routinized and negotiated between state officials and society	Low as personal networks divert resources to their own use	High but declining over time. Resources are gathered using coercion so there are no strong, positive incentives for citizens to be productive	Low as personal networks divert resources to their own use

state formation, and is now trying to construct a modern democratic system akin to the constitutional-bureaucratic state formations of the 'West'. Second, describing these three types of state formation enables us to develop two ideas of state strength: we will be able to see that only the constitutional-bureaucratic state is strong over time because it is more adaptable, but that absolutist state formations can be strong because they can achieve specific tasks quite well at certain historical junctures. Realizing this, we can say something about our fourth form of state formation, constitutional-patrimonialism. This is an unstable type of state formation. Its evolution to the constitutional-bureaucratic type is not guaranteed because politicians may decide that the short-term strength of an absolutist state is better suited to their interests and to dealing with problems of social management and the provision of security.

The chief difference between constitutional-bureaucratic and an absolutist type of state formation is in the prevalent form of state power. All state formations have both despotic and infrastructural powers, but which form of power is most prevalent differs widely.[7] This means that the nature of state autonomy, capacity and organizational integrity also differ considerably. In a constitutional-bureaucratic state formation infrastructural power is more prevalent than despotic power. Infrastructural power exists where there is a cross-penetration of state and society so that decision making is not isolated from social concerns. The state's decision-making powers are created by a negotiation of its functions, rights and responsibilities that is carried out primarily through the interaction of the executive branch of government and representatives of social groups in legislative assemblies. A state with infrastructural power is thus not isolated from society, but nor is it dominated by any particular interest from within society, or by society as a whole to the point where officials cannot sometimes take action that they think necessary.[8] The state and its autonomy are 'embedded' in society, and the state's power is exercised evenly over all of the territory of the state and is not effectively challenged in any part of its territory.[9] Within the territory for which it claims to make rules, a state with infrastructural power can thus work to satisfy the common interest or general will that was mentioned above. The general will is defined – imperfectly – and redefined by elections, debate, lobbying, social protest etc., which work through the constitutional division of responsibility for legislative activity between executive and representative assembly. Of course, social inequality does have an impact on policy: the economically powerful have more chance of making their interests heard than the poor; the state takes action to preserve an economic system in which there are social divisions; the reproduction of social division with the connivance of the state naturally favours the rich. The state's embedded autonomy is thus relative: there is only 'fairly strong', rather than an absolute, 'institutional differentiation of formal collective decision making from the overall system of inequality', rather than an absolute differentiation.[10]

Relative state autonomy is facilitated by the complexity of the modern democratic state and their organizational integrity. State officials and departments might share concerns with social groups that they deal with on a regular basis. For example, farmers may be close to bureaucrats from a ministry of agriculture, or bankers might have common cause with civil servants from a finance ministry. But the complexity of a democratic state prevents any one interest from dominating the whole: state officials may thus reflect social interests in constitutional-bureaucratic systems, but they generally do not do this at the cost of bureaucratic neutrality in the state at large. Moreover, there is a social expectation that state officials will work according to legal norms that are neutral. This means that there is coincidence between the organizational norms of the state and social norms. This organizational integrity is not perfect – state officials fall from grace just like the rest of us – but where it breaks down, the polity itself at society's demand rectifies it. Corruption, for example, is prosecuted and rectified through the regulation of the bureaucracy by law. Organizational integrity, like autonomy, is therefore never absolute, but private interests do not break it down finally or irrevocably.

State autonomy and organizational integrity facilitate state capacity because the orders that emanate from the state are viewed as generally being legitimate and are implemented. Capacity is also constantly under review in a constitutional-bureaucratic state formation and what the state 'does' and what society 'does' is negotiated between them and by such things as elections changing what society asks the state to do through its elected politicians. The need for coercion is therefore low since the state does not generally demand more of its citizens than they are prepared to do. The need to coerce bureaucrats is also relatively low. They require supervision, but organizational integrity and the social legitimization of power facilitate the practical aspect of policy implementation, the actual process of getting things done. Orders are respected as they are passed down bureaucratic hierarchies and both those who give orders and those who seek to fulfil them expect that bureaucrats will obey the orders given them. Since state orders are accepted as legitimate, the range of supervisory tasks that bureaucrats have to undertake is limited and the ability of the state to gather resources to create capacity is great. Since the responsibilities of the state are defined by negotiation, society accepts that resources have to be passed over to the state on a regular basis in order that it may fulfil its responsibilities. Infrastructural power thus ensures that the extraction of resources from society by the state is efficient and that the state can expect a regular, routinized flow of resources from society that can be deployed to ensure security and welfare for society.[11] There is also less waste of resources since the state does not have to use a large part of the revenue it collects to coerce resources from its citizens in the future. All this means that in comparison to other state formations, administration in a constitutional-bureaucratic state formation is able to encompass a wider range of tasks without stretching the capacities of state officials. Alternatively, if such stretching occurs, the constitutional order facilitates reconsideration of bureaucratic and social responsibilities so that either state capacity is increased by the provision of more resources, or responsibility is passed from state to society so that the state is not overloaded.

Finally, the durability of constitutional-bureaucratic states has been increased by their ability to regulate their relations with other constitutional-bureaucratic states cheaply. Military force plays little part in the relations between constitutional-bureaucratic states, which can coexist in a situation of 'democratic peace'.[12] Their effective systems of administration enable them to make international agreements and expect that those agreements will be implemented without recourse to military threats. Shared democratic norms also enable them to believe that other constitutional-bureaucratic states are trustworthy. Resources can thus be directed towards a narrower range of security threats from other types of state, and international agreements can be made between constitutional-bureaucratic states that spread the cost of ensuring security, or that help to manage such things as international economic relations.

Infrastructural power thus enables constitutional-bureaucratic states to be flexible and to adapt, whilst helping them to direct resources with relative efficiency to deal with social management and security problems. In contrast, despotic power, which prevails in absolutist types of state formation, creates rigidity. Despotic power exists where there is a high degree of centralization of decision making so that most of society is excluded from decision making. Consequently, a state (of whichever type) in which despotic power prevails over infrastructural power is isolated from the society that it administers and in large measure relies on coercion to manage society. How this occurs in absolutist-patrimonial and absolutist-bureaucratic state formations is very different so that they have different forms of state autonomy, capacity and organizational integrity, and different problems in recreating these features of the state.

Absolutist-patrimonial states are administered through networks of personal affinity and loyalty created by patronage. Most often, these states are monarchical and dominated by aristocracies, who share control over legislative activity. The basic form of patronage in such states is between monarch and aristocrat, with the aristocracy in turn having clients dependent upon them. State autonomy in such systems is high because policy making is exclusively the preserve of the monarch and the noble elite. There is little substantive difference in a state organized by patronage between state and personal interests; the will of the despot is declared to be the same as the general will of the state's subjects as in Louis XIV of France's famous dictum that 'l'état, c'est moi' ('I am the state'). Proprietary officeholding in absolutist-patrimonial states therefore starts at the top. It spreads through the rest of the political system because monarchs, in the absence of developed modern bureaucracies, have to rely for administration on the small number of people in society with the skills to act as administrators because of military prowess, social standing, financial resources etc. These people in return for obedience to the monarch demand privilege and security of status in face of the monarch's arbitrary authority, and the best way to achieve this security is to take personal possession of political office so that it is held by right and can be passed on to one's heirs.[13]

States with this mixture of patrimonialism and absolutism are most successful when the tasks before them are relatively straightforward: they can oversee basic agricultural production, tax agrarian surpluses and use this tax to support noble privilege and a simple military machine under noble command. Managing such tasks does not require a complex bureaucratic organization beyond patronage networks organized around individuals and that stretch from court to village. Nonetheless, this form of administrative hierarchy often lacks organizational integrity because of disputes about the rights and duties of patrons and clients. Such disputes are common in this type of state because the exercise of power is often arbitrary and violent as the will of the monarch changes, and the state's control over its territory is often limited. An absolutist rulers control over the state is only as good as their ability to coerce all of their clients to obey their instructions and implement their orders throughout the territory of the state. Since an absolutist ruler may be far away and communications between capital and province are generally poor in underdeveloped societies, proprietary officeholders have much scope to implement policy as they please. Moreover, both state capacity and organizational integrity may decline if an absolutist-patrimonial state is required to undertake tasks that require technical skills not possessed by the aristocracy, or if international competition requires that the state do things that run counter to the interests of the patronage networks that are its main administrative resource. In such cases – as we will see how in Chapter 2 when we look at the failure of Tsarism as an absolutist-patrimonial state formation – the state may become increasingly inefficient at managing the tasks before it. Traditional officeholding groups resist the spread of meritocracy, or the state may fall behind its competitors as patronage networks resist policies that are needed to modernize and match rivals.

A strong despot or monarch might attempt to override opposition and force the pace of change. However, the despot's chances of success are often limited because it is difficult to gather resources for modernization and because it is difficult to accommodate political reform within an absolutist-patrimonial system. Much of the state's revenue in an absolutist-patrimonial state is distributed to the networks that the despot relies on for support and it is difficult to divert monies to new purposes. Political reform is often half-hearted. Attempts to expand political participation through the creation of legislative assemblies or to build up greater infrastructural power by developing more modern forms of bureaucratic administration are compromised where despots maintain substantial powers of appointment to public office or control legislative activity to the detriment of representative assemblies. The result of reform in absolutist-patrimonial state formations, therefore, is often mixed. Reforms may have to be coerced and where they fail, or are only partially successful, the state remains enfeebled and social control increasingly becomes a matter of coercion since the absolutist-patrimonial state does not have the machinery to manage the demands generated by international competition or domestic change.

Absolutist-bureaucratic states differ from absolutist-patrimonial states in that they organize the exclusion of the mass of society from legislative activity and decision making by vesting power in bureaucratic organizations. Modern bureaucratic organization is founded on impersonal principles that are deemed to be rational and therefore of best service to society. In absolutist-bureaucratic states, what is deemed rational is generally the product of an ideology, of a set of ideas about how the world works and how it should work if properly ordered; ideology is, in other words, a guide to the construction of a better, more perfect society.[14] In an absolutist-bureaucratic state, the definition of ideology and how its prescriptions should be implemented to transform society is the prerogative of the bureaucracy. This ensures a high degree of state autonomy in an absolutist-bureaucratic state: the mass of society is excluded from decision making because it does not possess the 'knowledge' necessary to guide social development as officials of the state do. But although officials interpret ideology, they are not free to interpret it suit its own material interests; they are also one of its subjects since the ideology of an absolutist-bureaucratic state claims to define everything, even the position and functions of state officials.[15] Consequently, the absolutist-bureaucratic state should not become the possession of an individual or class in the same manner as an absolutist-patrimonial state; officeholding should not become proprietary. The role of ideology also makes absolutist-bureaucratic states very different to constitutional-bureaucratic states. In the latter, what is deemed best for the sake of social, economic and political organization is deduced through political contest and the clash of interests and summarized in legal norms to which all are held accountable, even state officials. In absolutist-bureaucratic states, there is no such accountability. State officials 'know best' and other forms of ensuring that the regulation of social life is carried out impersonally – with regard to the general good of society and not in the advantage of a small number of individuals – such as the law are secondary to ideological considerations.

The desire to create a perfected society under bureaucratic tutelage is supposed to create a particular form of infrastructural power. Social acceptance of ideology and participation in the construction of a perfect society should lead to the mobilization of the people and the direction of their energies towards fulfilling policy without great bureaucratic effort. The paradox of absolutist-bureaucratic states, however, has been that creating infrastructural power based on mobilization has never developed without coercion. Despotic power has thus always been more prevalent than infrastructural power in absolutist-bureaucratic states despite the claims that such states have made about popular participation. The ideology of an absolutist-bureaucratic state projects a vision of a perfect society and the means towards it rather than actual social needs or aspirations. An absolutist-bureaucratic state will try to manage this dissonance between ideology and social needs by indoctrination (persuading the population that their actual desires are reflected in official ideology), but it will also use terror to destroy social groups that it deems to be in opposition to its new society, or that it considers to have no place in such a society. Since ideology in an absolutist-bureaucratic state claims to interpret and judge the entire social world and the actions of individuals therein, the range of actions, thoughts and social positions that can be classified as deviant and punished as being dangerous to the good of society is potentially very wide. Violence – both real and threatened – is thus integral to absolutist-bureaucratic states to an extent that is far beyond what is normal in absolutist-patrimonial states.

However, violence is not just inflicted on enemies of the perfect society to be by bureaucrats. Officials too are coerced when they fail to implement policies that are deemed essential by political leaders, or as organizational integrity breaks down. An absolutist-bureaucratic state ought to have a large degree of capacity and organizational integrity since its officials are supposed to work to common ends as defined by its ideology. However, as will be noted from Table 1.1, capacity and organizational integrity in an absolutist-bureaucratic state are not always high. Certain tasks are fulfilled with ease because they are deemed necessary for political reasons and resources can be diverted to them without social complaint and progress closely monitored. Examples of this would be the USSR's rapid development of nuclear weapons and a space programme because of the political prioritization of these projects and their consequent funding regardless of cost. However, and in the main, state officials have too many tasks in an absolutist-bureaucratic state because ideology demands the regulation of aspects of social and economic life to a degree beyond that found in other state formations. Moreover, many of the multiple tasks before a bureaucrat in absolutist-bureaucratic states are difficult to fulfil properly because they demand high levels of resources that the state cannot provide. This results from the fact that the absolutist-bureaucratic state exercises a high degree of control over economic life and takes so much from the population that it creates few incentives for its citizenry to be productive, and because the range of activities that the state has to take on stretch the economy too far.[16] A corollary of this is that an absolutist-bureaucratic state has to coerce resources from its citizenry and uses up a considerable proportion of the resources that it accumulates in developing an administrative capacity in coerce further resources from its population.

The overloading of bureaucracy with regulatory tasks and the inefficient collection of resources means that officials are often unable to reach the goals that are set for them by political authorities. This means that capacity is nearly always a problem in absolutist-bureaucratic states since not all orders emanating from political authorities can be fulfilled; more is sought of officials and they achieve less; state officials have to choose which state orders to fulfil and which they may ignore safely. In trying to compensate for this low capacity, an absolutist-bureaucratic state creates high penalties for non-compliance with state orders; non-compliance with orders is, after all, a betrayal of the perfect society that is being built for the good of humankind and therefore deserving of harsh punishment. Coercion is thus central to the character of absolutist-bureaucratic state formations not only with regard to society, but also to manage political relations within the state itself. But this reliance on coercion also erodes the character of absolutist-bureaucracy since it attacks bureaucratic impersonalism. The fear of failure and punishment leads officials to seek some protection from censure by making alliances with other politicians. This weakens organizational integrity since it creates political loyalties that rival those to the state and ideology. Alliances can be used by officials to protect themselves as they pick from the wide range of demands made of them by political leaders and implement only those that they think central authorities will check up on. This selective implementation of policy and protection also has the effect of making officeholding less impersonal and more proprietary; what policies are implemented is a matter for individual decision and the search for protection from censure leads to patronage and clientelist relations between bureaucrats. It also weakens the territorial control of the state because as in an absolutist-patrimonial state, the implementation of central directives and laws will be uneven across the territory that the state nominally controls.

The response of an absolutist-bureaucratic state's central political authorities to failure to implement its instructions is sometimes reform, sometimes terror against bureaucrats deemed to be disloyal. Whatever the method, the result is usually the same; both the dovetailing of reform with ideology and the forced compliance with ideology created by terror limit the effectiveness of efforts to improve state capacity. Reforms very often do not deal with the source of a problem for ideological reasons; fear of repression creates further informal bonds between officials desperate for some protection. Moreover, capacity and organizational integrity are subject to decline overtime. Like absolutist-patrimonial states, absolutist-bureaucratic states can find it difficult to modernize and manage social complexity. This is because ideology may adapt at a slower rate than social evolution and a bureaucracy trained to conform to an ideology may lack the technical skills needed to adapt to new challenges. Again, shifting resources to modernization can prove difficult because certain areas of spending by the state have to be protected for ideological reasons, and because changes in policy increase the economic demands made of citizens without necessarily increasing their incentive to be productive.

States with absolutist forms of power thus suffer from problems of adapting to change. Consequently, and despite the fact that both absolutist-patrimonial and absolutist-bureaucratic state forms have dominated human history, these forms of state power have historically been weak in the longer run. Absolutist-patrimonial states have been overtaken by states that manage to develop infrastructural power. Absolutist-bureaucratic states have become less efficient as their organizational integrity is worn away by patronage and the political will to use terror is weakened by bureaucratic connivance. States with despotic power, in whatever form that it takes, have thus been less able to adapt to change than those with infrastructural power created by constitutionalism and bureaucracy. Constitutional-bureaucratic state formations have failed in the past and been replaced with other types of formation such as when Weimar Germany collapsed in the early 1930s to be replaced by Nazi dictatorship. However, where such constitutional-bureaucratic state formations have existed for some time they can develop a facility to endure – as in the USA and the United Kingdom – and this type of state formation has become increasingly common over time, as democracy has developed across the globe.

Does this mean that constitutional-bureaucratic states are strong and the absolutist states are weak? If we take strength to equal survival then the answer to this question is yes. However, we should bear in mind that absolutist states can be strong too and that developing absolutism and patronage, rather than constitutionalism and bureaucracy, can enable political leaders to resolve some of the problems of social management and international competition that face a state, especially if they do not have the resources necessary to build up bureaucracy, the skilled personnel necessary to staff it, or the time needed to create impersonal administration. As a result, constitutional-bureaucracy might not always be seen as the best solution to the problems of our fourth type of state formation, constitutional-patrimonialism. This type of state formation is a hybrid system. Neither form of state power is well developed within it. The constitutional regime checks despotism since it forces some negotiation over access to decision making, but at the same time there will be an imbalance in power between executive and legislature so that effective social control over the state is compromised. State autonomy will be relative, rather than high as in an absolutist system, but it will not be embedded since patrimonial practices will mean that proprietary office-holders use the powers of the state for private ends and public trust in politicians and political institutions are low, and social willingness to comply with state orders is weak. A corollary of this is that politicians are often unwilling to honour constitutional norms because their power is based as much on patronage as it is on popular support channelled through a representative assembly, or direct elections to executive office. Indeed, control over patronage can often be turned into electoral support by using the state's resources to buy political support from the powerful. Since this happens at a regional, as well as at national, level, the territorial basis of state power is undermined by the development of regional fiefdoms where national laws and directives are often unfulfilled as regional elites please themselves and use office for personal gain. Infrastructural power in such a system can only be weak. State capacity and organizational integrity remain low since policy implementation becomes a matter of choice and convenience, and powerful social groups can pressure officials for policies that suit them, and corrupt them to get exemptions from things like taxation, or to receive favours from the state. In turn, this makes it difficult for the state to act in the public good, command social respect and provide services to the public. Social management is thus haphazard, and there is always the danger that coercion will have to be used in the absence of more pacific means of regulating society and political disputes.

Constitutional-patrimonialism is thus an inherently unstable type of state formation because laws and bureaucratic impersonalism regulate competition between elite groups and society only weakly and are subverted. How countries with such systems may develop is uncertain. Some states that have been constitutional-patrimonial in form have developed into constitutional-bureaucratic states through slow processes of transformation, such as the United Kingdom.[17] Elsewhere, constitutionalism, bureaucracy and patrimony have coexisted for shorter historical time periods before some shock to the polity has enabled bureaucracy to begin to gain an upper hand over patrimonialism. An example of this would be modern Italy, which has been undergoing a legal revolution against political patronage and corruption over the last decade. Common to both these cases, however, was the fact that a constitutional regime was secure. Either no one had an interest in seeing absolutism return or the power to force such a return, and/or external commitments and alliances guaranteed the constitutional regime.[18] This, however, is not always the case in cases of constitutional-patrimonial state formations. Constitutional-patrimonial state formations may endure whilst the political, social and economic conditions develop that may create constitutional-bureaucratic state formations. But this may take a long time, if it happens at all. A danger thus exists that some form of absolutism may become attractive to politicians because in the short term it helps them deal with an immediate problem of social breakdown, economic failure, or because it simply suits their interests to hold on to power by eliminating their rivals through repression and the abandonment of constitutionalism.

Unfortunately, the country we are interested in – modern, post-communist Russia – is closer to a constitutional-patrimonial state formation than it is to a constitutional-bureaucratic one. The state is weak and barely able to support democracy, let alone to deepen and consolidate it by promoting a uniform, impersonal administration across the territory of the Russian Federation. The Russian state has had difficulty adapting to changing circumstances because of a lack of resources and has not been able to stabilize the national economy, fund itself, or provide some welfare to its citizens. Consequently, there has been no real safety-cushion for democracy. Since the state is weak and unable to enforce a common set of rules throughout Russia, the rules that it makes and the institutions that make them are held in low esteem. Distributional conflicts over who gets what from the state have not been kept separate from arguments about how politics is ordered and what progress has been achieved in building democracy is constantly threatened by politicians seeking some short-term advantage for themselves and their followers.

Most of the rest of this book is concerned with these failings of the contemporary Russian state. They are discussed in more detail in Chapters 3 to

5. This discussion needs to take place in context, however, and that is provided in Chapter 2. In this chapter, we will look at the failures of the Tsarist and Soviet states. Both of these states were absolutist, although in very different ways. Their despotism did not mean that they were always weak. For a time they were able to create effective organizations, coerce resources from the population and sustain the rule of the Romanovs and the CPSU. However, as absolutist states they were less able to adapt to the pressures to which they were subject. A combination of international competition, the effects of modernization, ideological rigidity, leadership intransigence and organizational inflexibility exhausted any earlier signs of state strength that they had exhibited. As the pressures on them mounted, both failed dramatically.

Chapter 3 examines domestic political developments under President Yeltsin to see how Russia tried to cope with the legacies of Soviet collapse by building a new political order. It argues that Yeltsin did not develop a political strategy to cope with these problems. Instead, he placed his hopes in an economic strategy (rapid commercialization followed by privatization; the details of these policies can be found in Chapter 4), and in the emergency powers that he had been granted after the failed coup of August 1991. In the absence of a political strategy, and given the wide range of political problems faced by the new regime, Yeltsin's emergency powers were not enough to ensure political stability whilst economic transformation was carried out. Yeltsin became embroiled in a battle over the Russian Constitution and the powers and responsibilities of the presidency and the legislatures. Although Yeltsin was to win this battle with the forced closure of the parliament in October 1993 and the introduction of a new Constitution in December 1993, he compromised control over government and policy and this set a pattern for politics under the new Constitution. Yeltsin ruled Russia by dividing his opponents and creating a confusing array of institutions. This increased Yeltsin's personal importance in the Russian political system since he was able to mediate between rival interests and institutions, but it meant that the Russian state became permeated by interest groups so that it lost autonomy; policy formulation and implementation was weakened as state capacity was compromised and organizational integrity broke down. Officeholding became proprietary and patronage rife, and the 1993 Constitution gave too much power to the President, especially as political parties are weak, and the representative assembly, the Duma, could not exert great influence over the executive.

One consequence of these political failures was the continued weakness of economic reform in Russia. This is detailed in Chapter 4. The reform plans adopted after the collapse of communism in 1991 were very ambitious and their success was never guaranteed. However, as political turmoil and competition grew, economic reform became impossible to carry out as the reformers intended. Chapter 4 details the economic plans of the reformers and their failures and how they produced a new hybrid form of economy. This has been named a 'virtual economy' by some observers since it is an economy based on barter rather than monetary exchange. The nature of this economy and the new forms of social inequality and power it has produced are analysed, as are the Russian government's efforts to deal with it. These efforts were unsuccessful for both political reasons and because of the weakness of the Russian economy in the international economic system. The state was too weak to act as the guarantor of economic reform and could not gather enough taxes to meet its own debt repayments. The result was the collapse of the rouble in August 1998 and the default on debt repayments. Ironically, this crisis left the Russian economy in what seems to be a healthier state since it has witnessed some growth in industrial output and GDP since August 1998. However, appearances are deceptive in Russia and the chapter argues that Russia is still in a weak position with poor economic prospects.

Domestic political chaos and economic decline have made it difficult for Russia to act as a superpower in the same way that the USSR did. Russia's foreign policy problems are analysed in Chapter 5. The end of the USSR also posed fundamental questions about Russia's national interests. The Cold War between the USA and the USSR had defined national interests very simply as victory or accommodation with the opposing side. The end of the Cold War meant that Russia had to rethink who its friends were and what its responsibilities and powers in the world were. Moreover, the collapse of the Soviet Union created a Russian state free of empire for the first time. Being free of empire, however, meant coping with its legacies. Russia has not been able to resolve its relations with either the former Soviet republics or with the rest of the world in ways that might have helped it to deal with its domestic political and economic problems. Relations with the West, which were supposed to be co-operative and to support democratization and marketization, became increasingly fraught under Yeltsin. Relations with the other Soviet successor states have not been stable since neither they nor Russia is quite sure of how their common problems should be resolved, through multilateral or bilateral negotiations. Consequently, Russia has not had stable, predictable relations with the outside world since the end of communism in 1991 and its unsettled foreign relations have highlighted its weakness as a state.

Finally, with the development of modern Russia described in Chapters 3 through 5, we will sum up the Russian experience of post-communist state-building and its results and assess what its prospects over the next few years might be. This means first, revisiting some of the questions that have been raised here about constitutional-patrimonialism as a form of state and assessing the prospects for change from this system. The next few years are vital for Russia. Although President Putin was shy of making promises during his election campaign in 2000, expectations that something should change and a desire for change are high. Chapter 5 looks at the rise of President Putin and his first government in the context of the post-Soviet state-building experience and tries to assess whether popular expectations and desires will be met. Of course, nothing may happen, but this too would be of momentous importance. It would confirm that Russia and its people will be a long time getting out of their current state of uncertainty and escaping governmental malaise, their ambiguous relationship with the rest of the world and their economic hardships, and that the dangers of a move away from democracy will remain alive in Russia for some time to come.

Notes

1 V. Putin (1999) 'Rossiya na rubezhe tysyachiletii', http://www.pravitelstvo. gov.ru/minister/article-vvp1.html.
2 M. Mazower (1999) *Dark continent. Europe's twentieth century*, Harmondsworth: Penguin.
3 S. Holmes (1996) 'Cultural legacies or state collapse? Probing the postcommunist dilemma', in M. Mandelbaum (ed.) *Postcommunism: four perspectives*, New York: Council for Foreign Relations.
4 B. Jessop (1990) *State theory. Putting capitalist states in their place*, University Park, PA: Pennsylvania State University Press, p. 340.
5 This is a composite definition based on J.A. Hall and G. John Ikenberry (1989) *The state*, Milton Keynes: Open University Press, pp. 1–2; Jessop, *op. cit.*, p. 341; in M. Mann (1988) 'The autonomous power of the state: its origins, mechanisms and results', in M. Mann, *States, war and capitalism. Essays in political sociology*, Oxford: Blackwell.
6 The distinction between these types of regime and state organization is made in T. Ertman (1997) *Birth of the Leviathan. Building states and regimes in early modern Europe*, Cambridge: Cambridge University Press, pp. 6–10. For an alternative discussion of the concepts in relation to the USSR see, G.M. Easter (2000) *Reconstructing the state. Personal networks and elite identity in Soviet Russia*, Cambridge: Cambridge University Press.
7 The distinction between infrastructural and despotic forms of state power is drawn in Mann, 'The autonomous power of the state ...'. Discussions of the two categories can be found, *inter alia*, in Hall and Ikenberry, *op. cit.*, and L. Weiss and J.M. Hobson (1995) *States and economic development. A comparative historical analysis*, Cambridge: Polity.
8 For an analysis of the ways that autonomy is constructed and exercised in democratic states see E.A. Nordlinger (1981) *On the autonomy of the democratic state*, Cambridge, Mass: Harvard University Press.
9 P. Evans (1995) *Embedded autonomy: states and industrial transformation*, Princeton, NJ: Princeton University Press
10 D. Rueschemeyer, E. Huber Stephens and J.D. Stephens (1992) *Capitalist development and democracy*, Cambridge: Polity, p. 63.
11 Weiss and Hobson, *op. cit.*, pp. 6–7.
12 On the idea of 'democratic peace' see M.E. Brown, S.M Lynn-Jones and S.E. Miller (eds) (1996) *Debating the democratic peace. An International Security reader*, Cambridge, MA: The MIT Press.
13 Ertman, *op. cit.*, pp. 8, 27
14 Sometimes these ideas are held as beliefs, sometimes they are adopted by people for career reasons and sometimes they are just honoured out of fear. It does not matter why people adhere to an ideology in an absolutist-bureaucratic state, only that they have to.
15 For a fuller description of how this worked in the USSR, see N. Robinson (1995) *Ideology and the collapse of the Soviet system. A critical history of Soviet ideological discourse*, Aldershot: Edward Elgar, pp. 13–29.

16 For a more substantial treatment of this point, see M. Olson (2000) *Power and prosperity. Outgrowing communist and capitalist dictatorships*, New York: Basic Books.

17 In the United Kingdom, a rough political settlement between monarch and parliament in the seventeenth century gradually became established as a constitutional order, albeit without a written constitution, and patrimony was slowly transformed into bureaucracy in the nineteenth and twentieth centuries.

18 An example of the former would be the United Kingdom, where neither monarch nor parliament had the desire or ability to supplant the other totally so that over time bureaucracy came to be seen as a more effective form of organizing administration than patrimonialism. Italy, where factors such as membership of the European Union, participation in NATO and the involvement of the USA helped to secure a constitutional regime, albeit one staffed by political cronies for much of the post-War period, would be an example of the latter.

2 The limits of absolutism

Tsarism and Soviet socialism

The history of Russia in the twentieth century is bound up with that of two other, greater, political entities: the multiethnic Tsarist empire and its replacement, the Union of Soviet Socialist Republics (USSR) that was born in the chaos of revolution in 1917 and formally constituted by the Union treaty of 1922. Russia was the largest part of both of these states and their history is its history to a degree that would not be true of other parts of the Tsarist empire or USSR, many of which enjoyed brief periods of independence from the USSR, or retained stronger independent political traditions than Russia. For many Russians, Russia was (and for some still is) coterminous with the Tsarist empire and the USSR. In administrative terms this was certainly the case: the Tsarist state was the chief political authority in Russia; the most important political body in the USSR, the Communist Party of the Soviet Union (CPSU, known before 1952 as the Bolshevik Party and the Communist Party), had branches in all of the republics of the USSR except Russia, where regional party organizations reported directly to the central party leadership. It is therefore impossible to tell the story of Russia without telling that of the Tsarist empire and the USSR. It is only towards the end of the USSR, in 1990 when the newly elected Russian parliament declared 'sovereignty', that a specifically Russian polity began to emerge and the Russians – that is the people of the Russian Federation, rather than just ethnic Russians – found themselves in a state that was separate from the states inhabited by the peoples of Ukraine and Belarus, Transcaucasia, Central Asia and the Baltic littoral.

This chapter reviews the fate of both the Tsarist and Soviet states. It is necessarily schematic in approach, concentrating on internal political developments and efforts at building a state that could deal with change and the challenges of building a modern economy.[1] International affairs were very important in shaping the way that Tsarist and Soviet authorities dealt with these challenges. Tsarism, as will soon be apparent, was laid low by international events that prompted its modernization and downfall. Fear of invasion between 1917 and 1941, and international competition in the Cold War after 1945, greatly shaped the USSR's development and fate. However, for reasons of space and because international competition was a constant pressure on

Russian and Soviet political leaders (see Chapter 5), we will concentrate on how internal political forces and processes produced state formations that ultimately lacked the capacity to adapt to new circumstances and therefore failed to survive through to today.

The failure of the Tsarist state

Tsarism's failure was revealed by its inability to compete with its international rivals. This failure was first apparent when Russia fought and lost a war – the Crimean War of 1853–1856 – against France, the United Kingdom and Turkey on its own territory. The Crimean War exposed the inadequacies of the Tsarist state and Russian economy. The army was in need of modernization and Russia needed to develop its industrial and transportation infrastructures if it was to be able to both defend itself and act as a great power in the world as its rulers desired. Ironically, the roots of failure in the Crimean War and subsequently were the product of earlier state building successes. If Russia was backward in comparison to its competitors by the mid-nineteenth century, if it had a rigid autocratic system of government and an entrenched nobility that was resistant to change and jealous of its privileges, this was because of the Tsars' earlier successes in building an absolutist-patrimonial state to control the vast territories that comprised the Russian empire by the 1850s.

The Tsarist state developed as an absolutist-patrimonial empire out of the principality of Muscovy. Muscovy rose to pre-eminence amongst the competing principalities of Russia in the fifteenth century when it annexed its main rivals, and in the sixteenth century, became the centre of an empire through the conquest of the Kazan, Astrakhan and Siberia, and the start of its expansion into the southern steppe and towards the Pacific Ocean (reached in 1639). The initiation of empire building posed several problems for the Tsars. The vast territory they controlled was surrounded by hostile states like Poland and Ottoman Turkey, and by 'empty' steppe inhabited by nomadic tribes and other self-governing peoples like the Cossacks. Both sets of neighbours posed military problems for Russia's rulers. Russia's state rivals sought to control territory deemed to be Russian, whilst nomadic tribes and the Cossacks were prone to raid Russia's settled areas. Moreover, the steppe was an area to which people – like the Russians and Ukrainians who formed the Cossack bands – might flee and put themselves beyond the political and economic control of the Tsar.

The Tsars' need to control this vast territory created a series of social and political institutions that were classically absolutist-patrimonial in form and that enabled the Tsars to fend off their foreign rivals, consolidate their control over the Russian people and territory, and extend their Empire over the Eurasian landmass. Tsarist success was based on two social institutions: serfdom and the service nobility. The service nobility was created to staff the army and the bureaucracy and was rewarded with territory conquered in the

South. Serfdom was founded to limit population movement and took two forms: peasants were either owned by nobles, who were given grants of land in return for service, or by the state (that is the Tsar) who taxed them for revenue and used the monies raised to support the court and the army, which for much of the Tsarist period was the main institution of the state. Serfdom developed between '1550 and 1650 ... at the very time when the monarchy ... emerged as the absolute master of the country. Like compulsory service for the landowning class, peasant serfdom represented a stage in the transformation of Russia into a royal domain.'[2] Russia's service nobility and serf peasantry thus emerged just as some societies in Western Europe were moving away from serfdom towards free labour and as new commercial and urban groups began the long struggle to secure property rights and civil liberties from the arbitrary depredations of autocrats

Change therefore came slowly to Russia in comparison to the transformation of Western Europe from the sixteenth century onwards. What passed for modernization in Russia, for example, the reforms of Peter II ('the Great', ruled 1689–1725) and Catherine II ('the Great', ruled 1762–1796) was directed at increasing the effectiveness of the Russian state in international competition by building up some native military industries, increasing political control over the Orthodox Church and improving the education of nobles who would serve the state. In short, modernization was to strengthen the capacity of the state to implement the Tsar's wishes and it shored up the absolutist-patrimonial system rather than laying the foundations of a modern bureaucracy. Even when the link between noble service and land tenure was broken in 1785, the basic shape of the absolutist-patrimonial state remained in place; the powerful, those with land and status, had little interest in systemic change. The nobility might turn against individual Tsars, but they depended upon the continuance of autocratic government to ensure their social position, and competed for imperial favour for social and economic advancement. Government was thus an activity of the few, who possessed office due to royal and noble birth and who used their proprietary officeholding to maintain the wealth and power of their families. The state was consequently isolated from the bulk of the population. Even the Russian word for state (*gosudarstvo*) derives from a word for owner (*gosudar*), that came to signify princely authority with the rise of Muscovy, and connoted that the state was the private property of the Tsar and his to command.[3] The range of policies that the Tsar could implement was infinite in theory since there were no institutional constraints on the monarch's power. In practice, and certainly by the end of the eighteenth century, most Tsars shared their nobles' outlook and concerns and were content to rule with their nobles and use noble patronage networks to supplement government agencies in their administration of the population.

This system received a shock with the loss of the Crimean War and underwent changes thereafter. But although the absolutist-patrimonial state was reformed it never fully disappeared and the contours of a replacement for it remained vague. Defeat in the Crimea brought a wave of reform as Alexander II (ruled 1855–1881) introduced, first, the emancipation of the serfs in 1861, and second, the 'Great Reforms', which attempted to reorganize local government and the law. Again, as with the earlier reforms of Peter II and Catherine II, Alexander's reforms, and the efforts to stimulate the Russian economy that followed later, were designed to increase the effectiveness of the Russian state as an autocratic system, in particular to augment its military power. The hope for serf emancipation was that it would produce a more prosperous peasantry, which would be loyal to the regime and would provide an agricultural surplus that could be used to invest in Russian industry and communications, and to modernize its armed forces. The Great Reforms were designed to improve the efficiency of the state and to increase its support amongst the population. Most important were the establishment of the *zemstvos*, local government assemblies established in 1864 and 1870 to give landowners and urban businessmen and professionals a voice in government.

The emancipation of the serfs and the Great Reforms both brought about massive changes to Russian society, but not necessarily in the fashion that Alexander II or his advisers had hoped. The problem in both cases was that the reforms did not satisfy expectations because they were bolted on to the existing system and thus only weakly moved Russia away from absolutist-patrimonialism. Change was limited because the Tsar and many of his advisers did not want to reform rapidly and because the Tsarist state lacked the administrative machinery and capacity to manage rapid change. The Great Reforms did increase the participation of some groups in the political process, but this liberalization did not legitimize state power generally. Indeed, the reforms and the emancipation often raised expectations that the Tsarist state then either could not, or would not, meet. In particular, many members of Russia's intelligentsia felt that they had no place in the Tsarist system no matter how it was reformed and saw the suffering of the people as only resolvable by the complete destruction of the autocracy and noble privilege. Alexander II's reign was thus marked by student protest and terrorism, which culminated in his assassination in 1881. Some of the progress in political reform made by Alexander was subsequently reversed by his more conservative successors, but terrorism and agitation for social revolution were never quelled. A liberal alternative to Tsarism was thus unable to develop fully from within the Tsarist system to become its credible replacement. Part of the intelligentsia turned away from any compromise with the Tsarist system, whilst 'within system' reformers were constrained by the half-heartedness of reforms, which meant that they had little chance of building a mass movement in support of change. The *zemstvos* were never able to develop into mass representative institutions because the number of people represented in local assemblies was very small. In Moscow, for example, only 0.5 per cent of the population was entitled to vote in the city assembly elections in 1912.[4] Although the franchise for elections to the nationwide Duma (parliament) introduced after the 1905 revolution was wider than this (see pp. 27–8), the

Tsar was to remain at the centre of government decision-making and moves to extend participation in governance were thus blunted. This limited the possibility of peaceful development away from autocracy and absolutism, but also meant that reform was unable to draw on the goodwill and energies of the Russian people to carry it through.

Emancipation was equally vague in its modernizing results. Freed peasants were granted land but had to make redemption payments on it to the state and to their landlords and they received less land on average than they had tilled before emancipation. Traditional village communes (*mir* and *obshchina*) were maintained in order to ensure continuity in tax payments to the state. This meant that there was little change in farming practices; land was distributed through the commune and peasants had little incentive to invest in it. Redemption and tax payments placed a heavy financial burden on the peasantry and many soon fell into arrears. It was only in 1907, after the 1905 revolution, that redemption payments were finally waived. The state was also slow to provide credit to the peasantry with which improvements in farming could be made. Finally, the rural population of European Russia rose between 1863 and 1897 from 50 to 79 million, increasing the strain on peasant households in some areas as they had to rent land or borrow money to buy more land. The lot of some peasants did improve after emancipation in some areas, but improvement was far from uniform and the peasant economy was a poor source of investment resources for industrialization and military modernization.

The results of Alexander's reforms were thus ambiguous. There was some growth in the Russian economy between 1861 and the 1890s, but it was not until the 1890s that the Russian state began a major effort at modernization under Count Witte, the Minister of Finance between 1892 and 1903. Witte's policies produced a major spurt of industrial growth by supporting the development of the country's economic infrastructure. In particular, Witte encouraged the building of railways and of industries that supplied the railways with locomotives, rails, metals etc., and of arms industries. Witte also endeavoured to stabilize the rouble by putting it on the gold standard. This was designed to facilitate foreign investment in Russia that would compensate for the state's poor revenue base (there were limits to what could be extracted from the peasantry), and consequent inability to maintain investment in Russian industry over any period of time. The state was the primary customer for capital goods (those goods used in production, as opposed to consumption by individuals) and the expense put a serious strain on the state's budget in the late 1890s and early 1900s.

The results of Witte's campaign to modernize Russia were impressive in many respects as industrial production rose in the 1890s by an average of 8 per cent a year.[5] However, despite this impressive period of growth Russian production per capita remained below that of the major European powers and the USA. Indeed, in some respects Russia was falling further behind its competitors despite the efforts of Witte. The per capita industrial output figures for Germany, another relatively late industrialiser in the nineteenth century, are far more impressive than Russia's, for example, and there is evidence that some other late industrialising states performed better than Russia in this period. Despite Witte, the gap between Russia and the more advanced world powers did not narrow between 1861 and the start of World War I: all of Russia's major European rivals, and the USA, then still an emergent superpower, increased their relative wealth in comparison to Russia during this period.[6] The Tsarist state thus promoted economic change but was not a particularly effective instigator of change in comparison to its rivals. Fatally, Tsarism's failure had both an international and a domestic dimension. It could not create either an effective military machine and compete in the power politics of the imperialist age, nor could it bring forth a more fully developed modern society that could support a political order to peacefully and gradually replace it.

Internationally, the failure of the Tsarist state to be an effective instigator of modernization was demonstrated by a military disaster that was as humiliating as the defeat in the Crimea: the Russo-Japanese War of 1904–1905. The cause of the war was an imperialist dispute over Manchuria and Korea, areas that both states sought to control.[7] Russia's path to war was eased by court politics: economic interests at court dissuaded Nicholas II (ruled 1894–1917) from compromising with Japan and military leaders flattered Nicholas's imperial ambitions and expected that their influence would rise with an easy victory over what was believed to be an 'inferior' enemy. Initially, there was popular support for the war, but this soon evaporated. The war was another example of the incompetence of the Tsarist system as well as its failure to restore the basis of the country's military power after the Crimean defeat. The army's weapons, commanders (appointed through royal patronage rather than because of proven competence), and tactics were all inadequate, and supply proved as much as a problem as it had in the Crimea 50 years previously. The Japanese inflicted a series of defeats on the Russians and Nicholas was forced to accept a humiliating peace treaty.

The defeat in the Russo-Japanese war marked the failure of the Tsarist system in its own terms; it was not what it desired to be, a major imperial power able to compete with its rivals in global politics. Its domestic failure was of another sort. In failing to be an effective instigator of modernization, the Tsarist state created a socioeconomic system that was dissatisfied with the political order, but which was unable to force change on it, or constrain it from further foreign adventures and disasters. The gap between state and people grew in Russia at the start of the twentieth century, rather than narrowed, as modernization did not create new sources of support for the Tsar, but gradually alienated all of society from him. Where modernization produced urban, capitalist economies in Western Europe in the years before World War I, Russia remained a predominantly rural and peasant society, with 83 per cent of the Russian population still living in the countryside in 1917.[8] Russia's drive towards modernization thus created a different form of capitalism to that of its main rivals. Capitalism did not replace traditional forms of social organization, but was laid on top of them to create a complex and instable society. Industrialization in Russia did not create a strong property-owning middle class able and willing to exert itself politically and socially because of its economic wealth. There were some very rich and prominent capitalists in Russia after the 1890s, and there was a large degree of regional variance in the fortunes and outlook of entrepreneurs. However, in general, Russian capitalists were dependent on the state and on foreign capital. As we have already noted, the government was the main market for much of Russia's industrial production and big businesses co-operated with the government and were supported by it as it attempted to modernize the armed forces.[9] Foreigners lent both to the government in the form of bonds and to Russian industry. Geopolitical considerations played a large part in this lending as from the 1890s onwards France sought to bind Russia to it in an anti-German alliance by becoming the main lender to the Russian government. Dependence on the government and the linkage between its borrowing and foreign policy thus ensured that both industrial development and the political activities of many industrialists were shaped by the aspirations of the Tsar and his advisers. Even when the Russian middle classes (for want of a better term) began to protest against the autocracy as they did in the first years of the twentieth century and especially after the military disasters of the Russo-Japanese war, they were not strong enough to deliver a credible political alternative to Tsarism. Instead they compromised with it out of fear of the anger displayed by peasants and workers in the course of protests against the Tsarist state and the disorder that these protests brought with them. Modernization thus only brought equivocal, and weak, support for the Tsarist system from new social groups.

The alienation of peasants and workers from the Tsarist system also had its roots in the weakness of the Tsarist state. Being administratively weak and possessing only a relatively small bureaucracy to rule a huge and diverse territory, the autocracy could not manage the social dimensions of modernization effectively. Despite the growth of its economy between the end of the nineteenth century and World War I, Russia did not develop mechanisms to redistribute some of the wealth created by development to ease the social pressures caused by the growth of its towns. The state, fixated as it was on military development, did not support redistribution to alleviate the poverty that much of the population lived in, and jealously guarded sources of revenue so that local authorities were hampered in any efforts that they made at improving the lot of the people. As a result, Moscow, for example, was 'the unhealthiest city in Europe'. It had a death rate of 26.9 per 10,000 of its population in 1910, at least 10 per 10,000 higher than the death rates in Paris, Vienna and Berlin, and infant mortality was 50–75 per cent greater than in Western Europe.[10] Where welfare was provided to the poor, it was either by the *zemstvos*, which were constrained in what they could do by a lack of resources, or by charities, and was an *ad hoc* and inadequate response to social deprivation.

The social costs of modernization that were borne by the mass of the Russian people meant the political distance that had existed between the state and people under serfdom was not closed in the late nineteenth century. Change and new forms of urban poverty that it brought exposed popular myths about the personal benevolence of the Tsar. These myths had previously excused the state in the person of the Tsar for responsibility for the excesses of his officials on the grounds that he did not know what they were doing in his name, and made some protest against the state possible since rebels could argue that disobedience was permissible if it alerted the Tsar to the failings of the state and enabled him to correct them. This mythic image of the Tsar fell apart under pressure from modernization. Traditional forms of social organization and regulation could not manage many of the new social problems created by urbanization. The weakness of representative institutions like the *zemstvos* – which did not represent workers or peasants who were not entitled to vote – meant that there were no institutions capable of mediating between the people and the state, or of controlling protest when it happened by assimilating popular demands and letting them have even some weak influence on policy. Protest brought the people face to face with the only state institution that could be brought into play by the Tsar and his advisers to control social protest, the military; the absolutist-patrimonial state's inability to manage change made it more reliant on coercion to manage social problems.

The clearest example of this, and the moment at which the myth of the good Tsar was finally dispelled, came on 'Bloody Sunday' January 1905, when an Orthodox priest, Father Gapon, led a peaceful demonstration of workers and their families to ask Nicholas II for a limit to the working week, some welfare rights for workers, an end to redemption payments, and some moderate political reforms such as equality before the law and an end to arbitrary government. The form that this demonstration took was conservative: 'no one believed more than Father Gapon in the bond between Tsar and people'.[11] The January 1905 march of workers and their families was like a religious procession, with the crowd displaying icons and portraits of the Tsar, and asking for the Tsar's intercession against the state in favour of 'his' people. Neither the Tsar personally, nor the state of which he was in charge, were prepared to countenance the demonstrators' demands since in parts, and unwittingly, they aimed at the very core of the absolutist-patrimonial system: the arbitrariness of autocratic rule, the dependence of legislative activity and decision making on royal whim and prerogative. Gapon was ordered to cancel the march and when he did not the response of the state, in the absence of other means of dealing with the protest, was to repress it violently with great loss of life.[12]

'Bloody Sunday' sparked the 1905 revolution as revulsion at the suppression of a peaceful demonstration and disgust at the military failures in the war against Japan combined to create a wave of strikes and peasant rebellion across Russia. The revolution of 1905 was a 'moment of truth' as both the failures of the Tsarist system and the weaknesses of the opposition to it were laid bare.[13] The peasantry endeavoured to seize the land that they thought had been denied them in the emancipation settlement and to destroy the property of landowners in the hope that this would prevent them from returning and taking up their position of dominance in rural society. Worker protests were concerned to improve their lot, to secure rights to representation by trade unions and the vote, and were for the creation of national representative institutions. A general strike in October 1905 led to the creation of Soviets (councils) in Russia's main towns. These were spontaneous creations of the working class and brought together workers and members of Russia's socialist opposition, including Lenin's Bolsheviks, and were chaotic attempts at self-rule and direct democracy. Liberal politicians from the *zemstvos*, and their supporters from the middle classes shared workers' political demands, although were less happy about the manner of their protests.

The revolution failed because these protests were not co-ordinated and because the army remained loyal despite the disasters of the Russo-Japanese war. The army's loyalty enabled the Tsar – or rather Witte to whom the Tsar finally turned – to pursue a strategy of divide and rule. At the same time that the workers were trying to create alternative political institutions to autocracy during their general strike, the Tsar issued the October Manifesto, which promised civil rights, an elected national Duma, and cabinet government. This promise of constitutional monarchy split the liberal and the worker opposition. The liberals could not control the strike movement and prevent its radicalization, and were disturbed by the threat of political violence as fighting broke out between the left and the Tsar's supporters in Moscow following the proclamation of the October Manifesto. The liberals therefore abandoned the strike movement; some of them joined the government at Witte's request, whilst others looked forward to the election of the national Duma and founded political parties, such as the Octobrist Party that was named after the manifesto, to compete for seats in it. Once liberal and worker opposition were divided, the Tsar was able to use the army to suppress urban revolt and the Soviets. The suppression of the workers' revolution was followed by the restoration of autocracy in the countryside. Although it was extensive and often more violent than the disorders in the towns, the peasant rebellion was against the emancipation settlement, rather than a positive political protest in favour of a new order. It therefore had no real political leadership or organization, and peasant protest was suppressed over the course of 1905 and 1906.

Although the autocracy had nearly fallen during 1905, Nicholas II learnt few lessons from the revolution. Witte, the architect of the compromise with the liberals that had brought the revolution to an end, was soon removed as Prime Minister. Nicholas was the personification of the limits to the adaptability of the absolutist-patrimonial state. He sincerely believed that there was a divine link between himself and the people and continued to do so even after the events of 1905 had disabused many Russians of any such notion.[14] Nicholas therefore continued to try to rule as an unconstrained autocrat after 1905 and preserve the autocracy for the 'good' of the people and the nation. He tried to emasculate the Duma and to support conservatives against his own ministers to prevent more extensive reform of government.

There was ample scope for autocratic interference in government under the terms of the October Manifesto. Despite the creation of a Duma, the Tsar still appointed the government, could veto legislation and appointed half of the upper house of the new legislature, the State Council. Nicholas refused to compromise with the first and second Dumas, which wanted compulsory land redistribution, and they were dissolved in July 1906 and June 1907. The new Prime Minister, Petr Stolypin, then changed the electoral law so that peasants, workers and national minorities had less say in the Duma's composition. The third Duma, convened in November 1907, was consequently more conservative than its predecessors and less representative of the nation. The fate of the first and second Dumas indicates that social and economic reform after 1905 were partial. Stolypin believed that the solution to Russia's problems was to create a stratum of land-owning private farmers who would be prosperous and loyal to the regime. To this end, Stolypin set about breaking up the peasant communes, the *mir* and *obshchina*. Since he could not get agreement from the first and second Duma on reform, Stolypin decreed that heads of peasant households could henceforth claim the land that they held under communal tenure as their private property.[15] Stolypin's reforms were, however, only a partial success. In 1916, 61 per cent of peasant households held their land communally; this was a drop of 16 per cent from 1905, but the peasantry was still a long way from being transformed into private landowners.[16] Nor was the countryside at peace during this time. Despite the brutal suppression of the peasant revolts of 1905, there were more than 17,000 rural disturbances in European Russia between 1910 and 1914.[17]

The changes that followed 1905 did not, therefore, lead to any expansion of the social base of the autocracy through the creation of a prosperous rural class of farmers, nor did they create a legitimate constitutional monarchy. The outline of a constitutional order was instead grafted on to the older forms of the Tsarist absolutist-patrimonial polity. In time this graft may have put down deep roots and served to constrain the Tsar and begin to limit his freedom of action. In the short time between 1905 and the outbreak of World War I, this did not happen and Russia remained a polarized society with the basic structures of absolutism intact. The outbreak of World War I temporarily healed some of Russia's divisions under a wave of patriotic feeling. Russia even scored some successes in the early battles of the war. Soon, however, Russian weaknesses resurfaced. Russia's troops were poorly equipped and supplied in comparison to their enemies and were frequently badly led. Russian industry could not cope with the demands of a modern war and yet again, its transport infrastructure proved unable to bring troops, weapons and supplies to the front. Nicholas's response was disastrous. In September 1915, he took personal charge of the Russian army and suspended the Duma; Nicholas was determined to rule as an autocrat once more unencumbered by any pretence at constitutional constraint. With Nicholas at army headquarters, power over the government in Petrograd (as St Petersburg had been renamed at the onset of war) passed to his wife, Alexandra, who was under the influence of Rasputin, a charismatic monk of dubious reputation (to say the least).

Rasputin's influence on Alexandra, the changes in government that were instigated by them, the disastrous conduct of the war split the autocracy from liberal support and from much of its conservative support. The hardships of the war – the loss of life, the shortages caused by the disruptions to trade and the inadequate supply system – exacerbated Russia's social divisions and urban poverty. Matters came to a head in February 1917 when protests against food shortages turned in to political demonstrations. Unlike in 1905, the army did not stay loyal: as the protests against the Tsar grew, the army transferred its loyalty to the demonstrators and troops ordered to go to the capital to resort order refused to go. Soviets were reformed at popular behest and Duma leaders created a Provisional Government under Prince Lvov. Nicholas tried to abdicate in favour of his younger brother, but when he declined power passed to Lvov and the Provisional Government.

The re-emergence of the Soviets at the same time that power passed from the Tsar through the Duma to the Provisional Government created a situation of 'dual power'. The Provisional Government and the Soviets divided political authority between them; moderates recognized the Provisional Government as the legitimate successor to Nicholas, but the Soviet enjoyed popular support from workers and soldiers in the important political centres of Petrograd and Moscow. In a way, neither was able to develop as the centre of a powerful set of institutions in 1917. The Provisional Government was unable to consolidate its grip on power because of the radicalization of the popular revolution over the course of 1917. The Soviets did not develop as independent institutions because they were dominated first by moderate socialists and then by the radical left. As a result, they were prisoners of the radicalization of the popular revolution; as popular support for moderates declined and radical socialist parties began to gain in support, the Soviets membership changed and they did not develop into stable institutions capable of effecting compromise between Russia's competing political camps.

The demands of the popular revolution in 1917 were multiple. Peasants – as usual – wanted land and over the course of 1917 took matters into their own hands. Property was redistributed through the communes, which reasserted their hegemony over village life. Workers wanted better conditions and were soon radicalized and calling for a democratization of the factories through worker self-management. Workers' primary loyalty was to the Soviets that they reformed in February and which they saw as the organs of government best suited to fulfil their demands. Nearly everyone wanted an end to Russia's involvement in the war and most soldiers wanted to return home, especially as the redistribution of land began in the villages. The Provisional Government did not try to satisfy any of these demands since the parties that formed it wished to honour its international commitments to its war allies and argued that reform should be delayed until the war was won. This was a disastrous position. The army disintegrated as both a defensive force against Germany and as a force for internal control as soldiers deserted. Peasant revolution and land seizures denied the government control over much of the countryside, robbed it of resources, and exacerbated the crisis in the towns as food supplies dwindled. Workers confronted their bosses over factory management and were radicalized.

The only success that the Provisional Government had was a negative one: it compromised Russia's moderate socialist parties, the Mensheviks (a rival socialist party that had split with Lenin's Bolsheviks in 1903) and the Right Social Revolutionaries (SRs). Initially, these parties dominated the Soviets that had reappeared in February. From this position, they moderated some of the demands made by workers and soldiers and constrained the workers' militias that had been formed in February. As the Provisional Government faltered, the moderates joined it in May 1917 to give it some popular legitimacy, but lost credibility with the masses as a result. The popular revolution began to take its lead from radical socialist forces such as the Left SRs, the anarchists, and especially from the Bolsheviks, whose slogans of 'All Power to the Soviets' and 'Bread, Peace and Land' neatly summarized the demands of the popular revolution and whose leader, Vladimir Lenin, had an unparalleled record of opposition to the war. The Provisional Government was nearly overthrown in July 1917 when mass protest broke out in Petrograd after the failure of an offensive organized by Alexander Kerensky, Lvov's successor as Prime Minister. One of the reasons that the July disturbances did not bring the Provisional Government down was that Lenin did not want to launch his party's bid for power until it commanded majority support in the Petrograd Soviet and all-Russian Congress of Soviets. In short, Lenin did not want to take power in the name of the Soviets when they were still dominated by moderates who supported the Provisional Government; he wanted a stark contrast between the Soviets and the Provisional Government so that 'dual power' could be resolved in favour of the Soviets with the Bolshevik party in a dominant position inside them.

Lenin did not have long to wait for his wish to come true. Like Nicholas II after 1905, Kerensky did not learn from his mistakes. Although the Bolshevik cause was set back by the party's suppression after July, it soon gathered fresh support as Kerensky failed to bring Russia out of the war. The ground for a Bolshevik seizure of power was laid by their attaining majorities in the Petrograd and Moscow Soviets and their expectation of commanding a majority at the all-Russian Congress of Soviets due to meet in October 1917. The party was further strengthened by its re-emergence from the underground and the arming of its supporters in response to the threat of a right-wing coup led by General Lavr Kornilov in August. The Kornilov revolt, although a fiasco, showed that the Provisional Government was detached both from the right and the left and had no social support base in Russia's polarized society. The threat from Kornilov led Kerensky to allow the recreation of the workers' militias, now labelled Red Guards under the command of the Petrograd Soviet's Military Revolutionary Committee. Kerensky thereby armed the very group that would overthrow him. At Lenin's urging, the Bolshevik party accepted the need to seize power in the name of the Soviets and proclaim it at the October Congress of Soviets, and the Petrograd Soviet's Military Revolutionary Committee under the leadership of Leon Trotsky, organized the seizure of power in Petrograd and the capture of the Winter Palace and the Provisional Government.

The formation of the Soviet system, 1917–1953

The Bolshevik seizure of power in October 1917 was a close-run thing. The Bolsheviks did not command the support of the majority of the Russian population, or the support of many of the subject nationalities of the old empire. Lenin was persuaded to allow elections for the Constituent Assembly (the representative body that was supposed to replace the Provisional Government) in November 1917 and the Bolsheviks gained only a quarter of the seats. Their lack of majority support did not concern the Bolshevik leadership. They had launched their revolution in the expectation that a socialist revolution could not work in an agrarian society like Russia's. The purpose of revolution in Russia, Lenin believed, was to break the chain of imperialism at its weakest link – Russia – and so stimulate revolution globally.[18] The global revolution would then come to the aid of the fledgling socialist state in Russia and help overcome resistance to socialism. Moreover, the Bolsheviks believed that they had taken power in the name of the Soviets and a higher form of democracy than could be guaranteed by a liberal constitution. They therefore regarded the revolution as morally legitimate even if only a minority of the population supported it.

Believing that help for the revolution was on its way from abroad meant that the chief task before the Bolsheviks after they had taken power was to survive. Some room for manoeuvre was gained by delivering some of the demands of the popular revolution; peace was made with Germany and the Bolsheviks decreed that the land belonged to peasants. But these policies did not solve the problems of how to rule and fight a civil war. The Bolsheviks had little experience of administration; they were revolutionaries not bureaucrats. The old state machinery of the Tsarist system had largely collapsed in 1917 and although some of the old bureaucracy and its personnel were taken over by the new regime this was not possible across Russia as a whole. The party did not have strong organizations in large parts of the country. Both party and state had to be created from scratch, therefore, as Bolshevik control over Russia grew with the rolling-back of White armies. The first steps at building a new state were thus taken amidst confusion and chaos. However, four basic traits of a new order soon emerged to ensure survival and establish the basic characteristics of the Soviet regime as an absolutist-bureaucratic state formation.

First, the party secured its hold on power by ruthlessly suppressing threats. The Cheka, the first version of the Soviet secret police, was established in December 1917. In January 1918, the Bolsheviks closed down the Constituent Assembly at its first session, in June they removed the Right SRs and the Mensheviks from the all-Russian Central Executive Committee of Soviets, and in July they suppressed their allies, the Left SRs, when they protested the growing dictatorship and the peace with Germany. From mid-1918, the Bolsheviks ruled alone. Moreover, as the Civil War spread, political repression grew into the 'Red Terror', mass social control through the suppression of 'class enemies'. Despotic power was therefore the first major creation of the Soviet state and it relied on violence for social control in the face of widespread political, social and military opposition.

Second, the party expanded its role after October 1917 to become the manager of the economy and supervisor of all state bodies from the army and secret police, to local councils, educational establishments, and of all other public associations and institutions, like trade unions.[19] An expansion of the party's roles after the revolution had always been implicit in Lenin's ideas on political organization; he believed that there were limits to what people could achieve in revolution without leadership, and his idea of Soviet 'democracy' did not entertain the idea of political pluralism.[20] The party's role post-revolution was therefore always going to involve the ideological policing of both state and society to ensure that socialist development took a correct path. The Civil War enlarged this ideological inclination into an effort at making the party omnipresent: from the Civil War onwards the party was a dominant presence in all state institutions and its will prevailed in decision making in all state bodies. The party thus developed into 'the nucleus' of the Soviet political system as Article Six of the 1977 Soviet Constitution was to describe it.[21] The means by which the party spread its control were not just ideological. It also controlled all job placements through the *nomenklatura* system to ensure the loyalty of all important public officials. Literally, the *nomenklatura* system was a list of important jobs filled by party appointees, although in popular and academic parlance it has come to stand for the Soviet elite more generally. The development of the *nomenklatura* system eroded the distinction between party and state. The unification of the two was not finalized until the 1930s, but from the outset of Soviet power, the party's expanded roles meant that there was a concentration of both executive and legislative/decision-making power in the hands of the party and its leadership. This gave the USSR an absolutist system despite the fact that from 1923 onwards it had a series of constitutions that delineated the legislative and executive responsibilities of party and state bodies.

Third, the party changed the character of the revolution. The popular revolution and its democratic spirit faded away after 1917 as its energy was diverted though mass mobilization by the Bolsheviks and stifled by a concentration of decision-making powers in the party. Soviets declined as effective representative institutions due to party control over their membership and activities. The Red Army, organized by Trotsky, replaced the popular militias and Red Guards of 1917 as the military organization of the revolution and military discipline replaced the rough soldiers' democracy of 1917. Likewise, the reintroduction of one-man management and the suborning of trade unions to help organize production instead of protecting workers' rights curtailed democracy in the factories. Economic activity became dedicated to the war effort and was centrally directed (where possible in the chaos of the war years) by VSNKh, the Supreme Economic Council. The distinction between military and civil policy blurred. The Bolshevik policy style was the same in both their efforts to defeat the Whites and their foreign allies on the battlefield, and in their struggle to gather resources for war; the people were mobilized through military-style campaigns to confront a problem whether civilian or military, and once it had been 'defeated', the next pressing problem was selected and 'attacked'. The party itself became militarized with party members adopting military style dress – such as the uniformed garb favoured by Stalin and some other leaders into the 1950s – and bearing arms.

Finally, party oversight of all economic and political activity stretched its administrative capacity. As a result, party workers were forced to improvise administration and decide which orders from the centre they would implement and which they would pay lip service to. With a deficit of personnel and resources, they had to find ways of bypassing the bureaucratic hierarchy when it stood in the way of fulfilling important central demands and ensure that there were people they could call on to help them when they needed to switch resources from one task to another to fulfil an assignment from the centre. In short, and despite the fact that they were supposed to work uniformly, party workers adapted policy to local conditions and filled the gap between the party's actual administrative capacity and that needed to win the Civil War by building on personal connections developed during their years of underground struggle against the Tsarist regime.[22] The implementation of policy frequently took place not through bureaucratic hierarchies, but through the delegation of tasks to 'trustworthy and reliable personal associates'.[23] These personal connections developed into networks of linked officials, or 'family circles', as they spread out to control the Soviet state's expanding territory.

The policies of terror, party control and mass mobilization could all be easily justified by the party's ideology: the victims of terror were class enemies, the union of the people and party was deepened through mass mobilization and party control ensured that there was no ideological deviation. Indeed, it was hoped that the mobilization of the people by the party would create a particular form of infrastructural power by breaking down the barriers between political decision making and society, and drawing the mass of the people into the implementation of policy. Improvisation and administration based on networks of officials were not so easy to reconcile with ideology or with the intentions of Soviet leaders. Working through informal channels was not totally alien to the spirit of the party, which portrayed itself as an elite organization that defended the revolution without concern for petty bureaucracy. However, whilst the party could tolerate a degree of informality, too much created a danger of the party losing its identity as an impersonal servant of ideology and hence threatened its organizational integrity. Working through networks of trusted cadres encouraged personal loyalties beyond those to the party and networks based on personal affinity; patronage had the potential to alternative centres of power and could cover for corruption. There was thus a tension in the Soviet system from the first between norms of bureaucratic impersonalism, that were supposed to ensure organizational integrity and lay the basis for state capacity, and patronage and clientelist practices, which created the administrative capacity to implement policies in the midst of crisis and material want.

This issue constantly returned to haunt Soviet leaders and we will examine it again at length below (see pp. 39–41) since it was shaped most fully by developments under Stalin. However, even in the early 1920s it had a direct effect on the development of the Soviet system. Party discipline looked very poor to the central leadership at the end of the Civil War. Shortages and the expansion of the party had created opportunities for corruption and brought opportunists into the ranks of the party. Political divisions were also rife. A series of organized opposition groups – the Left Communists, the Military Opposition, the Democratic Centralists and the Worker's Opposition – emerged during these years to protest some of the actions taken or proposed by Lenin and the central party authorities.

These developments stimulated Lenin to consolidate the power of central party organizations at the end of the Civil War. This involved weakening internal party democracy and helped to set the scene for Stalin's rise to power. Lenin targeted internal party democracy because he thought it necessary to tighten discipline in the party so that it could cope with its domestic and international isolation. Domestically, the party was isolated by the depredations of the Civil War. The working class that had been its bedrock of support in 1917 was dispersed and broken as a social force by the demands that the Bolsheviks had made of them and the hardship of urban life during the war. The peasantry, even where it was not in open revolt as in Tambov province, was distrusted the Bolsheviks. Supplying the towns and the Red Army had involved the coerced expropriation of crops from the peasantry. The whole country had been ravaged by famine and disease, which killed more people than died in the fighting. Popular anger against the party and its policies had been demonstrated by the revolt at Kronstadt in February–March 1921, when previously loyal sailors rebelled and called for the establishment of 'Soviets without communists'. The global revolution that Lenin had expected in 1917 never materialized so that the Soviet state found itself surrounded by hostile capitalist powers. Although there was some rapprochement between the USSR and its capitalist rivals in the early 1920s as diplomatic relations were established, the Soviet leadership saw the world around them as implacably hostile and dedicated to their destruction.

Lenin's solution was to retreat from socialism in economics (there being no resources from abroad to support the building of socialism), but to tighten discipline in the party to ensure its political control over the country. Even as the Kronstadt revolt was being suppressed, he announced the New Economic Policy (NEP) at the 10th Party Congress. NEP allowed some private enterprise to ensure food supplies to the towns and stimulate industrial production. However, Lenin warned that retreat from control over the economy demanded that the party be ever more vigilant in guarding against harmful deviations in political work. To this end the 10th Party Congress adopted a resolution banning factional activity in the party and tightening the subordination of party organizations to the central party authorities. The ban on factions and the increased subordination to the party centre built on efforts to institutionalize party work more effectively that had begun during the Civil War with the creation of the Politburo and a central party apparatus. These measures received a further impetus in 1922 when Joseph Stalin was made General Secretary of the Central Committee of the party and measures where taken to cleanse the party's ranks of careerists, the incompetent and the corrupt, who had joined in the Civil War years. These measures were not always successful as patronage networks and corrupt practices were often firmly entrenched and were only investigated when things reached crisis point.[24] Since Stalin oversaw the administration of the party, efforts to improve the quality of its personnel and increase compliance to central authorities gave him a great deal of power.

NEP improved the supply of goods to the towns and created a slight upturn in the Soviet economy after the ravages of the war years. However, it was not a popular policy with many party members since it was seen as benefiting the peasantry and market traders rather than the workers in whose name the revolution had been made. Party cadres were particularly fearful of the peasantry since the party was weak in the countryside and it was believed that NEP might make the peasantry independent of political control by boosting its economic power. The fate of NEP was thus always in the balance since for many it was not an appropriate answer to the question of how the party might build socialism and how should it govern itself and Russia. Following Lenin's death in 1924, NEP's future became entangled with the question of who should succeed him. The succession struggle was resolved in Stalin's favour by 1929 by guile, policy and the use of the party machine, despite the fact that Lenin's last political testament had advised Stalin's removal from office.

Guile played its part in Stalin's rise to power as Stalin first allied himself with other party leaders against Trotsky and what was dubbed the 'Left Opposition', and then changed tack and picked his former allies off one by one as members of what he labelled the 'Right Opposition'. Policy influenced the succession struggle as Stalin presented himself as the best defender of the revolution. The 'Left Opposition' insisted on the need to wait for international revolution before building socialism. Stalin argued that whilst it was impossible to move to communism (the highest stage of social development in Soviet thinking) without the support of international revolution, it was possible to build 'socialism in one country' because the party could change the social structure of the USSR and construct an urban, industrial economy appropriate to socialism. Indeed, Stalin argued, it was imperative that the party work on these tasks to protect the revolutionary gains made in 1917 and to keep faith with those who had died for the revolution.[25] Adopting this position, Stalin first won support against the 'Left Opposition' from party members who wanted to taste the benefits of revolution without delay, and then defeated the 'Right' by claiming that they were too soft on internal enemies of socialism such as the peasantry and were thus impeding the construction of socialism. The party's weakness in the countryside and the slow growth of industrial production played on all of the party's fears and gave Stalin's arguments substantial support. Party workers believed that the peasantry was withholding grain deliberately to weaken the regime and the economy and that the slow growth of industrial production made the USSR vulnerable to foreign enemies: fascists and virulent anti-communists took control in Italy and Japan in the 1920s, and Hitler – who viewed the Russians as 'sub-humans' and desired their lands for a new German empire – had begun his rise to power. Finally, Stalin's control over the central party machinery helped to weaken his opponents since it gave Stalin control over appointments and linked him to the regional party leaders and their patronage networks.[26] This allowed Stalin to dominate the party at the centre because it gave him support at party Congresses and on the Central Committee.

A mixture of domestic and international concerns thus sealed NEP's fate and Stalin's rise to power. However, the weakness of the party and the state meant that to stimulate the economy it had to fall back on the methods of the Civil War years – terror and mass mobilization directed by a central plan and carried out through military-style campaigns to collectivise agriculture and forcibly industrialise the economy. The peasantry was the first target of the drive to create 'socialism in one country' in 1929. Party workers were dispatched from the cities in a nationwide campaign to destroy private farming and replace it with collective farms. The weakness of the party-state in the countryside meant that it had no other means of confronting and controlling the peasantry except through a military style campaign of collectivization.[27] The campaign was organized around a simple slogan, 'destroy the kulaks [rich peasants] as a class', but whom the kulaks actually were was unclear since distinctions between peasant households were often not great. As a result, kulaks were defined politically: anyone who objected to the seizure of their livestock and the collectivization of their land was classified as a kulak or a kulak sympathizer. The collectivization campaign involved the mass deportation of several million peasants as kulaks or kulak sympathisers and the killing of many others in what was in effect a class war against the peasantry. The basis of the peasant economy was destroyed as grain was seized for delivery to the towns and peasants slaughtered their livestock rather than hand it over to the new collective farms. More livestock was lost in the first year of collectivization than in the whole of the Civil War; between 1928 and 1934 over half the USSR's cattle and pigs, and two-thirds of its sheep and goats perished.[28] Grain requisitions by the state reached record levels, but the destruction of the rural economy was followed by famine in the villages – during which grain was still seized to feed the towns – with the loss of several million more peasant lives.

Terror was not quite so immediately evident in the campaign to industrialise the economy, but it was an equally chaotic process. Nominally, industrial development was planned. The party leadership determined general economic priorities and state agencies such as Gosplan (the State Planning Committee, the successor to VSNKh) and economic ministries divided up responsibility for meeting the general aims of the party between enterprises, taking account of what resources they would need to meet their plan targets, and instructing them as to what investment they could expect and where their output should be delivered. In practice, planning was far more disordered, especially in the early years. This was because Stalin desired spectacular industrial growth to create a military machine capable of resisting foreign intervention and laying the basis of socialism. Five-year plan targets were therefore set high to squeeze the maximum amount out of production from the population and were then raised during the plan period.

The targets for the end of first plan period in 1932 can be seen in Table 2.1 (these are Soviet figures and should therefore be taken as indicative rather than definitive). Since the aim of industrialization was to lay the basis of an industrial economy and to provide for defence production, emphasis was laid on capital goods for use in the new factories that Stalin ordered built; the production of capital goods was to increase threefold and the plan (at least on the figures in Table 2.1) was exceeded. Plan targets in other areas were generally not met, but the increase in so short a period of time was impressive nonetheless. The chief areas that the USSR fell behind in at this time were consumer goods production and the provision of accommodation and services to the population of the rapidly expanding towns.

The main resources used to create the massive growth of the early 1930s were human capital and vast amounts of raw materials that were pumped into the economy. This meant that Soviet economic growth was – and was to remain – extensive, based on increasing the quantity of labour and materials used in production, rather than intensive, based on increasing the productivity

Table 2.1 Selected indicators from the first five-year plan

	Production in 1927–28	Plan target for 1932–33	Actual production in 1932
Capital goods (billions 1926–27 roubles)	6	18.1	23.1
Electricity (billion kwhs)	5.05	22	13.4
Coal (million tons)	35.4	75	64.3
Oil (million tons)	11.7	22	21.4
Iron ore (million tons)	5.7	19	12.1
Pig iron (million tons)	3.3	10	6.2
Steel (million tons)	4	10.4	5.9
Machinery (million 1926–27 roubles)	1822	4688	7362
Total employed labour force (millions)	11.3	15.8	22.8

Source: adapted from Alec Nove (1982) *An economic history of the USSR*, London: Penguin, p. 192.

of labour, or improving the efficiency with which materials are used.[29] Vast labour armies of volunteer and prisoner labour were organized to carry out huge construction projects such as the Volga–White Sea canal, or the building of giant metallurgical plants at Magnitogorsk. The reliance on large increases in workers to ensure growth is reflected in Table 2.1 in the bottom row. The size of the labour force grew far greater than was planned, with particularly high rises in industry and construction, where the numbers employed doubled and trebled in size.[30] This created a problem from which the USSR never resolved: poor labour productivity.[31] Factory managers hoarded labour so that they had spare workers to deal with any new orders coming from above and workers expended a minimum of effort due to the lack of incentives since even where pay was good, there were few goods to buy because of the under-investment in consumer good production. Forced industrialization was also wasteful of raw materials. The plans called for a huge surge in natural resource production, shown in the figures for coal, oil and iron ore production in Table 2.1. These were used profligately by managers since there was no real attempt in the plan to force them to be efficient, or take account of what it cost to produce a good. Output mattered, not what it cost in terms of labour or raw material inputs; the aim of production was to fulfil the plan, rather than to make profit. Factories that were technically bankrupt were not shut down, but were extended further 'soft' credit and investment by the state, monies that did not have to be repaid with interest under threat of closure. Consequently, Soviet factories were never as productive or as efficient as their Western counterparts (see Chapter 4 for a longer discussion of some of these problems).

The problems posed by extensive growth were compounded by other, political problems that the first five-year plan and the collectivization of agriculture created for the Soviet leadership. The demands made of party workers from the late 1920s onwards were immense and they were generally not able to fulfil them. They had to ensure that the areas under their control met economic plan targets that required more skilled labour, more invest- ment and more time than they had at their disposal. Failure in some policy areas was inevitable but there was no possibility of effectively objecting orders and the demands made by the centre because internal party democracy had been destroyed by the changes made at the 10th Party Congress and by the defeat of the 'Left' and 'Right' Oppositions. Moreover, challenging orders would have meant challenging the party and its claim that the orders it issued were rational responses to social needs based on an objective assessment of the situation and the need to build socialism and later communism. Party leaders were thus increasingly put in an untenable position: they could neither fulfil the orders they were given, nor refuse to fulfil them. As a result, they were always in a position where the centre, if it desired, could review their activ- ities, find fault with them and punish them.[32] Moreover, although party workers were supposed to be the ideological vanguard of society, the demands of collectivization and industrialization were such that they spent their time untangling the chaos of the planned economy and acting as bureaucrats.[33] Consequently, party officials saw no difference between their interests, the interests of society, and the interests of the bureaucracy. This left party offi- cials open to censure from their leaders because they were failing to fulfil their role of political leadership and not acting in the interests of socialist construc- tion.

To ward off the threat of censure for either failures of policy implementa- tion or bureaucratic behaviour, party officials once more improvised admin- istration, reinterpreted policy priorities locally and built informal networks to facilitate this and cover it up from higher authorities. Informal networks, as we have seen, had first emerged during the Civil War. In the 1930s the dependency of party and state officials on networks increased. Local party leaders used their patronage networks and 'family circles' of trusted cadres to deal with the demands of forced collectivization and industrialization in the absence of a well founded and resource rich administrative machine.[34] The expansion of party responsibility for economic affairs also extended the reach of patronage as managers sought to 'protect them[selves] from exposure by installing their own clique in strategic positions'.[35] The extension of informal networks and their use to reinterpret policy locally enabled the diversion of resources and effort to those policy areas that were most important to the centre since these were the areas were plan fulfilment would be checked. This increased the tendency to be economically wasteful that the plan created and exacerbated the plan's uneven distribution of resources. Party-state officials robbed low priority projects – generally social welfare projects and consumer goods industries – to over-invest in high priority ones – military and heavy industrial production – and ensure their completion. This reallocation was, of course, illegal since it was not provided for by the plan. However, party officials could interfere freely in the economy to ensure that resources were delivered to high priority projects, covered for those who lost resources and hence could not meet their plan targets, and in turn were covered for by their superiors who were interested in reporting success in important areas rather than failure in unimportant ones; 'both controlled and controllers not infrequently cover[ed] up for each other's sins and omissions in discharging tasks for which they [were] held jointly responsible'; in this way, administrators tried to ensure that they had a 'collective guarantee' that their mistakes were not punished.[36]

The reinterpretation of policy and the cover-ups it entailed were often facilitated by corruption and was always possible because resources could be redistributed around the Soviet system without consideration of their economic value: no one had to make a profit under the plan so resources could be freely used without fear of being caught out as a bankrupt. Consequently, Soviet officials often saw corruption and misuse of office as necessary to making the system work since its 'formal rigidities could only be overcome by informal understandings'; it was also difficult to distinguish in the Soviet system between an action taken to make up for some shortfall in the plan and a corrupt practice.[37] The dangers of this for the Soviet system of absolutist-bureaucracy were that corruption and informal networks weakened state capacity, the effective autonomy of large parts of the political system, and organizational integrity. The latter was impaired as the reinterpretation of policy and corruption meant that sections of the party acted independently of the centre so that the party as a whole lacked a common purpose.[38] Formally, the party-state was autonomous of society in that it worked to fulfil goals set by ideology, but practically large parts of it were 'captured' by the private interests of corrupt bureaucrats. Over time, and as we shall see later, this corruption gradually spread to the highest ranks of the Soviet political system. Capacity was diminished because the centre, by virtue of demanding so much, did not see all its instructions fulfilled. Consequently, it was not able to redistribute resources as it wished; its main priorities were met, but there was a constant shortfall in some area of economic growth, which then impacted in the economy as a whole. Finally, as time progressed, the diminution of autonomy and organizational integrity meant that it was harder to get officials to go along with policies that were designed to reverse this fall in capacity. There was a terrible irony to this. The centre demanded too much of its cadres; this led to the creation of informal political relations that were flexible and capable of delivering some of the policy outcomes desired by the central leadership; cadres involved in these relations were guilty in the eyes of the leadership of failing to work as it required and of acting autonomously in picking out which of its policies to fulfil; the centre tried to correct tendencies to informality by issuing more orders and increasing pressure on its cadres; in doing this it recreated the incentives to improvise administration, work informally and concentrate effort and resources on what were regarded as central priorities. The Soviet system thus forced its cadres to be adaptable by trying to restrict flexibility. Gradually this led to the spread of what Soviet leaders were to condemn as 'formalism': party organs pretended to honour policy whilst in fact they acted in their own interests.

These problems were apparent very early on in the 1930s. In 1934, at the Party Congress called to celebrate the successes of collectivization and industrialization, Stalin complained that 'bureaucrats and red-tapists long ago became skilled hands at demonstrating their loyalty to party and government decisions in words whilst in practice pigeonholing them', and attributed particular blame to regional leaders, 'who have given great service in the past, [but] have become magnates and consider that party and Soviet laws are not written for them but for idiots'.[39] However, even though the problems of the Soviet system were apparent early on, the problem of state capacity developed gradually between the early 1930s and the 1960s. The sheer tempo of development in these years and the vast resources that could be drawn on meant that problems of state capacity, autonomy and organizational integrity was perceived not as structural problems of the Soviet absolutist-bureaucratic state, but as a problem of discipline and incorrect party management. For these reasons, the structural problems of the Soviet absolutist-bureaucratic state also impelled it to turn its coercive apparatus on its own cadres.

The ground for mass terror had been laid in the early 1930s when Stalin expounded a theory that class struggle intensified as socialism was built. Socialism's enemies, Stalin argued, became more dangerous as socialism consolidated because to stop its progress they had to take radical action and because the great expansion of state property through collectivization and industrialization meant that enemies found themselves inside the Soviet state and hence able to work against it from within. This obviously increased the likelihood of repression as the USSR developed, legitimized the use of terror against the party-state itself and made it possible to classify failures of policy implementation as the actions of 'enemies of the people'. After Stalin had faced threats to his power in 1934, theory and paranoia combined with administrative chaos to create a wave of terror that swept through the party, state and society.[40] Millions were arrested, imprisoned and sent to labour camps, or executed on fabricated charges in the 'Great Terror' of 1936–1938. Artistic and intellectual communities were also ravaged in the name of orthodoxy and obedience to the party line, and ordinary people were caught up in a frenzy of denouncements as people tried to prove their loyalty and opportunists settled petty scores. However, and proportionately, the party and state suffered most as Stalin and the NKVD (as the secret police was now known) attacked any independent power base that might act to disagree with Stalin such as the military high command, destroyed the leadership of the party in the provinces, and obliterated the party's Central Committee and the central government.[41]

The terror and the cowed population that it produced marked the high point of the USSR as an absolutist-bureaucratic system. Stalin and the party-state leadership had unparalleled power to allocate resources to their favoured projects and ensure that their orders were met as long as the task at hand was specific and could be closely monitored (a good example would be the rapid construction of the Soviet atomic bomb after World War II). The autonomy of the party-state from social influence was almost total in that the party leadership listened to no voices save their own when making policy. There was thus no possibility of the party being accused of failing to serve the people except when Stalin might indicate that some minion was too much of a bureaucrat as a prelude to their extermination.

However, even at the height of terror there were constraints on the leadership's power. Terror never fully destroyed informal political organization within the party-state, or the reinterpretation of policy locally. Moreover, the party-state's ability to force people to produce more was thwarted by people's retreat into their private worlds. People feared to show initiative and reacted to the pressure put on them to produce by avoiding work where possible, by not caring about the quality of the goods they produced, by changing jobs to try and find an easier life etc. All these actions only provoked the party-state to increase its controls over workers and to launch more campaigns to raise labour productivity and expose 'wreckers' and saboteurs so that the USSR was locked into a vicious circle of repression and control breeding more repression and more efforts at extending control. The purges and the camp system of the Gulag were not only a human tragedy and an abomination, they were also an ineffective solution to Soviet problems. The terror created slave armies that were thrown into the battle for production in the most hostile climates of Siberia and the Far North, and added an extra incentive for workers to fulfil their plan targets for fear of accusations of 'wrecking'. This probably had some temporary positive effect, but the problems of plan and polity were systemic; it was the tempo of the plan and the unreasonable demands that it made that created waste, poor labour productivity and uneven policy implementation. It might even be argued that Stalin's policies did not enable the USSR to survive the German invasion of 1941. The USSR did achieve a high level of industrialization throughout the 1930s and was able, after some serious reverses, to organize the economic means to fight off the German invasion of 1941. However, it was not just the plan and the way that it enabled economic activity to be directed towards the war effort that produced this victory. An immense surge of patriotism – World War II is better known to Russians as the 'Great Patriotic War' – and self-sacrifice on the battlefield and in the factories played a major role in fighting off the German invasion between 1941 and 1945, and in reconstructing the country after 1945. Moreover, the unrestrained power of the party-state and Stalin were responsible for some of the horrendous losses of the 'Great Patriotic War' (around 26 million Soviet citizens died). Stalin interfered in military decisions and the Soviet military was unprepared to fight in 1941 because of the purge of the military in the 1930s and Stalin's refusal to believe that Germany would break the pact it had made with the USSR in 1939.[42]

The continuation of repression and the tightening of many political controls between 1945 and Stalin's death in 1953 were a betrayal of the hopes of many that their efforts in the war would be rewarded by some small measure of liberalization. However, the Stalinist system was impervious to change whilst Stalin was still alive. The onset of the Cold War between the 'West' and the new Soviet bloc of the USSR and Eastern Europe recreated the fear of foreign invasion, and the communist parties of Eastern Europe had to be controlled by purge. Stalin still feared political opponents at home and regional communist party organizations, such as the Leningrad party, which was purged in 1948–1949, were attacked to prevent their being used as alternative power bases. On the eve of his death, new purges, this time with anti-Semitic overtones, were in preparation. The terror of Stalin's last few years, although less dramatic than the terror of the 1930s, showed that the problems of political organization that had crystallised in the 1930s had not been resolved; purges had not produced a pure, compliant socialist society and polity and could not. Stalin had changed the face of Russia and the Soviet Union, but he did not leave a political system that was well ordered thanks to the administrative efforts of a capable, impersonal bureaucracy, and able to develop economically and socially under its leadership. Instead, the USSR had a political system that relied on arbitrary terror to force the tempo of economic development and iron out inconsistent policy implementation, which was wasteful of human life and economic resources, and staffed by bureaucrats who were more concerned with personal survival, and twisting policy to ensure it, than they were with the collective interest of the people they were supposed to lead to a brighter future.

The decline of the Soviet system: the diminishing capacity, autonomy and organizational integrity of an absolutist-bureaucratic state, 1953–1985

Stalin's death in March 1953 further unsettled the Soviet polity since it created a succession crisis. Stalin's post as General Secretary of the Central Committee of the CPSU was taken by Nikita Khrushchev. Khrushchev's chief rival for power, Georgii Malenkov, allowed Khrushchev to take this post since he thought that being head of the government, rather than the party, would be the best route to power. This was a tactical mistake. The arrest and execution of Lavrenti Beria, Stalin's security chief, and the purging and downgrading of the secret police, now named the KGB (the Committee for State Security; previously the MGB, the Ministry for State Security), increased the power of the party over the state and Khrushchev used his position as General Secretary to consolidate his support within the party. Most dramatically, Khrushchev decided to take the lead in breaking with Stalinism to secure his position.

Khrushchev's position at the apex of the party aided him in this. Delegates to the 20th Party Congress in 1956 were called to a special closed session at which Khrushchev made what came to be known as the 'Secret Speech' (in fact it was only secret for a few months). In his speech, Khrushchev denounced Stalin's theory that class struggle intensified as socialism was built and argued that this had led to the purging of loyal party members and to the construction of a 'cult of personality' around Stalin. The party had been displaced from its proper role of leadership because of this, Khrushchev claimed, and Stalin's rule had been erratic and arbitrary. Khrushchev's speech was a political act, rather than an attempt at determining historical fact. He glossed over the sufferings of the people in the first waves of collectivization and industrialization and concentrated on party and state officials who had been purged in the 1930s. He did not seek to rehabilitate the peasants suppressed as kulaks in the early 1930s, or leaders such as Trotsky or Bukharin. This was not accidental. Khrushchev's speech was aimed at winning support from the party and state leaders in his audience. By labelling Stalin as in error from the mid-1930s onwards he was reassuring them that Stalin's managerial style was at fault, not the system he had built and which they relied on for their positions, privileges and power. Central planning, the system of factories and collective farms that had been built in the early 1930s were all as they should be, Khrushchev argued, only their regulation by terror was to change. Terror was to be replaced by 'socialist legality'. This promised that the management of politics would be based on impersonal principles (legality) with absolute power over decision making vested in the party, which would decide what was legal and what was not.

The impact of the 'Secret Speech' was immense. Political violence and repressive police control did not fully disappear from Soviet political life. Popular protest was suppressed violently under Khrushchev with great loss of life at Novocherkassk in 1962, dissidents were arrested and sent to camps and mental institutions under Brezhnev, and under Gorbachev elements of the Soviet state reacted brutally and bloodily to protests in Georgia in 1989, Azerbaijan in 1990, and in Latvia and Lithuania in 1991. Nonetheless, Khrushchev ended the arbitrary nature of mass terror and the use of terror as a means of settling political disputes. The new style of settling disputes was demonstrated by Khrushchev's handling of dissent towards his rule. In 1957, Malenkov and two other survivors from Stalin's Politburo, Lazar Kaganovich and Vycheslav Molotov, attempted to have Khrushchev removed from office. Khrushchev could not win a vote in the Politburo and appealed to the Central Committee to prevent his ouster. The Central Committee, which was staffed by representatives from local party organizations and representatives from the state, supported Khrushchev. Instead of executing his defeated rivals, Khrushchev removed them from the Politburo and gave them jobs outside of Moscow. The plotters were labelled the 'Anti-Party Group' by Khrushchev as a sign that they had intended to rule the party by repression once more, and as a reminder that the party's dominance of the political system was only guaranteed under his leadership.

More widely, the end of terror was felt through the release of many of the prisoners who had been falsely accused under Stalin and by what became known as 'The Thaw'. The frozen intellectual order of Stalinism melted a little between 1956 and Khrushchev's removal from office in 1964 and there was some discussion of the Soviet past, including the publication in 1962 of Alexander Solzehnitsyn's *One day in the life of Ivan Denisovich*, a story about an ordinary Russian in Stalin's prison camps. There were limits to the Thaw and it was conducted to suit Khrushchev's political ends. Lenin's reputation was untouched, there was no comment on the Soviet system as the source of repression and the publication of more critical works by Solzhenitsyn and others was prohibited. The Thaw and the clampdown on cultural life after Khrushchev's ousting both helped to stimulate the dissident movement in the USSR in the late 1960s and 1970s. This movement did not bring down the Soviet system, but it did throw up some intellectual figures like Solzhenitsyn and Andrei Sakharov, the dissident nuclear scientist, and it punctured the USSR's claims of possessing a morally superior form of society to that of the capitalist 'West'.

The end of terror was a humanitarian advance, but its end did not resolve any of the basic problems of Soviet power and economy. Khrushchev was still faced with the problems of how to generate economic growth and get orders that he issued fulfilled. His response was a mixture of innovation and traditionalism. Tradition was maintained by the use of campaigns to force up economic growth. From 1959, Khrushchev asserted that the USSR had entered the stage of 'full-scale construction of communism' and in 1961 a new party programme was issued in which it was stated that communism would 'in the main be built in the USSR' by 1980.[43] Like Stalin proclaiming the possibility of building 'socialism in one country', Khrushchev's intention with these pronouncements was to force the pace of economic development. If communism were a state of material abundance, moving towards it would have to entail increased economic effort from the party and society to create a wealthier society: industrial output was supposed to increase fivefold and national income was to quadruple by 1980.[44] However, as with Stalin before him, Khrushchev's ambitious plans posed the problem of how to get the party-state machine to fulfil orders from the central leadership.

Campaigns for production created some pressure on the party-state machine to fulfil orders since they gave the party goals to organize around and compensated for the end of terror. Khrushchev launched a series of economic campaigns to raise production: the 'Virgin Lands' campaign, an attempt to increase grain production by putting new land under the plough in Western Siberia and Kazakhstan; the maize campaign that sought to emulate the maize production Khrushchev saw on his visit to the USA; the campaign to end the housing crisis by launching massive construction projects; the campaign to overtake the USA in meat and dairy production. However, whilst campaigns to raise production forced the party to work harder, they also relied on the party diverting resources to new priority areas so that growth was unbalanced, facilitated by corruption and involved other orders going unfulfilled. Campaigns were not enough, therefore, to regulate the behaviour of Soviet officials. Indeed, they could make things worse. A good example of this, and a paradigm of the Soviet problem generally, was the A.N. Larionov affair. Larionov was first party secretary of Ryazan' province. In 1959, he responded to Khrushchev's call for more meat production by promising a 280 per cent increase in meat deliveries from his area. He delivered his promise and was praised by Khrushchev: other areas were instructed to emulate Ryazan' success in meeting, and overfulfilling, campaign targets. However, Larionov had only achieved his spectacular promise by slaughtering breeding stock. Consequently, the production of meat in Ryazan' fell dramatically in 1960. Larionov diverted resources to buy in livestock from other areas and stole from neighbouring areas, and falsely claimed that it had been bred in Ryazan'. This was not enough to compensate for the lost breeding stock and maintain production: meat deliveries from Ryazan' dropped from 150,000 tons in 1959 to 30,000 tons in 1960. Faced with failure, exposure and disgrace, Larionov committed suicide.[45]

The Larionov affair was an extreme case, but it demonstrates that although the leadership could use campaigns to force local party organizations to divert resources to areas that the leadership declared to be high priority, campaigns were actually a weak means of controlling party workers and building up state capacity. The perennial problem of controlling party workers was exacerbated by the fact that the USSR was now a more complex society after World War II. Even after the huge changes brought about by collectivization and industrialization in the 1930s, 54 per cent of the Soviet population still worked in agriculture in 1940 and 67 per cent of the Russian population lived in the countryside in 1939. By 1959, 52 per cent of Russians lived in towns and only 39 per cent of Soviet citizens worked in agriculture.[46] These trends continued throughout the rest of the Soviet period and they made economic and social regulation ever more complicated. The range of goods and services produced by the economy for urban populations, and the number of shops, factories, educational establishments, hospitals etc. grew. Social problems changed with the shift from rural to urban life and demanded fresh policy responses and agencies to deal with them. The party's ability to oversee all of these developments stretched it and increased its propensity to ignore the centre's demands that it oversee all policy areas and implement central directives across the board in favour of concentrating on priorities and crisis management.

Khrushchev's response to the control problem, now that terror was not an option, was to try to devolve administration and increase the numbers of people responsible for it. Khrushchev broke up economic ministries and delegated responsibility for economic management to regional economic councils (*Sovnarkhozy*). It was hoped that these would be able to respond better to local needs than ministries in Moscow and that they would break down the 'departmentalism' of ministries to create efficient links between enterprises that had previously reported to different central authorities.[47] Increasing popular participation was justified by the fact that the building communism involved more than economic development: it was also supposed to see the withering away of the state as society was empowered to administer itself without any special political machine. Khrushchev thus sought to draw the Soviet population into political work and make local party organizations closer to the people. He called for public organizations (such as the Komsomol, the youth wing of the party, and trade unions) to take over the management of culture and leisure from the party, and established new bodies like the *druzhinniki* (basically vigilantes) and the comrades' courts, to act as part-time enforcers of public order and to administer some local justice. The party was to be reformed by 'bifurcation' (dividing it in two sections), one responsible for agricultural administration and one for industry. Khrushchev also suggested that there be a higher turnover of party officials. He called for limited terms of office to party posts and for non-party personnel to take part in party work. This, Khrushchev believed, would increase experience of management and party work. It would bring the party closer to those that it oversaw by increasing specialization within it and would create checks on officials since their behaviour would be moderated by popular participation.

As with earlier efforts at mobilization of the population, Khrushchev's reforms aimed to create a Soviet version of infrastructural power by drawing more people into the implementation of policy to increase the capacity of the Soviet state. This was, however, far from the same as democratizing or liberalizing the USSR by creating greater popular freedom. Khrushchev presumed that the party would remain in charge of society and that power over basic decision making would reside with top party leaders. He only wanted to improve administration by increasing the pressure on party officials to deliver the policies he desired and increasing the capacity of the party-state by involving more people in its work. Nonetheless, these policies were still not popular with party officials. Khrushchev's use of traditional campaign targets continued to generate orders that were difficult to fulfil without improvisation and adaptation. The 'Virgin Lands' were not suitable for grain production and after a short time needed massive investment to stop environmental degradation and to enable modest production to continue; the USSR as a whole was unsuitable for growing maize, and both maize and traditional crops were lost. Khrushchev arbitrarily raised building targets and threw the construction system into chaos. His administrative reforms threatened party officials' status and interfered, or threatened to interfere, with the party's ability to improvise solutions to some of these problems and his instructions. The territories covered by the *Sovnarkhozy* were created arbitrarily so that they did not create any greater economic efficiency. Reforms like bifurcation attacked the powers of local leaders that allowed them to direct resources around the Soviet economy and compensate for the vagaries of policy changing according to the leader's whims. Khrushchev's call for 'socialist legality' thus came to nought. The CPSU was still charged with ensuring economic growth and had to use its power to try to meet its leaders' goals. It therefore did not settle into routinized administration, but improvised solutions to calls for ever-greater economic effort. Khrushchev encouraged this by his campaigns and calls for communism to be built, but at the same time weakened the party's ability to respond by tinkering with administration.

Khrushchev's attacks on the party's methods of work eroded the support that his earlier denunciation of terror had built up. Failures in foreign policy (most notably the Soviet climb-down during the Cuban Missile Crisis in 1963) and domestic policy (such as the failed maize campaign) led to a coalition of party and state leaders conspiring to remove him from office in 1964. Khrushchev appealed to the Central Committee for support as he had in 1957, but he was forced from office in October 1964 on the charges of creating disorder in the party and the state through his administrative reforms, launching 'hare-brained schemes', building his own 'cult of person-ality', and ignoring expert advice over policies like the 'Virgin Lands' scheme. Khrushchev was guilty of all of these things, but if he was guilty, it was with mitigating circumstances. His errors were in no small measure caused by his trying to get an unworkable system to function, and moreover, of getting it to work without mass terror. His removal from office, whilst a relief to party, state and society, did not cure the Soviet system's problems, as his successors hoped, but allowed them space to develop.

Khrushchev was succeeded by a collective leadership. Leonid Brezhnev took over as General Secretary of the CPSU Central Committee, Aleksei Kosygin became Prime Minister, and Nikolai Podgorny was Chairman of the Supreme Soviet (and formally head of state). As with the collective leadership after Stalin, power was to become concentrated on the General Secretary, Brezhnev, especially after he replaced Podgorny as Chair of the Supreme Soviet in 1977. Brezhnev's consolidation of power was thus gradual; he never enjoyed the free rein that Stalin, and to a lesser extent Khrushchev had. The gradual build-up of power by Brezhnev and the limits on his free-dom of action were partly a result of the new leadership's promise of 'stability of cadres'. This policy did away with Khrushchev's idea of limited tenure for party offices and combined with Khrushchev's curtailment of terror as an instrument of everyday politics ensured that party workers and state officials stayed in place until retirement or natural death. This slowed down the circulation of elites so that there were fewer opportunities for Brezhnev to build up his power through appointments as Stalin and Khrushchev had done. It also meant that the power of party workers to build up their personal power bases and fiefdoms was unchecked. The collective leadership also abol-ished the *Sovnarkhozy*, re-established central ministries in Moscow and unified the party by ending its bifurcation into agricultural and industrial wings. The reunification of the party consolidated the power of local party leaders and was another factor that constrained the power of the new General Secretary. Finally, the big push towards communism that Khrushchev had announced was called off. The USSR, Brezhnev announced, was not in the stage of the 'full-scale construction of communism', but had entered the stage of 'developed socialism'. This was to be a long stage of historical development during which there would be no rapid change in society, but rather the 'perfection' of socialism. Mass mobilization and campaigns still occurred under Brezhnev, but they were ritualized events and were not aimed at wrenching the economy to a new level of development. The party was to lead this process of 'perfection' unencumbered by non-party workers and without giving up any responsibilities to public organizations as Khrushchev intended. The inviolable position of the CPSU in the Soviet system was enshrined in Article 6 of the 1977 Constitution, which stated that the CPSU 'directs and guides Soviet society, [is] the nucleus of its political system'.[48]

These new policies gave the USSR its most settled period of administration, but also allowed those features of the system that weakened it as an absolutist-bureaucratic state formation to develop so that the Soviet state's strength was dissipated.[49] All of the means utilized by Stalin and Khrushchev to try to control the activities of local leaders disappeared, or were weakened. Terror was not restored, campaigns became less effective, Khrushchev's efforts at boosting popular participation dropped off, and no major upsurge in economic activity was planned for most of Brezhnev's period in office. Change under Brezhnev was incremental. There were some attempts at economic and administrative reform under Brezhnev, but the policies that were introduced concentrated on technical issues of organization. Kosygin attempted to reform the economy in the 1960s by creating a better incentive and pricing system. In the 1970s, there were reforms to the administration of the economy as enterprises were brought together to form production associations, the aim of these mergers being to reduce costs and improve efficiency. The 1970s also saw some efforts at reforming local government administration, the intention being to remove some responsibility for welfare provision from enterprises and the party to local Soviets so as to enable factory managers to concentrate on production and party officials to focus more on political work. The effect of all these policies was blunted, however, by the intransigence of party officials who had settled into a pattern of administrative behaviour since the fall of Khrushchev, did not intend to be shifted from it and were not forced to by the leadership and its policy of 'stability of cadres'. Reform initiatives were taken on and formally honoured by the party-state bureaucracy, but had little practical effect.

With little pressure on them from above, networks of party-state officials stabilized and very often developed into corruption networks. Corruption became systemic under Brezhnev as resources were moved around the system to compensate for breakdowns in the planning system and as people took advantage of Brezhnev's loosening of the political bonds to take personal profit. Huge amounts of resources were siphoned away from the state budget during this time, and the networks of corruption reached into the upper echelons of the party and state. Party leaders misreporting cotton production figures stole millions of roubles in Soviet central Asia. Caviar was exported as smoked herring and the hard currency (as opposed to the soft rouble that could only be spent in the USSR) earned pocketed by officials; a deputy minister of the fishing industry was implicated and executed after the exposure of the fraud. A Deputy Minister of Culture was arrested for diamond smuggling in 1982.[50] Brezhnev's daughter, Galina, and son-in-law, Yurii Churbanov, were heavily involved in bribe taking. Churbanov was a Deputy Minister for Internal Affairs in charge of parts of the USSR's police service and received huge bribes to cover up corruption. Officeholding under Brezhnev thus became truly proprietary since it became possible not just to divert resources to fulfil tasks that the centre might check on, but to divert them to personal consumption. Clientalism and patronage began to make the USSR look less like a state governed by an impersonal bureaucracy fulfilling ideological aims, and more like a patrimonial system run to personal advantage by a self-selecting elite.[51] The power of some party bosses was such that they ran their republics and provinces like personal fiefdoms, as 'magnates' who Stalin had complained of back in 1934.

Corruption at the top of the party-state under Brezhnev was matched by the growth of a 'second economy' that involved most Russian citizens and petty influence peddling throughout the political system. The extent of influence peddling and the second economy are difficult to estimate because being illegal they were hidden. Some indication of the extent of influence peddling can be gleaned from surveys of Soviet émigrés, which shows that there was an increase in influence peddling as terror declined and the Soviet system settled into a more stable administrative pattern. For example, the results of one such survey (conducted in 1983) show that 17 per cent of people used political connections to circumvent the official system of job allocations under Stalin compared to 41 per cent of people under Brezhnev.[52] This is a notable rise and denotes that influence peddling was having an effect on the state's ability to mobilize and dispose of its citizens' labour under Brezhnev. The extent of the second economy was also difficult to gauge. Some estimates claimed that it accounted for about 25 per cent of Soviet GDP, that it involved 17–20 million workers (many part time) or 15 per cent of the labour force in 1984, and that it was a vital source of services such as home and automobile maintenance.[53]

The growth of corruption and the weakening of the party's ability to mobilize the population had detrimental affects on the economy. The decline in the economy is recorded in Table 2.2, which shows the slow down in the rate of growth in the economy for five-year plan periods between 1961 and 1985. Two sets of figures are provided: the official statistics and the figures as recalculated by two independent Soviet economists in the late 1980s. Both show that the general rate of economic growth slowed. On its own this means very little. Many economies have high growth when they begin to industrialize and in the first bloom of urban development, and then witness a slowdown to a steadier rate of growth. This was not the case in the USSR where

Table 2.2 Soviet economic growth rate, 1965–85 (average annual growth, comparable prices, per cent)

	1961–5	1966–70	1971–5	1976–80	1981–85
Official statistics	6.5	7.8	5.7	4.3	3.6
Unofficial recalculation	4.4	4.1	3.2	1.0	0.6

Sources and note: adapted from Anders Åslund (1989) *Gorbachev's struggle for economic reform*, London: Pinter, p. 15. The unofficial recalculation figures were produced by Grigori Khanin and Vasily Selyunin.

the decline in growth rates was symptomatic of larger problems. Soviet economic slowdown was caused by the exhaustion of possibilities for extensive growth. The two sources of extensive growth – labour and raw materials supply – began to decline under Brezhnev, or became very expensive. The increase in labour supply to the economy fell from 6 per cent in the five-year plan period 1971–1975 to 2 per cent in 1981–85; the increase in production of fuels and raw materials fell from 25 per cent in the five-year plan period 1971–1975 to 7 per cent in 1981–1985.[54] These changes were caused by a fall in population growth as family size shrank in response to housing shortages and the pressures of urban life, and because the wastefulness of Soviet industry quickly exhausted easily available and cheap sources of raw materials. Moving to intensive growth could have compensated for this, but the USSR was unable to squeeze much more out of its labour force or plant. The leadership lacked the political will to introduce radical reform, and the planning system worked against technological innovation and management reforms that might have increased productivity. Soviet labour productivity rose in the 1970s, but it did so at a declining rate, whilst capital productivity fell consistently under Brezhnev, declining by 1.9 per cent between 1966–1970, 3.8 per cent in 1971–1975 and 2.9 per cent in 1976–1979.[55] This meant that although output from Soviet industry grew, it did so at increased cost: the USSR was using more raw materials to get less than other economies. The material wealth of the USSR was literally being eaten away to support inefficient economic growth.

The decline of its economy made the USSR a less effective competitor in global politics. By the 1980s, the Soviet Union was a military giant but an economic midget in world affairs. The Soviet economy was far smaller than that of its capitalist rivals. In 1986, Soviet Gross National Product (GNP) was only 55 per cent that of the USA's, and per capita GNP was only 47 per cent that of the USA's.[56] The Soviet economy lagged far behind the West's in efficiency and technology. The USSR used three times as many inputs as Western economies to produce a similar physical good. The quality of Soviet products and industry were also of much poorer quality: only between 6 and 10 per cent of Soviet industrial production was saleable on world markets at the end of the 1980s, and only 4 per cent of Soviet industry was technologically equivalent to global standards.[57] The technology lag and the poor quality of Soviet production weakened its ability to trade with the outside world. By the late 1970s, the USSR primarily exported energy products raw materials, rather than finished goods, and imported high cost finished products from the West. This was the pattern of trade of a developing state, rather than of a superpower. The income earned from the sale of energy and raw materials was then pumped into the Soviet economy to maintain its modest rate of growth. Even this could not be guaranteed, however, since the revenue from raw materials and energy depended on high world market prices. If these fell, as they did in the early 1980s, the flow of resources to the Soviet economy dried up.

Economic backwardness relative to its competitors strained the one area in which the USSR was strong: its military. The amount taken out of the economy, and thus diverted from consumption and investment, by the party leadership to fund defence did not decrease as the economy declined. Since the economy was smaller than that of its rivals and less efficient, the amount spent by the USSR to keep up with its rivals was far larger relative to its economic strength. By 1987, US defence spending was about 7 per cent of GNP, whilst Soviet defence spending accounted for about 40 per cent of GNP.[58] The defence burden was also growing as the Soviet economy slowed down. Relations with the West, which had improved gradually under Khrushchev and in the early 1970s during the period of *détente*, were upset in the late 1970s. Changes in the balance of power in the third world, the coming to power of Ronald Reagan and Margaret Thatcher in the USA and the United Kingdom, the Soviet invasion of Afghanistan in 1979 and the deployment of intermediate nuclear forces in Eastern Europe led to the outbreak of the 'second Cold War' in the early 1980s and a new, expensive round of the arms race began. Finally, the decline in the Soviet economy weakened its hold on Eastern Europe. Maintaining its 'empire' was increasingly costly to the USSR since it subsidized their inefficient economies. This strained the USSR's budget and brought only poor returns as Polish protest over Soviet influence and for independent trade unions in the early 1980s showed. The USSR's ability to cope with these changes in the early 1980s and maintain its superpower status was in doubt. Although no state was likely to challenge it militarily, it was losing position and influence in the world and would not be able to maintain its military might relative to the USA without economic reform.

Finally, the defence burden of being in superpower competition with the more prosperous USA and its wealthy European allies deprived the USSR of vital resources that it could have used to stimulate production in other areas and fund social services. It thus contributed to what Mikhail Gorbachev, who was to become General Secretary of the CPSU Central Committee in March 1985, described as the 'pre-crisis situation' created by the 'stagnation' of political and economic life under the Brezhnev era. Economic decline, corruption in the party and the failure of the leadership to counter decline firmly had weakened the legitimacy of the CPSU. The party had allowed what Gorbachev called a 'gap between words and deeds' to grow up: under Brezhnev, Gorbachev argued in 1987, 'the world of day-to-day realities and the world of feigned prosperity were diverging more and more'.[59] Whilst the CPSU leadership talked of equality and social progress and used the slogans of socialism to proclaim their right to rule, social justice, defined by Gorbachev as equality of access to services, education and the wealth produced by society, had declined and social problems had mounted. The difference between the party's 'words' and its 'deeds' was, Gorbachev argued, eroding the moral base of socialist society. The party was to blame for this. Corruption and bad working practices under Brezhnev had diminished its influence in society as a political force. The party needed to abandon its role as economic manager and renew itself as a Leninist party to restore confidence in the socialist system and bring about an end to the economic malaise of the Brezhnev era. By 2000, Gorbachev argued, the USSR should have attained what he termed 'the highest levels of social productivity in the world'. In short, Gorbachev wanted the citizens of the Soviet Union to enjoy comparable living standards to citizens of wealthy industrial states.

Perestroika, the end of the USSR and the re-emergence of Russia

Gorbachev was not able to begin reforms to try to restore social justice and faith in the Soviet system for two and a half years after Brezhnev's death in November 1982. Yurii Andropov, a former head of the KGB, first succeeded Brezhnev. Andropov made moves towards reform by exposing some corruption in the party and state and trying to tighten labour discipline. He also promoted some younger, honest officials, like Yegor Ligachev to the central party apparatus and gave Gorbachev, who was already a member of the Politburo, a more prominent role. Andropov's appointments policy and promotion of Gorbachev set him on the road to take over as General Secretary. Reform was set back, however, when Andropov died before Gorbachev could be confirmed as his successor. An old ally of Brezhnev's, the ailing and uninspiring Konstantin Chernenko, took over as General Secretary for just under a year.

The interregnum after Brezhnev's death shaped the Gorbachev reforms very subtly, but very importantly. Gorbachev was supported by Andropov's appointees when he came to power in March 1985. This gave him the strength to move quickly against remaining political opponents so that he was able to build his personal power up very quickly, but it also meant that Gorbachev had to follow some of the same reforms that Andropov had favoured. Chief among these policies were efforts to tighten labour discipline and raise the quality of Soviet production. Andropov had tried to improve labour discipline by cutting down on absenteeism from work by having the police raid shops, bars and other public places to round up absent workers. In May 1985, this campaign was extended into a full-scale campaign against alcohol consumption, which was blamed for absenteeism as well as for many of the USSR's social problems. The strongest supporter of the campaign in the leadership was Ligachev, one of Andropov's appointees. Other campaigns were launched to 'accelerate socio-economic progress' (in contrast to Brezhnev's idea that socialism only needed 'perfecting') by investing in new technology, the creation of 'state quality control' auditors in factories to force up the quality of production, and campaigns against 'unearned income', in other words against the second economy.

The main effect of these measures was probably to persuade Gorbachev beyond doubt that the campaigning policy style of the past was not enough to shake the USSR out of its malaise and restore social justice. The results of the campaign against alcohol were less than impressive. Despite great effort involving the promotion of temperance societies, the closure of alcohol retailers and the destruction of vineyards, Russians kept on drinking. Alcohol production went underground as black-marketers supplied popular demand and at the same time deprived the state of tax income and made the campaign against 'unearned income' something of a joke. Local party branches initially reported impressive figures for the closure of shops selling alcohol, sanctions against party members who drank excessively, membership of temperance societies etc., but once the centre's attention shifted slightly, the campaign was put on a backburner.[60] The fate of the anti-alcohol campaign demonstrated that the party's style of administration was a problem; the fate of other campaigns showed that the economic system was too rigid to create growth or improve quality. Changes in investment priorities to emphasis on technology caused confusion, increased waste as some existing projects were abandoned for lack of funds, and only achieved modest returns: a 15 per cent rise in investment in machine building only led to a 3 per cent increase in new assets. The moves to increase the quality of production only caused a slump in production as large amounts of industrial output were condemned as substandard. The slump in production hit workers' pay packets as they were penalized for failing to fulfil plan targets, but this did not lead to any rise in quality since defective supplies were the cause of most quality problems.[61]

A further sign that more radical change was needed came in April 1986 when an accident at the nuclear reactor at Chernobyl' in the Ukraine spread radioactive material over large parts of the Western USSR, Scandinavia and Eastern Europe. Gorbachev was embarrassed by this international demonstration of the faults of Soviet industry and by the fact that the USSR had not been able to react to the accident effectively because of the culture of official secrecy. Chernobyl', Gorbachev wrote in his memoirs, 'was graphic evidence, not only of how obsolete our technology was, but also of the failure of the old system'.[62] After Chernobyl', Gorbachev began to change tack and talk more and more of *perestroika* (restructuring). Reform, he proposed, needed to involve radical change and had to be directed not just at the economy and public morals, but also at the political system. Only when the political system became more flexible and better able to draw in the people to support its policies, Gorbachev argued, would the economic problems of the USSR be resolved.

The first sign of this was a change in the policy of *glasnost'* (openness). More information had begun to be given out to Soviet citizens about social problems under this policy in 1985, but from mid-1986 onwards *glasnost'* began to tackle more substantial political issues to build support for reform and demonstrate why it was needed. It was not Gorbachev's initial intention, but over time the loosening of media controls developed into the beginnings of a free media. Greater tolerance of discussion was signalled by the release from internal exile of the dissident Andrei Sakharov in December 1986. The real start of *perestroika* came in 1987 with the January and June plenums of the CPSU Central Committee. At these two meetings, Gorbachev turned his attention to the party and its functions and related success in economic reform to changes in the party's roles. He argued that Soviet socialism had lost its way and degenerated into bureaucratic formalism because the party spent too long on administration and not enough time on political work with the people. It was necessary, Gorbachev claimed, to separate the party and the state, for each to fulfil its functions properly without interference from the other.

These were not new themes in Soviet political discourse, but the solutions that Gorbachev proposed were different to the policies of the past. In economics, a new 'Law on Enterprises' proposed that businesses should have more independence from the party and from ministries, should operate according to calculations of profit and loss, and that workers should have the right to elect their factory managers. This was not completely free industrial democracy since elections had to be approved by higher authorities, but Gorbachev was trying to break down the barriers to economic reform and innovation. Independence from party and state ministries and the need to take account of losses was supposed to do away with inefficient work practices and waste. It would also create incentives because factories would have the right to dispose of profits and could reward their workers if they did well. Party branches in factories were to work as political leaders, supporting political educational work amongst the labour force and convincing them of the need to work in line with national party policy. This would increase party activism at grassroots level. To facilitate this further, Gorbachev proposed that party members should play more part in the administration of the CPSU to break down its internal bureaucratic mindset. Party management should be democratized, Gorbachev argued, with the leaders of local party organs and the central committees of the republican communist parties elected by secret ballot. The democratization of party life, Gorbachev argued, would serve as an example to the rest of society, remove party workers who were not capable of implementing reform policies from office and make party leaders focus on political leadership to support the ordinary party member.

The problem with these ideas was a simple and classical: how to get them to work? Both political authorities and economic managers were being asked to take steps into the dark. A factory manager might, for example, think that more independence was a good thing and try to implement the policy line. However, if the manager did so and broke away from the local party and the relevant ministry, who would the factory turn to for help if things went wrong, if suppliers failed to deliver necessary raw materials and components, or payments were not made for goods delivered? The USSR had no effective system of commercial law to which a manager could turn. In the absence of an administrative system designed to support managerial independence it was better to keep working with the ministry in Moscow and asking for assistance from the local party. Party work thus did not change greatly; party leaders continued to see themselves as responsible for economic management and prioritized it above other tasks.

Gorbachev's reforms were thus blunted in their effectiveness because they had to break down bureaucratic resistance that preferred traditional ways of administration to new methods. Gorbachev's hope was that agitation 'from below', from ordinary party members, would break some of this bureaucratic resistance down. However, democratization of the party was blunted by opposition in the party leadership and because of mixed signals about reform. Gorbachev did not set specific goals for the party to achieve; he wanted the party to find the answers to Soviet problems through its own political work so as to close the 'gap between words and deeds'. The party, Gorbachev believed, had to make its ideological message real by demonstrating that it reflected the interests of the people; in the process, the party would discover on its own what the best way of implementing reform was and would be able to renew its political leadership by drawing on the support of the people. The key to success and socialist renewal for Gorbachev was not to command the party to fulfil specific tasks, but to get it to interact with the Soviet people, learn from this interaction where the Soviet system was failing, work out how to mend failure and lead the people in the resolution of problems. *Perestroika* as Gorbachev conceived it was not about setting out specific targets for the CPSU to strive to fulfil as Khrushchev had done: the party would only formally obey orders as it had done in the past. To be successful *perestroika* had to increase pressure on the party to limit its roles to political activity and create mechanisms through which party and people could interact. Gorbachev's vision was of the CPSU continually engaged with the Soviet people, of it working with them to develop new policies and implement them so that the Soviet system would become efficient and productive. Again, and as with the Khrushchev reforms of administration, the hope was that this would develop some sort of infrastructural power by involving more citizens in the implementation of policy.

There were several problems with Gorbachev's vision of a Soviet system with greater infrastructural power. Whilst Gorbachev set out a vision of the CPSU as the leader of the people, party leaders were unsure of what they were to do practically. This meant that reform developed spasmodically. It also meant that there was scope for divisions in the party leadership to emerge over the style of party work and the USSR's problems and generate uncertainty over the fate of reform. Boris Yeltsin, who had been appointed as first secretary of the Moscow city party organization by Gorbachev, was committed to rapid reform and the reorganization of the Moscow city party organization to remove corrupt and ineffective bureaucrats from office. For Yeltsin, a central plank of this reorganization was a campaign against the privileges of party leaders. Yeltsin justified his campaigns against privilege by linking it to the restoration of social justice that Gorbachev argued was an aim of *perestroika*. Ligachev, on the other hand, saw attacks on party privilege as dangerous because they diminished the authority of the party. In 1986, Ligachev and Yeltsin clashed at the 27th CPSU Congress over the question of party privilege, and subsequently Ligachev's power in the CPSU Central Committee enabled him to interfere in Yeltsin's efforts at bringing change to the capital. Eventually in October 1987, and frustrated with what he perceived to be the lack of support for his work in Moscow, Yeltsin attacked party conservatives at a Central Committee plenum that had been called to discuss Gorbachev's speech commemorating the seventieth anniversary of the 1917 revolution.[63] Yeltsin's speech was a political mistake. Instead of rallying support for his work, Yeltsin found himself abandoned by Gorbachev and attacked on all sides, first at the Central Committee and then at a meeting of the Moscow city party committee where he was removed from office.[64]

Yeltsin's removal showed the dangers of pursuing reform too vigorously if you were a party official; reform's lack of definition meant that you could easily be attacked for radicalism. However, Yeltsin's problems also demonstrated that the party had to be pushed more and more if it was to break with the past as Gorbachev hoped. This need to push the party towards reform meant that although Gorbachev was vague about what the party should do, at the same time he demanded more of it. This contradiction could only lead to confusion and was to have fatal consequences for the party and hence for the Soviet system as a whole. In 1988, Gorbachev used a CPSU Conference (the first since 1940) to launch an ambitious set of political reforms that were designed to force the CPSU to work with the Soviet people, but which in practice created the possibility of organized opposition to party rule. Gorbachev announced the creation of a new two-tier parliamentary structure. The Supreme Soviet, previously a large and ineffective body that rubber-stamped party directives, would in the future be a smaller, full-time legislature with 542 deputies. Instead of being directly elected by the people, it would be elected by a new parliamentary body, the Congress of People's Deputies (which would have 2250 deputies). This new body – which would in part be popularly elected by multi-candidate elections – would meet twice a year and set out the strategic goals of policy. The Supreme Soviet would transform these goals into legislation. Elections for the new Congress of People's Deputies were set for March 1989. The new Supreme Soviet would be elected when the Congress met in June 1989. Gorbachev saw the Congress of People's Deputies as representing two things: it would be a symbol of what he called the 'socialist pluralism of opinions', and it would be the pinnacle of a new 'socialist law-based state'.[65] The CPSU, through the election campaign to the Congress of People's Deputies, would illustrate to the people that although there were different opinions in Soviet society, it represented all of them. It would thus demonstrate that there was a rough unity that underpinned pluralism in the USSR based on support for socialism. By interacting with the people, the CPSU would also learn about how the different approaches to socialism could be strengthened through developing policies to integrate them further and perfect the unity of the Soviet people in support of the party. The creation of a 'socialist law-based state' would help party workers concentrate on this political work. The Congress of People's Deputies was legally charged with the determination of state policy. Party workers would have to secure their control over politics by winning election to the Congress. This would automatically turn party workers away from administrative to political work (in the form of electioneering) and demonstrate to them how they would in future control politics via elected representative institutions at all levels of the Soviet system.

Gorbachev's plan was thus not for the CPSU to lose power, but for it to exercise power in a new way. It would rule through a constitutional order, ratifying its power to control legislative activity by dominating a new representative assembly. The party, however, did not prove equal to the task. Gorbachev was partly at fault for this failure as he sent the party contradictory messages. Gorbachev insisted that the CPSU needed to interact with the people, but also told it that it alone represented the unity at the heart of the 'socialist pluralism of opinions' and had to ensure that this unity was represented in the new Congress and Supreme Soviet. Gorbachev was thus asking the party to change the way that it worked, but at the same time ordering it to intervene in politics and produce a loyal parliament by shaping popular initiative. However, the party could not both change its methods of work and continue to dominate the Soviet population, as the elections of 1989 made apparent. Something had to give, and as the party failed to change it would be demonstrated that the CPSU was actually an unrepresentative body and people could begin to argue that its rule was the cause of Soviet problems, not the solution to them.

Gorbachev was thus caught in a trap. In endeavouring to make the party strive for a general goal, rather than specific ones, he exposed it to criticism when it publicly failed. Two-thirds of the deputies to the Congress were elected by popular vote in single-mandate constituencies, the rest were nominated by 'public organizations' such as the party and trade unions. The nominations from public organizations caused scandal as they failed to respect the wishes of ordinary members of public organizations. Deputies were chosen by the central plenary meetings of public organizations, rather than by popular vote. In the CPSU, 31,500 nominations were received for the party's 100 congressional seats from the party membership. However, the CPSU Central Committee voted on 100 nominations for these 100 seats: a no-choice, undemocratic election, which subverted internal party democracy and mocked democratization in the party and initiative 'from below'. Gorbachev was elected to the Congress in this way. Direct elections to the Congress were marred by the actions of electoral commissions that frequently blocked names from going on to ballot sheets. Over two-thirds of the names put forward by public meetings for candidacy never made it on to the ballot sheet as electoral commissions sought to ensure that many party leaders stood unopposed for the Congress and to bar candidates that the party saw as too troublesome. Despite these efforts at limiting competition, many party leaders failed to get the necessary 50 per cent of the vote needed to secure election and 'troublemakers' like Yeltsin made it on to the ballot paper and scored striking successes against officially approved candidates.[66]

The elections thus proved a moral defeat for the party and for Gorbachev. The CPSU still controlled the state and the country, but the elections demonstrated that it did so through bureaucratic manipulation as much as through popular acclamation Although Gorbachev was elected as Chair of the new Supreme Soviet, an opposition group, the Inter-Regional Deputies Group, emerged and began putting forward alternative political proposals. This new group was the first organized opposition group inside the Soviet state since the 1920s and its membership included Boris Yeltsin, who was emerging as the popular figurehead of anti-CPSU protest, and the veteran dissident Sakharov (who was to die in December 1989). The unity of a 'socialist pluralism of opinions' that Gorbachev had hoped the CPSU would summon forth instead dissolved into very ineffective parliamentary politics. Gorbachev did not receive unanimous support for *perestroika* and the opposition saw their proposals rejected by the CPSU majority.[67] The failure of Gorbachev's vision of a new unity between party and people was further demonstrated as the first convocation of the Congress of People's Deputies was followed by miners' strikes in Russia and Ukraine that rapidly developed from protests about economic and welfare issues to address political issues, including calls for the revocation of the Article 6 of the 1977 Constitution which enshrined the CPSU's 'leading and guiding' role.

The Congress of People's Deputies marked a turning point in the development of *perestroika*, and hence in the history of the USSR. Before the elections, Gorbachev had been subject to some criticism from below from the 'informal groups' that had begun to emerge with the liberalization of *glasnost*.[68] However, he had by and large been free to develop policy as he saw fit, only constrained by opposition from within the party leadership and by his own unwillingness to be specific about *perestroika* in the hope that this would lead party members to take up the reins of political leadership. After the elections to the Congress, Gorbachev continued his efforts to force the party to act as a political leader, but he was subject to criticism from within the party as it began to fragment and from increasingly organized nationalist and democratic opposition leaders and groups.[69] Gorbachev's solution was to create a new post, President of the USSR, to which the Congress of People's Deputies elected him in March 1990. The new presidential post gave Gorbachev strong executive powers and he hoped that he might use these to push reform forward. Gorbachev also hoped that the CPSU would be freed of bureaucratic activity and would be able to concentrate on political work by his taking on personal executive powers and responsibility for reform. To reinforce this, Article Six of the 1977 Constitution was revised to remove the legal guarantee of the party's right to rule at the same time that the new presidential post was established.

Gorbachev's hopes were, however, to be disappointed. Despite the creation of the USSR presidency and the revision of Article Six, the Soviet political space began to disintegrate. Between the March 1989 elections to the Congress of People's Deputies and establishment of the USSR presidency in March 1990, Soviet power entered its terminal stage: Soviet politics as the struggle to control both population and officials of the party-state began to draw to an end. *Glasnost'* had weakened the threat of coercion that had bound the people to the state since the Civil War and had remained a threat even after Khrushchev's denunciation of Stalin. The CPSU's ability to mobilize the population to the goals set by the leadership began to evaporate when people had a political choice in elections and when party officials were uncertain as to what the point of mobilization was. Subsequently, the CPSU began to fall apart as an organization. In December 1989, the Lithuanian communist party organization declared its independence from Moscow and other republican communist parties increasingly began to ignore the orders that emanated from the Kremlin. Across the USSR, party membership declined as party members quit and the flow of new entrants into the party's ranks dried up. In January 1990, party members associated with the Inter-Regional Deputies Group formed the 'Democratic Platform' to argue that the party should be transformed into a political party that had no other function but to fight elections and no other means of ruling but via elected assemblies. In June 1990, a Russian communist party organization was established. Previously local party organizations in the Russian Federation had been subordinate to central, all-Union party bodies. The establishment of a party organization for Russia was a move by conservatives to take control of party resources as the Soviet Union began to disintegrate, and as a vehicle to oppose Gorbachev's democratization of the party.[70]

However, the main threat to the Soviet system came not from conservatives, but from the election of republican legislatures in March 1990. In Russia, the experience of the 1989 elections and the fate of radical proposals at the Congress of People's Deputies prompted the organization of an umbrella group, Democratic Russia, to support candidates who were pro-democracy, in favour of limiting CPSU power and economic reform. Although Democratic Russia was only founded in January 1990 and never managed to develop a mass membership, local party organizations and a concrete political platform, candidates aligned with it managed to take enough seats at the March 1990 elections to control the city councils of Moscow and Leningrad, and to elect Yeltsin as Chairman of the Russian Supreme Soviet.[71] Yeltsin's grasp on power was slight since Democratic Russia did not command a majority in either of the two chambers of the new Russian parliament (like the USSR, Russia had a directly elected Congress of People's Deputies, which was a part-time body and which elected a smaller, full-time chamber, the Supreme Soviet). This, as we shall see at the start of the next chapter, was to have a profound effect on post-Soviet Russian politics. Nonetheless, under Yeltsin's leadership Russia was able to declare its 'sovereignty' in June 1990. This meant that the Russian parliament and government under Yeltsin's general leadership regarded laws passed by the Russian parliament and instructions issued by the Russian government to take precedence over those issued by the USSR parliament and government.

The proclamation of 'sovereignty' in Russia and other republics started a 'war of laws' as Gorbachev and the central Soviet government struggled to assert their authority. The result of this struggle was administrative chaos; the state as a uniform system of administration began to disintegrate. The Soviet and Russian governments issued contradictory instructions and economic reform plans were caught up in squabbles over authority. With the CPSU disintegrating and popular protest growing, the need for effective administration and decisive action to replace Soviet economic structures was imperative. In the absence of effective administration, the slow decay of the economy sped up. The economy was stuck between the old planning system and a market. Table 2.3 shows how Gross Domestic Product, industrial growth and retail prices (consumer inflation) changed between 1990 and 1991: prices rocketed as industrial production slumped because of the breakdown in the system of state orders, and the economy contracted.

The absence of effective administration enabled something else: spontaneous privatization. As control over party workers and economic administrators weakened, and as the contest between the Russian and Soviet government's grew, local authorities and economic managers were able to

Table 2.3 Selected Soviet economic statistics, 1987–1991 (percentage changes)

	1987	*1988*	*1989*	*1990*	*1991*
Gross domestic product			3.0	−2.0	−17.0[a]
Industrial growth rate over previous year	3.5	3.8	1.4	−0.1	−14.7
Retail price increases	1.3	0.6	2.0	5.6	86.0[a]

Source: Karen Henderson and Neil Robinson (1997) *Post-communist politics*, London: Prentice Hall, p. 106.

Note:[a] All of the USSR except the Baltic republics.

begin to claim and use state and party property as their own. The economic *nomenklatura* did not do this collectively as a social group aware of its interests; individuals and groups simply took advantage of opportunities as they presented themselves and as they faced the challenge of economic disintegration in the last years of Soviet power. They were helped in this by reformist legislation. The 'Law on Enterprises' from 1987 enabled factory managers to separate themselves from control by industrial ministries so that they became the *de facto* owners of the plants that they managed.[72] Other privatizations occurred as ministries were broken up in efforts to reduce economic bureaucracy, but re-emerged as giant corporations and 'concerns' (such as the Gazprom company that replaced the Ministry of Gas) under the control of former ministers.[73] Party officials were no less active in setting up private companies using party property and resources.[74] These actions of spontaneous privatization meant that the Soviet state did not so much collapse as disappear; its resources were 'stolen' from it by its officials when they realized that Gorbachev and central party-state authorities no longer had any power left to prevent them from using property and resources as they wanted.[75] The transfer of resources from central control to local elites deprived Gorbachev and the central state of the power to resist the encroachments of republic governments and made local authorities indifferent to the fate of the central government. 'Spontaneous privatization' thus helped to neutralize large sections of the *nomenklatura* in the struggle to free Russia from the USSR and promote democracy in 1990–1991. However, it also left a legacy of elite economic power that was to have considerable influence on both the choice and outcome of post-communist economic reform (see Chapter 4).

The collapse of the economy, the fight with the republics, the quickening disintegration of the CPSU and the weakening of the state as resources were transferred to private hands, reduced Gorbachev's reform plans to a chimera of idealistic aspirations. As a result, from the end of 1990 onwards, he was as concerned to survive politically and to pull something from the wreckage of the collapsing Soviet state, as he was with reform. In the winter of 1990–1991, he allied himself with conservatives in the Soviet state and promoted them to positions of responsibility in the hope that their loyalty to the USSR would shore up the Soviet state and halt the flow of power to the republics. This period has been labelled Gorbachev's 'drift to the right', i.e. to conservatism. However, after attacks on the Baltic republics and as moves against Yeltsin in Russia failed (see Chapter 3), Gorbachev changed tack and drifted 'back to the left'. He called a referendum in March 1991 that asked whether or not people thought it necessary to 'preserve the Union of Soviet Socialist Republics as a renewed federation of equal and sovereign republics'. The Russian authorities under Yeltsin added a question to the ballot paper in the Russian Federation asking if people thought it necessary to introduce a new office of Russian president. Both questions were supported by about 70 per cent of voters. People did not want to lose the USSR entirely, but they wanted more effective and local leadership such as a president of the Russian republic might provide to tackle economic and social collapse. The division of opinion amongst the people reflected the political stalemate between Gorbachev and Yeltsin. The central state was not powerful enough to restore order against the popular Russian leadership under Yeltsin and as its powers faded because of spontaneous privatization. However, it was powerful enough to prevent the Russian authorities from taking action to halt economic collapse. Yeltsin was able to extend his personal power by securing election to the new post of Russian president in June 1991 with 57.3 per cent of the vote, but he was not able to rule Russia whilst the USSR still existed.

Faced with stalemate, Gorbachev and Yeltsin put aside their differences and with other republican leaders negotiated a new Union treaty to replace the 1922 Union treaty. This broke the stalemate, but in a way that neither Gorbachev nor Yeltsin expected. Faced with the transfer of some powers away from the central state to the republics, the conservatives, who Gorbachev had only months before appointed and supported, turned on him and launched a coup attempt on the day before the new treaty was signed in August 1991. The plotters, who formed a State Committee for the State of Emergency (SCSE), imprisoned Gorbachev in his holiday home in Ukraine, but failed to arrest Yeltsin or to fully mobilize the Soviet security forces behind them. Incompetence, drunkenness and popular resistance around the Russian parliament building, the White House, brought the downfall of the SCSE within three days. In falling, the plotters also brought the USSR down with them. What Yeltsin, the Russian democratic movement and the nationalist movements of the other Soviet republics could not manage on their own was achieved for them by the Soviet state itself: the Soviet state ceased to exist practically with the coup's failure since it could no longer threaten to coerce Russia or the other republics of the USSR, and was formally wound up on 25 December 1991. Yeltsin and the Russian government stepped into the vacuum that it left behind to try to create a new Russia.

Conclusion

Absolutist political regimes failed twice in Russia in the twentieth century and on neither occasion did they lay the basis for a more stable polity to develop. Tsarism collapsed before creating the social basis that would have enabled the state to evolve into a democratic order as the Provisional Government and moderate socialists desired. The modernization of Tsarism had not created a large capitalist class that had the resources to support democracy as crisis swept away the old order; war and the destruction of the Russian imperial army therein, destroyed the coercive apparatus that might have shored up moderate political authority long enough for a compromise to develop over Russia's future. With no strong economic classes or institutions supporting democracy, it faded under pressure from popular demands and as moderate politicians compromised themselves by supporting the unpopular war effort. The state and political authority collapsed and in the ensuing revolution, the Bolsheviks, an organized political force able to mobilize the people and direct them through the party and the administration that it was able to improvise, emerged victorious.

Victory, however, had its own costs. Soviet history was a struggle to control both the people and administration to build a better society in conditions of internal weakness and external threats. This struggle was always chaotic, costly of human life and neglectful of human needs. The Soviet system only achieved the mobilization of the peoples of the USSR in the service of its developmental goals through coercion. In the process it destroyed as much as it created, and built a political system that was more self-serving than it was dedicated to the betterment of society. This in turn subverted the ability of Soviet leaders to command that socialist development take a specific course. The party leadership was locked into a constant battle to have its policies implemented in what it deemed to be the correct fashion. Neither political coercion nor efforts at reform resolved this problem and by the time that Brezhnev took power, the political will to deal with it had almost disappeared. Gorbachev's efforts at creating a more efficient state based on party leadership degenerated into chaos as he both undermined party power and tried to preserve it at the same time. Again, collapse took place before the basis of a democratic order was laid. There was some privatization of state property at the end of the Soviet period, but it was of dubious legality and involved the transfer of state resources into the hands of the *nomenklatura*. Control over property gave elite groups power at the end of the Soviet period, but they did not necessarily have in mind a positive end to which this power could be deployed. The resources that they controlled were often badly managed, unprofitable and technologically out of date. Russians with economic power at the end of the USSR were not, therefore, politically united in support of either democracy or the market, but would be concerned with their own survival if their control over property were challenged.

Such a challenge was, however, inevitable. Boris Yeltsin and the Russian government were catapulted into control of the Russian economy and state after the August 1991 coup failed, had only a weak grasp on power and little idea about what to do with it. Survival meant coping with economic collapse and developing social support; coping with economic collapse and developing social support required building effective administration; building effective administration meant taking some of the resources under the control of former elites and using them to build up the Russian state into a machine that could support the market and cope with the diversity of a society stratified by the market and expressed through democracy. There were high hopes after August 1991 that Yeltsin could manage this transformation of Russian politics and society. Unfortunately, as we shall see in the following chapters, these hopes were not met and many of the problems faced in 1991 remain to be solved by Yeltsin's successor.

Notes

1 Fuller reviews of Tsarism can be found in R. Pipes (1977) *Russia under the old regime*, Harmondsworth: Penguin; G. Hosking (1998) *Russia. People and empire, 1552–1917*, London: Fontana. For the revolutionary period see O. Figes (1997) *A people's tragedy. The Russian revolution 1891–1924*, London: Pimlico; E. Acton, V. Cherniaev and W.G. Rosenberg (eds) (1997) *Critical companion to the Russian revolution, 1914–1921*, London: Edward Arnold; G. Hosking (1990) *A history of the Soviet Union*, revised edition, London: Fontana; R. Service (1997) *A history of twentieth-century Russia*, London: Penguin. The Soviet era is covered in more detail in Service, *A history* ...; Hosking, *A history of the Soviet Union*; R.G. Suny (1998) *The Soviet experiment. Russia, the USSR and the successor states*, New York: Oxford University Press; J. Keep (1995) *Last of the empires. A history of the Soviet Union 1945–1991*, Oxford: Oxford University Press; P. Kenez (1999) *A history of the Soviet Union from the beginning to the end*, Cambridge: Cambridge University Press. A review of Soviet history through documents can be found in R. Sakwa (1999) *The rise and fall of the Soviet Union 1917–1991*, London: Routledge. Change in Russian society is examined in more detail in V. Andrle (1994) *A social history of twentieth-century Russia*, London: Edward Arnold. *Perestroika* and the demise of the Soviet Union are covered in the aforementioned general histories of the USSR and in A. Brown (1996) *The Gorbachev factor*, Oxford: Oxford University Press; D. Kotz with F. Weir (1997) *Revolution from above. The demise of the Soviet system*, London: Routledge; M.E. Urban with V. Igrunov and S. Mitrokhin (1997) *The rebirth of politics in Russia*, Cambridge: Cambridge University Press; S. White (1993) *After Gorbachev*, Cambridge: Cambridge University Press; J.F. Hough (1997) *Democratization and revolution in the USSR, 1985–1991*, Washington, DC: Brookings Institution.
2 Pipes, *op. cit.*, p. 100.
3 *Ibid*, pp. 77–8.
4 T.J. Colton (1995) *Moscow. Governing the socialist metropolis*, Cambridge, MA: The Belknap Press, p. 52
5 T. Skocpol (1979) *States and social revolutions. A comparative analysis of France, Russia and China*, Cambridge: Cambridge University Press, p. 90.
6 See P. Gatrell (1986) *The Tsarist Economy 1850–1917*, London: Batsford, p. 32; A. Nove (1982) *An Economic History of the USSR*, Harmondsworth: Penguin Books.
7 Figes, *A people's tragedy* ..., pp. 168–70.
8 *Rossiiskii statisticheskii ezhegodnik*, Moscow: Goskomstat Rossii (1995), p. 17.
9 Weiss and Hobson, *States and economic development* ..., pp. 105–6; Gatrell, *The Tsarist economy*, pp. 177–84.
10 Colton, *Moscow* ..., p. 57.
11 Figes, *A people's tragedy*, p. 174.
12 *Ibid*, pp. 173–9; Hosking, *Russia* ..., pp. 407–8.
13 T. Shanin (1986) *Russia, 1905–07: revolution as a moment of truth. The roots of otherness: Russia's turn of the century. Volume 2*, Basingstoke: Macmillan. See also A. Ascher (1988 and 1992) *The revolution of 1905*, 2 volumes, Stanford: Stanford University Press.
14 Figes, *A people's tragedy* ..., chapter one.
15 Shanin, *Russia, 1905–07*, pp. 236–51.
16 Hosking, *Russia* ..., p. 435
17 J. Channon (1992) 'The peasantry in the revolutions of 1917', in E. Rogovin Frankel, J. Frankel and B. Knei-Paz (eds) *Revolution in Russia. Reassessments of 1917*, Cambridge: Cambridge University Press, p. 117.
18 See N. Harding (1981) *Lenin's political thought: volume 2, theory and practice in the socialist revolution*, Basingstoke: Macmillan.

19 On the party and its operations see R. Hill and P. Frank (1986) *The Soviet Communist Party*, third edition, London: Allen and Unwin.

20 A.J. Polan (1984) *Lenin and the end of politics*, London: Methuen; N. Robinson (1995) *Ideology and the collapse of the Soviet system. A critical history of Soviet ideological discourse*, Aldershot: Edward Elgar, pp. 33–51.

21 *Constitution (Fundamental Law) of the Union of Soviet Socialist Republics*, Moscow: Novosti, 1977, p. 16.

22 G. Gill (1990) *The origins of the Stalinist political system*, Cambridge: Cambridge University Press, pp. 37–9.

23 G.M. Easter (2000) *Reconstructing the state. Personal networks and elite identity in Soviet Russia*, Cambridge: Cambridge University Press, p. 33.

24 M. Fainsod (1958) *Smolensk under Soviet rule*, London: Macmillan, pp. 48–52.

25 Robinson, *Ideology* . . ., pp. 52–4.

26 Easter, *Reconstructing the state* . . ., pp. 38–9.

27 M. Lewin (1968) *Russian peasants and Soviet power. A study of collectivization*, London: George Allen and Unwin, p. 487.

28 R.W. Davies (1980) *The socialist offensive. The collectivisation of Soviet agriculture, 1929–1930*, Cambridge, MA: Harvard University Press, pp. 412–13; Hosking, *A history*. . ., p. 166.

29 J. Kornai (1992) *The socialist system. The political economy of communism*, Oxford: Clarendon Press, especially pp. 180–86.

30 Nove, *An economic history* . . . , p. 196.

31 D. Filtzer (1986) *Soviet workers and Stalinist industrialization*, London: Pluto. On the problem of labour productivity in later periods see B. Arnott (1988) *Controlling Soviet labour. Experimental change from Brezhnev to Gorbachev*, Basingstoke: Macmillan.

32 For an explanation of these processes see M.E. Urban (1985) 'Conceptualizing political power in the USSR: patterns of binding and bonding', *Studies in Comparative Communism*, 18(4): 207–226.

33 See J.F. Hough (1969) *The Soviet prefects: the local party organs in industrial decision making*, Cambridge, MA: Harvard University Press; P. Rutland (1993) *The politics of economic stagnation in the Soviet Union. The role of local party organs in economic management*, Cambridge: Cambridge University Press.

34 Easter, *Reconstructing the state* . . ., especially chapter 6.

35 Fainsod, S*molensk* . . ., pp. 270–1. There was plenty of scope for this extension. Appointment of city and district party secretaries was not controlled by the Central Committee apparatus until 1935, and even as late as 1937 the number of party officials whose posts were subject to confirmation by the Central Committee numbered 'only 5860 of a national stratum of party secretaries and officials numbering well over 100 thousand'. The inspection and exchange of party cards, which was supposed to root out members of opposition groups and remove inactive party members to make the party more efficient, enabled local party leaders to protect their family circles by removing their critics from the party. J. Arch Getty and O.V. Naumov (1999) *The road to terror. Stalin and the self-destruction of the Bolsheviks, 1932–1939*, New Haven: Yale University Press, pp. 265–66, 205–11, 220–29.

36 M. Fainsod (1963) *How Russia is ruled*, London: Oxford University Press, pp. 388–89. See also, pp. 234–37; P.R. Gregory (1990) *Restructuring the Soviet economic bureaucracy*, Cambridge: Cambridge University Press, p. 67.

37 G. Gleason (1991) 'Fealty and loyalty: informal: authority structures in Central Asia', *Soviet Studies*, 43(4): pp. 613–28; Gregory, *Restructuring* . . ., p. 66.

38 K. Jowitt (1992) *New world disorder. The Leninist extinction*, Berkeley: University of California Press, chapter 4.

39 J. Stalin (1934) 'Otchetnii doklad XVII s'ezdu partii o rabote TsK VKP(b)', in J. Stalin (1952) *Voprosy Leninizma*, Moscow: Gospolitizdat, pp. 515, 517. See also Getty and Naumov, *The road to terror . . .*, p. 205.

40 On the threats to Stalin in 1934 see Service, *A history . . .*, pp. 212–14; Easter, *Reconstructing the state . . .*, pp. 142–3.

41 Classic accounts of the terror include Alexander Solzhenitsyn (1974–76) *The Gulag archipelago*, London: Fontana and R. Conquest (1971) *The Great Terror. Stalin's purge of the 1930s*, London: Pelican. Revisionist accounts can be found in J. Arch Getty (1983) *Origins of the great purge. The Soviet Communist Party reconsidered*, Cambridge: Cambridge University Press; J. Arch Getty and R.T. Manning (eds) (1993) *Stalinist terror: new perspectives*, Cambridge: Cambridge University Press; Getty and Naumov, *The road to terror . . .*.

42 Russia's wartime experiences are dealt with in Service, *A history . . .*, and Hosking, *A history. . . .* Detailed accounts can be found in J. Erickson (1975 and 1983) *The road to Stalingrad* and *The road to Berlin*, London: Weidenfeld and Nicolson; R. Overy (1998) *Russia's war*, London: Allen Lane.

43 Robinson, *Ideology . . .*, pp. 73–80.

44 Keep, *Last of the empires . . .*, p. 59.

45 *Ibid*, pp. 107–8; Fainsod, *How Russia is ruled*, p. 573.

46 D. Lane (1990) *Soviet society under perestroika*, Boston: Unwin Hyman, p. 128; *Rossiiskii statisticheskii ezhegodnik*, p. 17.

47 E. Hewitt (1988) *Reforming the Soviet economy. Equality versus efficiency*, Washington, DC: Brookings Institution, pp. 223–7.

48 *Constitution . . .*, p. 16.

49 For alternative accounts of the USSR as a weak state see Urban, 'Conceptualizing political power in the USSR . . .', and D. van Atta (1990) 'The USSR as a "weak state": agrarian resistance to perestroika', *World Politics*, 42(1): pp. 129–49.

50 M. Goldman (1983) *USSR in crisis. The failure of an economic system*, New York: W.W. Norton, p. 98.

51 See Jowitt, 'Neo-traditionalism', in his *New world disorder. . . .*

52 Calculated from the figures in W. Zimmerman (1987) 'Mobilized participation and the nature of Soviet dictatorship', in J.R. Millar (ed.) *Politics, work and daily life in the USSR. A survey of former Soviet citizens*, Cambridge: Cambridge University Press, 1987, p. 350. For an anthropological account of influence peddling in the USSR see A.V. Ledeneva (1998) *Russia's economy of favours. Blat, networking and informal exchange*, Cambridge: Cambridge University Press.

53 Goldman, *USSR in crisis . . .*, p. 55; Hewitt, *Reforming the Soviet economy . . .*, p. 180.

54 A. Åslund (1989) *Gorbachev's struggle for economic reform*, London: Pinter, p. 16.

55 Keep, *Last of the empires . . .*, p. 222.

56 R. Sakwa (1999) *Soviet politics in perspective*, London: Routledge, p. 223.

57 Åslund, *Gorbachev's struggle . . .*, p. 17; D. Kuzin (1993) 'Rossiiskaya ekonomika na mirovom rynke', *Obshchestvo i ekonomika*, (3), p. 33.

58 Hewitt, *Reforming the Soviet economy . . .*, p. 67; M. Gorbachev (1996) *Memoirs*, London: Doubleday, p. 215.

59 M. Gorbachev (1987) *Perestroika. New thinking for our country and the world*, London: Collins, p. 22.

60 The campaign is dissected in detail in S. White (1996) *Russia goes dry. Alcohol, state and society*, Cambridge: Cambridge University Press.

61 Åslund, *Gorbachev's struggle . . .*, pp. 74, 79.

62 Gorbachev, *Memoirs*, p. 189.

63 Brown, *The Gorbachev factor . . .*, p. 169.

64 Yeltsin's account of these events can be found in his (1990) *Against the grain. An autobiography*, London: Jonathan Cape. See also J. Morrison (1991) *Boris Yeltsin*.

From Bolshevik to democrat, Harmondsworth: Penguin; L. Aron (2000) *Boris Yeltsin. A revolutionary life*, London: Harper Collins.

65 N. Robinson (1992) 'Gorbachev and the place of the party in Soviet reform, 1985–1991', *Soviet Studies*, 44(3): pp. 423–43

66 K. Henderson and N. Robinson (1997) *Post-communist politics*, London: Prentice Hall, pp. 46–8. Detailed accounts of the election can be found in M.E. Urban (1990) *More power to the Soviets. The democratic revolution in the USSR*, Aldershot: Edward Elgar; S. White, R. Rose and I. McAllister (1997) *How Russia votes*, Chatham, NJ: Chatham House Publishers, pp. 22–9.

67 N. Robinson (1993) 'Parliamentary politics under Gorbachev: opposition and the failure of socialist pluralism', *Journal of Communist Studies*, 9(1): pp. 91–108; Urban *et al.*, *The rebirth of politics in Russia* ..., pp. 147–71.

68 For details of the informal movement see Urban *et al.*, *The rebirth of politics in Russia*...; M. Steven Fish (1995) *Democracy from scratch. Opposition and regime in the new Russian revolution*, Princeton: Princeton University Press.

69 The fragmentation of the CPSU is described in G. Gill (1994) *The collapse of a single party system. The disintegration of the Communist Party of the Soviet Union*, Cambridge: Cambridge University Press. Events in the Soviet republics are described in Henderson and Robinson, *Post-communist politics*...; Suny, *The Soviet experiment*...; G. Lapidus, V. Zaslavsky and P. Goldman (1992) *From Union to Commonwealth: nationalism and separatism in the Soviet republics*, Cambridge: Cambridge University Press; I. Bremmer and R. Taras (eds) (1996) *New states, new politics. Building the post-Soviet nations*, Cambridge: Cambridge University Press.

70 J. Barth Urban and V.D. Solovei (1997) *Russia's communists at the crossroads*, Boulder: Westview, pp. 37–46.

71 White *et al.*, *How Russia votes*, pp. 31–4; Henderson and Robinson, *Post-communist politics*, pp. 112–14.

72 S. Johnson and H. Kroll (1991) 'Managerial strategies for spontaneous privatization', *Soviet Economy*, 7(4): pp. 281–316

73 N. Amodio (1993) 'From ministries to corporations', *Journal of Communist Studies*, 9 (1): 227–39; S. Clarke (1994) 'Privatisation: the politics of capital and labour', in S. White, A. Pravda and Z. Gitelman (eds) *Developments in Soviet and Post-Soviet politics*, Basingstoke: Macmillan, pp. 166–70.

74 M. McAuley (1992) 'Politics, economics and elite realignment in Russia: a regional perspective', *Soviet Economy*, 8(1): pp. 46–88.

75 S.L. Solnick (1997) *Stealing the state. Control and collapse in Soviet institutions*, Cambridge, MA: Harvard University Press.

3 Russian politics under Boris Yeltsin

Democratic hopes versus political fragmentation

The problems facing Russia at the end of the Soviet Union were common to post-communist states. A decisive break with the communist past required the reconstruction of political power so that economic reform could be carried out and democracy consolidated.[1] The role of the state in securing changes and breaking with the past was paramount. Democratic consolidation and economic reform in a post-communist state should provide what are often called 'public goods'. A public good is something that everyone in a society enjoys the benefits of without exception. Democratic consolidation would secure such public goods as freedom from persecution and arbitrary political control, and legal rights of appeal against the infringements of civil, economic and political freedoms and rights. The public goods of economic reform were supposed to be freedom from economic uncertainty. This freedom would be provided by creating low inflation, a stable currency, greater access to consumer goods and the right to own property. Economic reform would create inequalities so that the enjoyment of these public goods would be differentiated. However, no matter what level of wealth an individual enjoyed they would still benefit from economic stability and the potential for economic growth that derived from it: no one, neither an unemployed factory worker nor a millionaire banker has an interest in economic uncertainty and potential economic collapse.

Public goods, however, are not easy to provide. Whilst all members of a society enjoy the benefits of a public good, they may lose more from the changes involved in providing a public good: the provision of a public good may harm an individual or group's interests if they have to give up privileges they had heretofore exclusively enjoyed. Alternatively, action to secure a public good requires an effort and sacrifice for the common good that many people are not prepared to make. The delivery of a public good may bring benefit to an individual, but they may not wish to incur the short-term costs of sacrificing their time, money, present relations with colleagues, society and elites, to secure it. This is especially the case where the eventual provision of a public good is not guaranteed: a personal sacrifice may well turn out to have been for nothing. The provision of public goods thus occasion what are called collective action problems. It is rarely in the interest of the majority of people who would gain from the provision of public goods to take action to secure them since they would be guaranteed to suffer personal loss for an uncertain gain. It is often in the interest of a minority who would lose some privilege to act to block policies and actions to create a public good because they would lose more as individuals than they would gain as members of society enjoying a public good. In other words, people have selective incentives to resist moves to secure public goods, and selective disincentives to get involved in actions to obtain them.

The problems of providing public goods in Russia meant that 'collective actors' (as opposed to individual citizens) such as state institutions and the politicians empowered by society to act on their behalf bore the brunt of responsibility for taking actions to secure public goods for society. This meant that the state would be the object of protest from groups threatened by the provision of public goods. Its officials and institutions would be attacked and policy subverted by the powerful groups fearful of the loss of resources that guaranteed their position as the economic system changed and privileged new forces, and as power was vested in new democratic institutions and an independent judicial system. Ordinary citizens impoverished by the disruption of traditional patterns of economic activity would also criticize it. The challenges of both the ordinary citizens of Russia and elite groups had to be resisted if democratic consolidation and economic reform were to be secured. Political institutions, leaders and movements had to learn to represent social interests, resist them and reconcile them within the state, and using the powers of the state. Society, and in particular elite groups, had to learn that the political system was not going to produce outcomes that were uniformly in their favour, that the provision of public goods would prevail over private interest. Democracy is a matter of subjecting one's 'interests to uncertainty', accepting that the outcomes of political processes may not suit your private interest and working to secure one's interests in a way that might bring victory, but equally, and more likely, will bring partial success through compromise. Acceptance of this is particularly important by elites since they have resources that can be used to try to buy policy outcomes that they prefer and because they occupy positions of responsibility and can try to change the rules by which politics are governed and decisions made.[2] In short, dealing with the problems of post-communism in a democratic fashion required that the state develop capacity (the administrative means of getting things done) so as to take reformist measures and secure public goods, some autonomy from powerful groups so as to implement reform, and that it cease to rely on despotic, coercive power to overcome opposition from political opponents.

Russia under Yeltsin never managed to balance these different aspects of democratic post-communist change to reform its economy effectively or consolidate democracy unambiguously. Part of the reason for this was economic and due to economic policy. Russia was in such a weakened condition economically at the end of communism that it was difficult for the state to accumulate resources necessary to break the power of old elites from the *nomenklatura* that had appropriated state property for their own use at the end of the communist period. The economic policy adopted by the government that was designed to reform state power provoked conflict rather than assuaged it so that the Russian government found its rule and the power of the state challenged from day one of reform. These issues will be discussed in Chapter 4. Economics does not explain everything, however, although we will have to mention it on more than one occasion in this chapter because economics and politics have been inseparable in contemporary Russia. Political and institutional factors also played a major role in the failure of democratic politics under Yeltsin and these are the main subjects of this chapter.

Politically, Yeltsin faced two tasks at the fall of the USSR: how to consolidate his hold on office and how to create an effective administrative machinery of government. Economic policy offered solutions to these tasks, but, and as we shall see in Chapter 4, it failed to deliver them. Ultimately, Yeltsin was to be successful in consolidating his hold on power because he compromised on economic policy and the construction of effective government. There were two dimensions to the compromise on creating effective government. First, Yeltsin compromised on the composition of the government, drawing powerful groups into government, dividing and ruling between them and creating new institutions in the government to make him indispensable to all but beholden (when possible) to none. Second, Yeltsin connived at the dispersal of power throughout Russia as he courted regional political elites and the support that they could give him in his struggles with, first, Russia's parliament, and second, to get re-elected. The consequences of Yeltsin's actions were that central administration was confused, local governments frequently acted independently of central control to pursue their own policies, and democratic procedures were subverted. Administration did not become impersonal and governed by law, but was shaped by patronage and the use of office proprietarily for personal political gain and sometimes also for personal financial advantage. In particular, policy-making came to be unduly influenced by Yeltsin's personal interests and those of the economically powerful. Yeltsin accumulated immense powers to his office, the presidency of the Russian Federation, and secured his tenure of office, but his ability to use those powers, or command the government to work for the general good of the Russian people, was limited by the compromises he had made. The balance of powers in the Russian constitution was heavily skewed in favour of the presidency both by design and because political parties in the legislatures were unable to effectively control government. An effective constitutional and bureaucratic system thus failed to emerge during the years of Yeltsin's rule and hopes for democratic development degenerated into popular distrust of politicians and political institutions. Ironically, the degeneration of democratic hopes had its roots in efforts to protect the first weak shoots of Russian democracy at the end of the communist period by creating a new executive institution to lead the fledgling Russian government, the Presidency of the Russian Federation.

Creating the fault-lines of Russian politics: the foundation of the Russian presidency

Presidents, according to one school of political science thinking, are bad for democracy. The charges laid against presidentialism are many. A presidency gives one person too much power and discourages consensus because politics becomes a game of winner takes all. Presidentialism leads to the neglect of party development and cabinet government. It divides the executive under the president from the legislature as they contest sovereignty and the right to rule. The concentration of power in their office leads presidents to suffer delusions of grandeur as they 'conflate' their 'supporters with "the people" as a whole' and define their 'policies as reflections of the popular will'.[3] The Russian presidency under Yeltsin was to come to display all of these failings, but the intention behind its creation in 1991 was the opposite: the new institution was formed to protect Russian democracy, to deliver further democratic consolidation and economic reform that Gorbachev had failed to supply, rather than to weaken it.[4] Regrettably, the way that it came into being had two unfortunate effects: it made Boris Yeltsin's political survival appear to be the same as the survival of reformism and democratic consolidation, and it created the office of president with little supporting political infrastructure to resolve or prevent conflict between president and parliament over government and policy.

Yeltsin's survival and the presidency were linked because of the weakness of the democratic opposition at the end of the Soviet period. Democratic Russia had enough adherents in the Russian parliament elected in March 1990 to elect Yeltsin as chair of the Russian Supreme Soviet, but it was not a stable party to be relied on for support in the long-term: it was a fluid group of like-minded individuals and it did not command majority support in parliament.[5] Yeltsin's position in the emerging Russian state was therefore precarious in 1990 and early 1991. He had been elected by a narrow margin by the Russian Congress of People's Deputies and was weak in comparison to Gorbachev, who had considerable executive powers as President of the USSR. At first, there was no prospect of creating a Russian presidency to isolate Yeltsin from conservative threats in the parliament because Yeltsin's supporters could not muster a two-thirds majority to vote through the constitutional amendments needed to create a Russian presidency.[6] A means of overcoming this hurdle was, ironically, provided by Gorbachev's efforts to legitimate the USSR. Yeltsin and his supporters added a question to the referendum on the Union in March 1991 in Russia asking, is it 'necessary to introduce the post of [Russian] President, who would be elected by a republic-wide popular vote?' Popular support for the creation of a Russian presidency weakened conservative attacks on Yeltsin in parliament and led to the establishment of the mechanisms for electing the Russian presidency (majority elections, with a run-off if no candidate got over 50 per cent of the vote in the first-round election). Yeltsin duly beat five other candidates in the first round of the election in June 1991, receiving 57.3 per cent of the vote.

The way that the presidency was created in the course of the struggle for sovereignty and his first round electoral victory created a particular image of the presidency for Yeltsin. He saw his post as based on general popular acclamation rather than the support of a proportion of the electorate, and assumed that his policies were the will of the people. The presidency was created to symbolize the rebirth of the 'nation' and its democratic course. This was explained in Yeltsin's inauguration speech in July 1991:

> ... for the first time in their history, Russia's citizens have made their choice. They not only chose ... a President, they above all chose the path that our homeland is to follow. It is a democratic path, a reformist path... The President is not a god, is not a new monarch, he is a citizen invested with enormous responsibility for the fate of Russia and his fellow citizens; he is above all the person the people have placed their confidence in.[7]

The link between President, people and the democratic path of development was something that Yeltsin was to turn to again in the coming years of conflict over the Constitution and he used referenda to shore up his position in the spring of 1993 and to ratify a new Constitution in December 1993. More immediately, the image of the presidency as guarantor of change and protector of hard-won liberties was reinforced by events. Successful resistance to the August 1991 coup made Yeltsin and his new position seem positively heroic, the only body that could decisively take action to save Russia from slipping back into the past. One consequence of this was that Yeltsin did not work effectively to establish a presidential party and was never to do so. Elected as a symbol of change and its protector, parties were, in his view, to align themselves with him and his programme. This was spelt out in his speech introducing economic reform in late October 1991 when he declared that those 'parties which support the proposals could consider creating a united political bloc ... a strategic political alliance with the President'.[8] The weakness of parties and party support for the executive reinforced the image of Yeltsin as President as heroic and dynamic protector of Russia's progress, and he soon linked the failure of parties to the need for strong executive power: 'a civil society is only now being born in Russia [and] a multiparty system has not developed fully... In these conditions, a strong executive can be a guarantor of Russia's integrity and of movement along the developing path of reform.'[9]

The birth and baptism under fire of the presidency created more than its image and the idea that in helping Yeltsin to survive politically the presidency was essential to the survival of Russian democracy. It also led to a lack of attention being paid to the development of the presidency as an institution and the relations between it and the parliament. Institutional design was at first hurried and compromised, and was subsequently chaotic, concerned with filling gaps rather than ensuring coherence and balance in the constitutional exercise of power. The result was that there was a large gap between the idea of the presidency held by Yeltsin and that of many parliamentarians. The 'Law on the President of the RSFSR' adopted by parliament in April 1991 was a compromise. The direct power of parliament over the formation of the government (it only ratified the President's nominee for Prime Minister) and the ordinary activities of government and President were weak. However, parliament could alter government policy by amending the budget and voting changes to the structure and powers of the President and government, and had control over some appointments (for example, the election of the Constitutional Court). Presidential veto power over parliamentary decisions was weak. The President could return legislation to the Supreme Soviet, but not to the Congress of People's Deputies, for reconsideration, but a simple majority (the same simple majority that had passed the law in the first place) could override the presidential veto. The President could not dissolve either of the houses of parliament.

Mechanisms to resolve conflict between President and the parliament were insubstantial. The Russian Constitutional Court was prohibited by law from dealing with political cases until December 1992 and until July 1994 it could deal only with one case at a time.[10] It was frequently unable, therefore, to pass judgements in favour of either parliament or President. The weakness of the presidential veto over Supreme Soviet legislation meant that parliament had little need to take account of the President's views, or the consistency of their legislation with government policy when drafting laws. Moreover, there was no clear demarcation of who was responsible for initiating policy. Both President and parliament saw themselves as the lead institution in policy-making and claimed this role was theirs because they represented the 'people'. The Constitution described the President as the head of the executive and highest official in Russia (Article 121.1), but the two chambers of parliament were the 'highest bodies of state power' (Article 104). Yeltsin, as has been mentioned, saw the office of President as combining representation of the people with the choice of a 'path that our homeland is to follow' and claimed he had 'enormous responsibility for the fate of Russia and his fellow citizens'. Parliamentary leaders justified its claims in much the same terms, adding that parliament was more representative than the President was because it contained a range of political opinions.[11] In the view of many parliamentary deputies, and constitutionally, the powers of the President and changes to them were granted by parliament, and what parliament had gifted to the President it could take away. The discrepancy between the lack of day-to-day parliamentary oversight over the activities of the government and the powers of parliament to change the structure of government and distribution of power within it increased the prospects of conflict between the branches of government becoming fundamental, about the sovereignty, rights and prerogatives of government.

The fault-lines exposed: surviving the constitutional conflict, weakening reform, 1991–1993

If Yeltsin associated his personal fate with that of reform in 1991, gradually, and after the initiation of economic reform in 1992 and when reform policies came under attack, he began to see his survival in office as the same thing as reform and sometimes as a substitute for it. The first two years of Russian politics were marked by a bitter struggle between parliament and President over sovereignty – the right to rule – in which Yeltsin was able to portray his cause as that of democratic and market reform against a parliament that was increasingly associated with the politics of the 'Red-Brown alliance', a peculiar and unpleasant mixture of neo-communist, neo-fascist and nationalist ideologues. As we have already argued, the conflict between Yeltsin and the parliaments was always likely because there was little in the Constitution or the political scene to prevent it.[12] It became inevitable, however, with the choices that Yeltsin made after August 1991 because Yeltsin chose a radical economic reform option – 'shock therapy' – that was politically divisive. At first, however, the choice of radical economic reform seemed to solve many short-term political problems as well as economic ones (which we shall deal with in the next chapter).

The adoption of radical economic reform with the consent of parliament established that the political lead would be taken by the President and the government, rather than by the parliament, facilitated the creation of a post-communist government and resolved the related issue of who controlled the Russian economy. The collapse of Soviet administration engendered by the August 1991 coup came before the presidency and its attendant institutions, such as the Presidential Administration (headed by Yuri Petrov) and the State Council (headed by the State Secretary Gennadii Burbulis), had established their relationship with the government, the Council of Ministers, under Prime Minister Ivan Silayev. No settled administrative routine had been created by the time of the coup, and after it a competition began to shape policy and take control from moribund Soviet state bodies. A key issue in this contest was control over the economy and the relation of the Russian economy to the post-Soviet Union. At the instigation of Burbulis, Yeltsin resolved the issue of economic control and the struggles that were growing between the agencies of the Russian government at the end of October 1991 by asking parliament to grant him the power to issue mandatory decrees to begin the process of radical economic reform.[13] The granting of decree powers and the subsequent reorganization of government resolved the power struggle in favour of Burbulis since he was the political patron of the Yegor Gaidar's team of reform economists, and created the basis of a government for Yeltsin in place of the remnants of the old Silayev government.[14] Yeltsin became Prime Minister, but Burbulis led the government, which included Gaidar and his colleagues, on a day-to-day basis.[15] Yeltsin's control over the executive branch of government was reinforced by his use of his decree powers to try to assert control over regional government. Elections for heads of regional administrations were cancelled so that the heads of regional administration and Presidential Representatives to the regions appointed by Yeltsin as the August coup collapsed to ensure compliance with Russian government laws and decrees were kept in place to implement economic reform.[16] In rapid order, therefore, Yeltsin had created what is often called the 'executive' or 'presidential' 'vertical', a hierarchy of administrative bodies responsible to the President and supposed to ensure the implementation of government policy throughout Russia.

On the face of it, then, the adoption of radical economic reform policies by Yeltsin should have consolidated administration. However, the reformers soon discovered the vicious irony of reform. The state needed capacity so that it could implement reform policies. However, to build capacity required reform; reform was the only way of weakening the power of reform's opponents so that the power of the state would grow. The only way out of this 'chicken and egg' conundrum was to convince people that the government was serious about reform and that compliance with the government's orders was ultimately going to be unavoidable. In the absence of strong state capacity to implement it, reform relied on what is called 'credible commitment': it would work if people were persuaded that the government was stable and would not deviate from its chosen course, if people accepted that its policies would be implemented. This front of credible commitment to reform was not to last for long because Yeltsin was not able to ensure that the executive was committed to reform, or to express his own credible commitment to change. In fact, the merger of the presidency and the government in the cause of economic reform at the end of 1991 and the start of 1992 was the apogee of the effective identification of the presidency with the movement of Russia towards capitalism. Thereafter, Yeltsin gradually began to move towards protecting the presidency through alliance building and the purpose of political activity increasingly became more narrowly focused on the maintenance of presidential power. Economic reform, and with it plans to reconstruct state power by changing the relationship of state to economy and society, were weakened.

The rot started at the top and was a product of the reform strategy chosen and the government/presidential merger. The 'presidential vertical' split over reform at the top. The radical economic policies that Gaidar and Burbulis favoured overlay both competition within the executive, and between the government and the parliaments: the chief strategy for rebuilding the Russian state therefore both fuelled and became entangled in institutional struggles. The most obvious sign of this at the end of 1991 was Vice President Alexander Rutskoi's criticism of the new government and its economic policies. Supreme Soviet Chair Ruslan Khasbulatov also felt excluded from decision making and began to drift towards opposition. Rutskoi and Khasbulatov's dissent would soon develop into come a complete break between them and Yeltsin, and lead to the tragedy of October 1993 and the physical destruction of the parliamentary cause, but in the short-term Khasbulatov's stance helped unify parliamentary opposition to the government.

Less visible, but equally important, were the growing divisions between the Presidential Administration and government. There was no broad agreement between the government and the Presidential Administration over economic reform and the consolidation of the government posed questions of how resources seized by the Presidential Administration from the Soviet party-state would be distributed, and how the Presidential Administration would manage access to Yeltsin as Prime Minister/President. For Gaidar and his ministers, the problem was Petrov, the head of the Presidential Administration. Under his control, the government claimed, the Presidential Administration interfered in the reorganization of the government's personnel service, delayed decrees on government reorganization, blocked access to the official communications network, provided resources for Rutskoi's political party and its anti-reform policies, pressed alternative advice on Yeltsin through the President's Council of Experts and used the General Management Office of the Presidential Administration to pursue economic policies at odds with the government's. In February 1992, a meeting of the government called for Petrov's removal. As intra-executive competition grew in the first few months of 1992, there was little policy co-ordination. Policies that would always have been difficult, perhaps impossible to implement, were weakened as 'lobbying' became an integral part of government and a successful means of altering policy. As Yeltsin notes in his autobiography 'lobbying in Russia is quite easy. Even against a staunch premier such as Gaidar was.'[17] (Gaidar became acting Prime Minister in June 1992.) Lobbyists came through the Presidential Administration in early 1992, working through Petrov and others. Their influence on policy was facilitated by Yeltsin's predisposition to listening to 'energetic representatives of the body of factory directors' admitted in his biography: 'if some middle-aged industrialist comes to me and ... says "I've been in Gazprom [the gas monopoly and successor to the USSR Ministry of the Gas Industry] for 40 years, what's your [minister] doing..." my heart, it goes without saying, cannot stand it.'[18]

However, for Yeltsin personally, lobbying was not all bad. Whilst the access of lobbies to government through the multiple and competing centres of executive power worked against Gaidar's reform plans, they also gave Yeltsin political options, enabling him to trade policy implementation for political support as the conflict between President and parliament over economic policy developed into a full-scale contest for power in the spring of 1992. Yeltsin also built up his political support by changing the way that power was balanced within the government and Presidential Administration. Together these two practices enabled Yeltsin to counter his low support in parliament; he constructed alliances with parliamentary forces at second hand, by favouring groups that had influence in parliament and could weaken votes against him by dividing his opponents. This allowed Yeltsin to survive politically, but at a cost to policy. He began to play reformers and political allies off against one another to maintain his position as the arbitrator between them. Coalitions were built that made it look as if one side had gained the upper hand over policy, and then subtly changed to equal out the balance of forces within government and enable Yeltsin to dominate government and choose between policy options.

This method of rule began in April 1992, when Viktor Chernomyrdin (from Gazprom and then in late middle age) and two other industrialists came into government and Burbulis resigned as First Deputy Prime Minister. In June, Yeltsin balanced this change in the government by making Gaidar acting Prime Minister and another reformer, Anatolii Chubais, a Deputy Prime Minister. In the autumn, the pendulum swung back away from the reformers as Yeltsin sought to ally himself to the industrialist centrist forces that were a part of Civic Union, the powerful association of industrialists and some political forces such as Rutskoi's People's Party of Free Russia, before the December 1992 Congress of People's Deputies meeting.[19] To do this Yeltsin distanced himself from the government's economic policy and he duly attacked the government's performance in a speech to the Supreme Soviet in October 1992. Gaidar was not confirmed as Prime Minister at the seventh convocation of the Russian CPD in December 1992 and Chernomyrdin was brought in to replace him. Burbulis also lost his post as State Secretary. The elevation of Chernomyrdin and the perceived change in economic policy that Burbulis and Gaidar's removal brought, split Civic Union in the spring of 1993 as its economic lobbies and politicians like Rutskoi parted ways over the issue of a referendum on the Constitution. Industrial groups (particularly the energy sector where Chernomyrdin had made his career) no longer needed a grand political alliance of parties and social movement to influence policy; struggle over economic policy was internalized in a government to which lobbies had ready access. In turn, Chernomyrdin's promotion in December 1992 was matched by the appointment of another economic reformer, Boris Fedorov, as Minister for Finance and the replacement of Petrov by Sergei Filatov in January 1993. Yeltsin thus ensured that no single interest gained too much power in government, but also that coalitions were not stable. The basic pattern of his 'pick and mix' personnel policy of appointing conservatives and then balancing them with economic liberals, and vice versa, was to continue after 1993 and the introduction of the new Constitution.

Yeltsin also benefited from coalition building because changes in the government meant it was a compromise and not strictly 'his'. This allowed him to disclaim responsibility for certain policies, direct blame for policy failure on to others, and choose which areas he wished to intervene in and which he wished to leave to the government.[20] This was reinforced by what Huskey calls the 'politics of institutional redundancy', the duplication of executive agencies.[21] As appointments were made to government and the Presidential Administration to ensure political support and options for Yeltsin, the number of agencies with overlapping competencies and their staff grew within government and the Presidential Administration, and between them. For example, by mid-1993 there were six different analytical centres in the Presidential Administration providing Yeltsin with information and advice, as well as the Presidential Council, which contained four specialist advisory groups. The creation of overlapping institutions hindered administrative effectiveness since clear lines of authority were not established and responsibility for policy formulation and implementation were blurred. The conflict between the Presidential Administration and the government over economic policy was one example of this. Not surprisingly, institutional redundancy also increased the number of bureaucrats. Moves to limit the growth of executive agencies only ever had a temporary effect as new bodies emerged to take the place of those closed down. The large number of overlapping agencies meant that political competition inside the state grew. When agencies have overlapping competencies their control over policy is a function of the political support that they can accrue. Under Yeltsin, 'the formal titles and powers of officials were not always reliable measures of their authority. Much depended on political ambition, skills and connections, especially with the central leader, in this case the President.'[22] Institutional redundancy thus stimulated competition for patronage and provided incentives to ally with resource rich lobby groups. Patronage and powerful allies provided protection when presidential needs changed, or as Yeltsin intervened in a policy area, scapegoating some agencies and promoting others.

The coalitions and administration that Yeltsin built were thus unstable. Whether this was by design or not is difficult to say. Instability as a style of rule was advantageous to Yeltsin in that it enabled him to divide his critics and rule over them, and there is a view that Yeltsin was psychologically predisposed to ruling by creating competing centres of power.[23] There is also an argument that this style of rule recreated some of the practices of the communist period so that it was a system that Yeltsin was used to as a former regional party leader and candidate Politburo member.[24] This would argue that Yeltsin deliberately ruled in this way to ensure his rule. On the other hand, it may be that Yeltsin was drawn in to this style of rule gradually, but inexorably, as one act of political survival led to another and created a system of patronage that Yeltsin could not escape and relied on not only for survival but to implement policy (such as it was). Building coalitions drew together political opposites who were not committed to alliance with one another, but to influence peddling and building their hold on power and access to Yeltsin. Consequently, Yeltsin drew to him people with resources that could support the fragile state and presidency, but the interests that permeated government were only loyal to Yeltsin whilst it was in their advantage. Yeltsin had clients and allies, rather than protégés, and he had to guard against their growing too strong or independent in the posts that he granted them and be wary that they might act against him if he did not satisfy them, and had to remove them or downgrade them as his needs changed.[25] Whatever the source of Yeltsin's style of rule, the effect was the same. The duplication of institutions and their linking up to powerful interests in order to increase their bureaucratic power compounded the Russian state's weakness. The muddle of institutions diminished state capacity as it was unclear whose orders should be obeyed, what bodies were responsible for generating policy and what organizations were responsible for implementing it. Connections with lobby groups created the impression that the state was not acting autonomously for the public good, but in the service of narrow, private interests, an idea that was strengthened by the corruption of public life and the use of *kompromat* (compromising materials) against political rivals by both the presidential and parliamentary factions. Together, corruption and the declining capacity of the state caused by institutional redundancy fragmented the organizational integrity of the Russian state: it came to be a series of competing institutions serving particular lobbies and reform agendas, rather than a site where the interaction of social interests sorted out popular preferences into a national policy agenda. Patronage demeaned bureaucratic neutrality and undermined possible sources of infrastructural power as the prestige of the state and its policies declined; influence peddling weakened constitutional channels of policy-making in favour of informal procedures that served private interests.

The dispersal of power at the centre between competing groups and institutions, and the compromising of the state, was complemented by a dispersal of power from the centre to the regions and republics (territorial units in which there is a sizeable, titular ethnic minority) of the Russian Federation. This meant that the state's power over its territory, one of the basic characteristics of being a state, was compromised. Although Yeltsin created the 'presidential vertical' in 1991, getting the provinces to abide by central policies was difficult. Many regional governments were under the control of old elites (an estimated 80–90 per cent of local officials retained their posts after the fall of communism[26]), and ethnic elites in the republics pressed for greater independence from Moscow. These groups often had links with industrialists opposed to government policy and sought to maintain their own power by isolating themselves and their peoples from the effects of economic reform. They were helped in this by the fact that the relationship between the President, the government and the republics and regions was not properly codified after the fall of the USSR. A Federal Treaty was signed in March 1992 by most of the republics and all of the regions (Chechnya, which had declared itself independent in September 1991, and Tatarstan, which wanted greater autonomy, refused to sign). The Treaty recognized all as having equal rights and obligations, but allowed the republics the trappings of statehood: constitutions, parliaments, presidents etc. However, the Treaty was too vague to properly regulate the relationship between centre and periphery for long. Republics and regions tried to negotiate concessions for themselves; the regions complained that the rights enjoyed by the republics were unjust and threatened to proclaim themselves republics; the republics threatened to secede from the Federation unless they were granted greater concessions and economic autonomy. The power struggle in Moscow between Yeltsin and the parliament made this administrative mess worse. Local elites took advantage of the weakness of central government to do what they pleased. President and parliament were played off against one another, and the power of local elites and industrialists over the regions and republics was strengthened at the expense of central government. The most visible outward sign of this was the compromise, and then loss of control, over the appointment of governors. Yeltsin was forced to concede that governors should only be appointed with the agreement of local Soviets, which had been elected in 1990 and were often under the control of old elites, and relented on some of the appointments he had already made. As a result, the majority of governors were chairmen of Soviets and members of the *nomenklatura*.[27] These governors had little sympathy with the reformers in Moscow. Taxes and contributions to the federal budget went unpaid and government economic policy was flaunted as elites cushioned their population from the effects of market reform by subverting the market and by aiding local industrialists' takeover of their enterprises.[28]

Politics under the new Constitution, 1993–1996: more of the same

Yeltsin's style of rule was successful in one thing: it enabled him to survive and defeat his political rivals in the Russian parliament. Parliamentary leaders had less to offer in the way of patronage to potential allies from either the old *nomenklatura*, or the new commercial elites that were emerging to dominate finance and media. The natural allies of the anti-Yeltsin forces were communists and nationalists; both disliked economic reform because they saw it as betraying the country to the alien, capitalist 'West' and neither could forgive Yeltsin his role in the destruction of the Soviet Union. Although Yeltsin and the governments that he headed either directly when he was Prime Minister, or indirectly as arbitrator between government factions, lost popularity as economic reform stalled and popular dissatisfaction with the political impasse in Moscow grew, the parliamentary cause was not able to gather sufficient support to defeat Yeltsin from these extremist sources. An attempt to solve the constitutional battle between parliament and President by a referendum in April 1993 saw Yeltsin victorious: 58 per cent of voters (or 37 per cent of the whole electorate) expressed confidence in him, 53 per cent (34 per cent of the electorate) approved of the executive's socioeconomic policies, and 67 per cent (43 per cent of the electorate) thought it necessary to hold early parliamentary elections. Only 49 per cent (31 per cent of the electorate) thought it necessary to hold early presidential elections.[29] This was not a strong enough victory for Yeltsin to settle the constitutional question peacefully, but it meant that the population broadly preferred Yeltsin to the parliament. When the crunch came and relations between President and parliament broke down into violence in October 1993 after Yeltsin, in violation of the Constitution, dissolved the parliament, parliamentary appeals for popular revolt were ignored and Yeltsin was able to organize the military suppression of the parliaments. The threat of civil war fizzled out in shocking, but localized, bloodshed around the parliament and Moscow's main television studio (over 100 people were killed).[30]

Yeltsin's victory over the parliament did not lay the basis for a new democratic politics. The defeat of the old parliament was followed by a referendum on a new Constitution, drawn up under Yeltsin and granting extensive formal powers to the president, and elections to a new, two-tier parliament, the Federal Assembly, comprising the State Duma and the Federation Council. The Constitution was approved, albeit narrowly, and the new parliament was elected on 12 December 1993. The formal powers of the presidency under the new Constitution are impressive. The President can appoint and dismiss ministers with the Prime Minister and nominate candidates for Prime Minister. The Duma cannot reject the President's candidates for Prime Minister more than twice; a third rejection leads to the dissolution of the Duma and the appointment of the Prime Minister by the President. The President also has extensive powers of appointment to the military, judicial and regional posts. The President has the right to initiate legislation and referenda, and to issue decrees that have the force of law until parliament legislates to supplant them. The President can veto legislation from the Duma and the Federation Council; to overcome a veto the Duma and the Council have to muster two-thirds support for a vetoed bill. Presidential power is reinforced by the fact that it is extremely difficult to change the Constitution, and there are few checks on it. Changes to those articles of the Constitution that define the division of power and the rights of the presidency and parliament have to be approved by three-quarters of the members of the Federation Council and two-thirds of the State Duma's deputies. However, constitutional amendments only come into force once they have been 'approved by the legislative bodies of power of at least two-thirds of the members of the Russian Federation' (Article 136). There is therefore little prospect of a quick, simple, constitutional transfer of power from the President to parliament or government. Checks on presidential power from the Federal Assembly are weak. The Federation Council ratifies presidential decrees on states of emergency and the deployment of troops outside of the Russian Federation. The Duma can vote no confidence in the government, but the President can reject its finding. If a second vote is held within three months and goes against the government, the President has a choice: he can disband the government or dissolve the Duma. Voting no confidence is, therefore, as much a threat to the Duma as to the government. There are some limits to the President's powers to dissolve the Duma: it cannot be dissolved until a year after its election if it rejects his candidate for Prime Minister, or for any reason during the last six months of the President's term of office, a state of emergency or impeachment proceedings. However, impeachment of the President is almost impossible. A charge of treason or some major crime has to be supported by one-third of Duma deputies and be verified by a Duma committee. If the committee's findings are supported by a two-thirds vote of all Duma deputies, and the Supreme and Constitutional Courts, a resolution to impeach the President is put to the Federation Council, where it has to be passed by a two-thirds vote of all deputies. All these procedures have to be brought to a conclusion within three months.

The powers granted by the 1993 Constitution to Yeltsin led some analysts to describe the presidency as being 'superpresidential' and having 'hegemonic decision-making powers' which are virtually unmatched amongst post-communist presidents.[31] Yeltsin's use of his formal powers after 1993 was slighter, however, than these appellations suggest. Yeltsin initiated legislation, vetoed laws passed by the Federal Assembly and issued decrees after 1993, but he did not use his powers to govern with a great purpose except to get himself re-elected and to maintain himself in office

The reasons for this relative lack of activity in constructing reformist policy was that Yeltsin did not need to be active and was unsure of how to be active. The results of the 1993 Duma elections did not indicate a clear popular preference for a particular set of policies that Yeltsin might pursue to secure re-election, or create a parliamentary majority that might have put concerted pressure on the government to follow a particular policy agenda. The results of the December 1993 elections can be found in Table 3.1. The 1993 elections signalled a partial failure of pro-radical reform politicians as Gaidar's new party, Russia's Choice, only gathered 15 per cent of the vote and the pro-government Party of Russian Unity and Accord only just secured the five per cent vote share necessary to win seats allocated by proportional representation (PR). Neither Russia's Choice nor Party of Russian Unity and Accord did very well in competing for seats in the single member constituencies either. Centrist politicians did little better. The liberal Yabloko electoral bloc and the moderate Women of Russia group secured over 5 per cent of the vote, but Civic Union, which a year earlier had appeared a powerful centrist force, failed dramatically at the polls. Yeltsin could obviously not follow the policies of the communists in the resurgent Communist Party of the Russian Federation (CPRF). One strain of nationalism appeared resurgent (the Zhirinovsky variety represented by the Liberal Democratic Party of Russia), but it did not offer a credible set of policies to follow (it being irrational to provoke world war three), and was not a guarantee of re-election anyway since it had attracted under a quarter of the vote in suspicious, and possibly unique, circumstances.[32]

Table 3.1 The 1993 Duma elections

Party	PR party list		Single member constituencies	Total seats	
	% vote	seats	seats	N	%
Russia's Choice	15.51	40	30	70	15.6
Liberal Democratic Party of Russia	22.92	59	5	64	14.2
Communist Party of the Russian Federation (CPRF)	12.4	32	16	48	10.7
Agrarian Party	7.99	21	12	33	7.3
Yabloko	7.86	20	3	23	5.1
Women of Russia	8.13	21	2	23	5.1
Party of Russian Unity and Accord	6.76	18	1	19	4.0
Democratic Party of Russia	5.52	14	1	15	3.3
Other parties (5)	7.96	0	8	8	1.8
Against all	4.36				
Spoiled ballots	3.10				
Independents			141	141	31.3

Source: adapted from Stephen White *et al.* (1997) *How Russia votes*, Chatham, NJ: Chatham House Publishers, p. 123.

Whilst Yeltsin was in something of a quandary about what policies to follow to secure re-election because of the mixed signals from the 1993 elections, his security of office under the new Constitution and the possibility of doing deals with the new parliament meant that he was not under the same pressures as before. One chamber of the Federal Assembly could be used to block the other on occasion. The divisions between the parties represented in the Duma could be used to play them off against one another; and many of the independent deputies elected from single member constituencies were representatives of local elites who were willing to treat with the government for material advantage. At worst, and especially in the Duma elected in 1993, party factions and committees of the Duma were unable to co-operate with one another to significantly influence policy.[33] At best, the Duma has been able to force some compromises with the government over policy.[34] This has given the Duma some influence over political affairs, but during the Yeltsin years it was not able to develop its own agenda through the creation of a parliamentary majority and implement policies from such an agenda so as to act as a channel for the transmission of electoral preferences into legislative activity. The existence of a large CPRF faction that was close to a simple majority in the Duma elected in December 1995 (the election results can be found in Table 3.2) did not change this. The CPRF's dominance of the Duma and its administration could have upset the legislative process. However, the CPRF also gained organizational resources as a party from its large Duma faction and power in the Duma administration, and could not be sure that constitutional crisis would not lead Yeltsin to dispense with parliament altogether. It therefore had an interest in backing down from giving him reasons

Table 3.2 The 1995 Duma elections

Party	PR party list % vote	PR party list seats	Single member constituencies seats	Total seats N	Total seats %
CPRF	22.3	99	58	157	34.9
Liberal Democratic Party of Russia	11.2	50	1	51	11.3
Our Home is Russia	10.1	45	10	55	12.2
Yabloko	6.9	31	14	45	10.0
Agrarian Party	3.8		20	20	4.4
Power to the People	1.6		9	9	2.0
Russia's Democratic Choice	3.9		9	9	2.0
Congress of Russian Communities	4.3		3	3	0.7
Women of Russia	4.6		3	3	0.7
Other parties taking single member constituency seats (13)	18.4		18	18	4.0
Parties taking no seats (22)	8.27				
Against all	2.8				
Spoiled ballots	1.9				
Independents			78	78	17.3

Source: adapted from Stephen White *et al.* (1997) *How Russia votes*, Chatham, NJ: Chatham House Publishers, pp. 224–5

to dissolve the parliament so that it might continue to develop as a party within parliament with the hope that it might gradually expand from its parliamentary base into the executive. Consequently, and despite its self-image as an anti-systemic party opposed to both Russia's constitutional order and emerging capitalist economy, the CPRF acted as a responsible opposition and negotiated over policy instead of continually confronting the executive.

The new Constitution thus brought little change in the sense that it led to new reform efforts from the Duma or from Yeltsin. Yeltsin's press secretary from this time argued that Yeltsin had 'no ideology of his own except the ideology of power'.[35] Yeltsin preserved his influence by playing off institutions and forces against one another. What was a problem in the early days of post-communist governance in Russia became almost an art form in 1994 and 1995 when Yeltsin balanced institutions and competing and shifting policy coalitions. During this period, Yeltsin managed what was at least a three-way divide at the apex of government: Viktor Chernomyrdin and his colleagues from Gazprom who were now in government and industrial and agricultural interests balanced Anatolii Chubais and economic liberals who balanced conservatives like Aleksandr Korzhakov, Yeltsin's bodyguard and close companion, and vice versa. Again, the balance within government gave Yeltsin choices and enabled him to disclaim responsibility for certain policies, direct blame for policy failure on to others, and choose which areas he wished to intervene in and which he wished to leave to the government.

Institutional development and personnel changes were mainly concerned with balancing Chernomyrdin's control over economic policy. Over the course of 1994, Yeltsin issued a series of decrees creating new bodies and posts in the Presidential Administration such as the Finance-Budget Administration and the special councillor to the President on economic affairs.[36] These gave Yeltsin political options to intervene in policy and mediate between competing groups in the government. Personnel changes in the government followed the rouble crisis of October 1994 (see Chapter 4). Lobby interests remained in the government, but were balanced by the removal of the Chairman of the Central Bank of Russia, the replacement of the Minister of Economics and the elevation of Chubais to First Deputy Prime Minister for a second time. Yeltsin balanced these liberal influences in turn with conservatives in his personal entourage (such as General Aleksandr Korzhakov, his personal bodyguard and head of the expanding presidential security service, and Nikolai Yegorov, head of the Presidential Administration from January to July 1996), and in the 'power ministries' (the ministries of Defence, Foreign Affairs, and Internal Affairs, and the security services).[37] Chubais's rise was also balanced by his replacement at the State Property Committee by a conservative.

The choices that Yeltsin made from between competing groups in the executive were influenced by the electoral cycle. Having balanced Chernomyrdin in the course of 1994 with the introduction into government of some economic liberals, the pendulum of influence seemed to swing to conservatives like Korzhakov and First Deputy Prime Minister Oleg Soskovets. Yeltsin was also less than able – witness his drunkenness on a visit to Berlin and failure to get off the plane at Shannon Airport to meet the Irish Prime Minister at this time – and perhaps more reliant on old cronies like Korzhakov. The decision to invade Chechnya in November 1994 is generally regarded as evidence of this. This decision and subsequent invasion in December 1994 can also be described as having an electoral dimension: Yeltsin was posing as a strong national leader, the defender of the territorial integrity of the Russian Federation, whose 'small victorious war' would distinguish him from his competitors in the 1996 presidential election.[38] The decision to go to war also showed that the government could not be constrained from arbitrary, despotic acts by the new Constitution and the Duma. However, Chechnya and electoral considerations weakened the conservative interest over time. Chechnya was a political and military disaster and there were more fundamental issues of economic redistribution to be settled that were of greater importance to the presidential campaign since they involved financial interests that could supply media and monetary support for re-election. These questions of economic redistribution underlay the development of the major alliance of 1994–1997, the political linkage between part of the government, the Presidential Administration/ presidency and the commercial banks and financial-industrial groups (FIGs). Government policy and mutual advantage promoted this linkage.

The banks gained from the government's move to deficit financing through the sale of treasury bills (GKOs) and developed their industrial holdings though the 'shares for loans' programme, described by one commentator as 'a transition from shapeless co-operation [between the executive and business] without fixed rules to highly formalized co-operation', in which vast swathes of valuable assets still held by the state were transferred to the banks at knockdown prices.[39] (More details on the 'shares for loans' scheme can be found in Chapter 4.) Once the basic relationship was established between the banks and the government, electoral factors shaped its fuller development into an alliance.

The crisis in Chechnya, the lack of a clear and effective economic policy and Yeltsin's health problems wore Yeltsin's popularity down over the course of 1995. The pro-government 'Our Home is Russia' party, formed to test the waters for the 1996 presidential election, captured only 10 per cent of the vote in the December 1995 Duma election vote (Table 3.2). Russia's Democratic Choice (as Gaidar's party was now named) slumped to under the 5 per cent threshold. The CPRF took 22 per cent of the vote and managed to take 58 seats in the single member constituency votes.[40] This gave them a plurality in the Duma, and close to a majority since they could count on support from the Agrarians and the 'Power to the People' group. Yeltsin panicked at the Duma election results, firing Chubais, the liberal Foreign Minister Andrei Kozyrev and Sergei Filatov, the head of the Presidential Administration, and naming Soskovets the head of his re-election campaign. This surge in the fortunes of the conservative faction was short-lived. To win the election, Yeltsin needed money, media support and support from Russia's regions. Money and media support could only come from the banks that were cash rich and had extensive media interests. Dismayed at the rise of the conservatives, a group of bankers (popularly known as 'oligarchs' from this point onwards), decided to finance Yeltsin's campaign and restore some balance by placing Chubais in Yeltsin's campaign team as a first step to pushing Soskovets to one side.

The relationship between Yeltsin and the banks/FIGs saved the election for Yeltsin. The banks bankrolled Yeltsin's campaign and their media outlets promoted him to the virtual exclusion of other candidates.[41] Under Chubais's general direction and using the media controlled by the banks, the campaign developed into a referendum on the communist past. The effect was startling. The battle in the 1996 election campaign was to persuade people that only Yeltsin was a credible opponent to the CPRF candidate, Gennady Zyuganov. As can be seen from Table 3.3a, b and c, this was an uphill struggle. At the start of the campaigning season in January 1996, only 8 per cent of people considered voting for Yeltsin, 14 per cent thought he might win and nearly half of the poll sample (43 per cent) did not want him re-elected as President under any circumstances. Gradually, the media coverage of Yeltsin's campaign, the scorn poured on the CPRF, Zyuganov's lacklustre performance, and Yeltsin's use of his office to make lavish promises to ordinary voters on the campaign trail and to do deals with regional leaders,

Table 3.3 The Russian presidential election of 1996: opinion polls and results

a. *Which candidate would you vote for if the presidential election were held next Sunday (%)?*

	January	February	March	April	May	June
Boris Yeltsin	8	11	15	18	28	36
Gennady Zyuganov	20	24	25	26	27	24
Alexander Lebed	10	8	10	10	6	10
Grigory Yavlinsky	13	9	11	10	9	8
Vladimir Zhirinovsky	10	12	9	8	7	6
Other	22	29	16	15	11	5
Against all/difficult to say	17	17	14	11	11	11

b. *Who will win the presidential election in your opinion (%)?*

	January	February	March	April	May	June
Boris Yeltsin	14	21	29	40	52	57
Gennady Zyuganov	18	22	24	23	21	19
Difficult to say	40	39	35	28	21	12

c. *Which candidate would you not like to be elected President under any conditions (%)?*

	January	February	March	April	May	June
Boris Yeltsin	43	40	37	37	36	29
Gennady Zyuganov	14	21	26	27	29	31

d. *Results of the Russian Presidential Election, June and July 1996 (% vote)*

	First round	Second round
Boris Yeltsin	35.28	53.82
Gennady Zyuganov	32.03	40.31
Alexander Lebed	14.52	
Grigory Yavlinsky	7.34	
Vladimir Zhirinovsky	5.70	
Others	2.16	
Against all	1.54	4.83

Source: Karen Henderson and Neil Robinson (1997) *Post-communist politics*, London: Prentice Hall, pp. 310, 313

began to have an effect. None of the other candidates could break through the media's barrage of pro-Yeltsin propaganda to present themselves as serious alternatives to Zyuganov. Gradually, people began to believe that Yeltsin would win the election (Table 3.3b) and then began to consider voting for him (Table 3.3a). The anti-communist tenor of the campaign made people turn against Zyuganov and consider Yeltsin's re-election more conscionable (Table 3.3c). This was vital since it meant that Yeltsin stood more chance of winning a second round contest against Zyuganov if he did not win a first round victory by securing 50 per cent of the vote; only firm CPRF voters and a small proportion of the rest of the population were totally against him. This duly happened in the two rounds of the presidential elections in June and July 1996, as Table 3.3d shows. Believing that Yeltsin could win and being persuaded of the danger of a CPRF victory, more voters transferred their votes to Yeltsin in the second round than to Zyuganov, and those who could not bring themselves to vote for Yeltsin either did not vote (turnout fell between the two rounds), or voted against both candidates.[42] An alliance between the two rounds of the election with Alexander Lebed, who came third in the first round vote, helped Yeltsin's cause. Lebed, a popular ex-general with a reputation for honesty and firm action, was made Secretary of the Security Council and was instrumental in the removal of Korzhakov and Soskovets from office before the second round vote.

The contest between the groups around Yeltsin for his ear in 1994–1996 meant that the institutional confusion at the heart of the Russian political system continued unabated. The new Constitution thus brought continuity rather than change. However, there was a qualitative difference under the new Constitution. Before 1993 and the destruction of the parliament, Yeltsin's manoeuvrings could be argued to serve reform because he could portray the parliament as being backward looking. After 1993, Yeltsin's actions came to look more venal and self-serving, and to be a major chief cause of the Russian state's problems. The deal with the bankers over 'shares for loans' seemed to associate the Russian state with private interests almost to the exclusion of all other considerations and funding the state through the sale of GKOs contributed to a demonetization of the economy (see Chapter 4). As supplies of money to the economy from the government dried up, this had a knock-on affect on the government: if money was in short supply it could not gather tax payments. The association of the state with the bankers that was so personally profitable to Yeltsin and his campaign for re-election thus weakened the state in two ways. Its autonomy, and people's respect for it, was compromised by the perception that it acted in the interests of the new rich; its capacity was eroded as the resources that it commanded from tax raising declined. The state's organizational integrity declined as its autonomy was eroded at least in the popular imagination and as it could not fund its activities. Corruption and misuse of office grew as officials acted in their own interest and took bribes to compensate for the government's failure to fund them.

Again, a weakening of the centre's ability to influence events in the provinces mirrored the dispersal of power at the centre. Although some regional leaders were removed in October 1993, in the main the power of regional leaders grew after the forced dissolution of parliament in October 1993.[43] New regional representative institutions were set up, but with fewer powers than the old Soviets. Regional governors and republican presidents were empowered to decide how regional assemblies were to be elected and the number of deputies that were to serve in them, and had the right to veto duma and assembly decisions. Electoral malpractice in the elections to the dumas and assemblies in 1994 and 1995 was rife. Gerrymandering and the distribution of a disproportionate number of seats to rural areas were particularly common. As a result, many regional dumas and assemblies are packed with local officials or their clients: the so-called 'party of power'. Yeltsin buoyed up the power of regional leaders by declaring a moratorium on their re-election until after the presidential elections of 1996 so that they might support him. Secure in office, regional leaders did little to promote democracy in the provinces; political parties were weak, local industries and media were suborned.[44] The hold of private interests over the local state was thus as pervasive as it was over the national; in places such as the Republic of Kalmykia, the boundaries between private interests and political power were completely eroded. Finally, central control over the provinces was further weakened by the growth of what is termed 'asymmetrical federalism'. The Federal Treaty of March 1992 – which had not been a particularly effective means of regulating centre-province relations – was increasingly superseded by bilateral treaties between the federal authorities in Moscow and local leaders. Whilst these agreements helped resolve some separatist tensions in republics like Tatarstan, they complicated the management of the Federation by providing exemptions for republics. Yeltsin then extended these to the regions as he sought support for his re-election. These agreements, and the power of provincial leaders, imposed a cost on the central state's revenues just as the connection with the banks did. Bilateral treaties frequently included tax exemptions that hit the central budget and regional leaders frequently either did not gather, or did not pass on, revenues for the Federation that they were supposed to collect.[45] After 1996, the autonomy of regional leaders from the centre was reinforced by their direct election, which potentially gave them greater legitimacy and authority.

The endgame of Yeltsinism, 1996–1999

In the aftermath of the 1996 election, Yeltsin paid off his debts. Chubais became head of the Presidential Administration and two 'oligarchs', Vladimir Potanin (from Oneksimbank), and Boris Berezovsky (a financier with wide media and industrial holdings), entered the government as, respectively, First Deputy Prime Minister with responsibility for economic policy and Deputy Secretary of the Security Council. However, and despite appearances, Yeltsin's victory destabilized the alliance with business even as this alliance triumphed. A new wave of reforms built up in late 1996 and early 1997 that were aimed at restoring the revenue base of the state and weakening power of private interests over government.

The roots of this reform wave lay in the needs of the state and of Yeltsin personally. The state required some reform because it was in dire financial straits by the autumn of 1996 and the continued financing of the budget through its relationship with the FIGs was no longer possible (see Chapter 4). The fall of Korzhakov and his allies between the two rounds of the presidential election opened the way for Chubais to become the new head of the Presidential Administration. Chubais's appointment and that of other ministers like Aleksandr Livshits and Yevgeny Yasin created a constituency in government for reform. The real push for reform began with a government reshuffle in March 1997. This saw the removal of Potanin, and Chubais and Boris Nemtsov (the ex-governor of Nizhny Novgorod region), were brought into government as deputy prime ministers with, respectively, responsibility for economic reform and the Ministry of Finance, and for energy monopolies. Reform, particularly a tightening of tax collection, was necessary to counter a possible further devolution of power to Russia's regions. Yeltsin's re-election as president was to be followed by the election of regional heads of administration from late 1996 onwards. As a result, heads of administration would be less reliant on the central administration for their positions and the relationship between centre and periphery shifted further from an administrative one to one of 'political interaction'.[46] There was a strong possibility that this might increase the amount of bargaining between centre and regions over tax payments, exemptions and concessions, and that the amount of tax paid to the centre would decline as more independent regional leaders appropriated tax due the centre, or colluded with local enterprises to evade federal tax payments.[47] One of the central planks of reform in 1997 was a presidential decree aimed at curtailing the independent taxation powers of regions and the appointment of a more reform minded government after March 1997 was supposed to signal the centre's commitment to tax collection and sovereignty.

Finally, promoting the economic liberals and some reform policies was also a way of strengthening the dependency of the government on Yeltsin personally so that reform served his personal needs as well as those of the state. The issue of who would succeed Yeltsin was forced onto the political agenda early in the second term when his victory was almost immediately followed by a quintuple heart bypass operation. The deal that brought Aleksandr Lebed into the executive as Secretary of the Security Council in return for his support for Yeltsin in the second round of the presidential elections boosted Lebed's hopes of succeeding Yeltsin. Yeltsin's ill health also raised the prospect of the succession of Prime Minister Chernomyrdin to the post of acting president so that he would have incumbency advantages in any electoral contest. Other politicians, such as Yurii Luzhkov, the mayor of Moscow, also began to act as potential presidential candidates.

Lebed was quickly removed from office as all sides ganged up on him to weaken his claims to succeed Yeltsin. His office was Lebed's greatest asset if he was to succeed Yeltsin; once he lost it he began to fade as a national political actor. Reform was supposed to help Yeltsin control the rest of the contenders. The promotion of Chubais as head of the PA and then to the government weakened the hold of Chernomyrdin over economic policy, the main potential area of policy activity for the Prime Minister. The 'political ministries' of defence, foreign and internal affairs report direct to the President so that the Prime Minister can have only a limited impact on policy in these areas. If Chernomyrdin did not have control over economic policy, then his potential to act as heir apparent to Yeltsin was that much lessened. Chernomyrdin was the big loser in the cabinet reshuffle in March 1997: he lost control of the ministry of energy to Nemtsov and associates such as Zaveryukha were removed from post.[48] Chubais and the economic liberals were dependent on Yeltsin. With the exception of Nemtsov, who had no national political base of his own, the economic liberals were unpopular. Their relationship to the commercial banks was also tenuous. Links with the banks were in part severed with the removal of Potanin in the March 1997 government shake-up. Although Chubais apparently continued to have close relations with Potanin (and these were in part responsible for his eventual loss of government office), the banks were soon to be struggling with the government and against their former allies.

The reform measures taken from late 1996 onwards and the break with the banks that they entailed were thus a combination of an attempt at restoring state autonomy by weakening the connection with private interests, and restoring state capacity by generating resources that the state could use to increase its effectiveness. However, in trying to reform, Chubais, Nemtsov, and their supporters rediscovered the vicious irony of reform. The state needed resources to build up capacity, but to get resources required capacity: the state needed organizations and administrators capable of collecting taxes and resisting corruption, and legal tools to punish defaulters, but needed resources to develop such institutions and personnel. As the Russian state lacked such institutions and bureaucrats, especially after the years of corruption, lobbying and institutional redundancy, reform was going to be difficult. In the absence of institutions to do the reformers bidding, they relied once more on their ability to convince people that they were serious about reform and that compliance with the government's orders was ultimately going to be unavoidable. Reform, therefore, depended once again on 'credible commitment': it would work if people were persuaded that the government was stable and would not deviate from its chosen course.

Credible commitment to reform proved no easier to maintain in 1997 than it had in 1992. The government rapidly became embroiled in a conflict with the banks in 1997 and the structural weaknesses of the Russian economy meant that the government's attempts to force more tax revenue out of it were only partially successful (see Chapter 4). The bank's loss of influence over economic policy led to the outbreak of the so-called 'bank wars' in the summer of 1997. Chubais was accused of favouring Potanin and Oneksimbank by Berezovsky (who was still a Deputy Secretary of the Security Council and close to Yeltsin's daughter and adviser, Tatyana Dyachenko) and others.[49] Yeltsin first tried to calm the media storm that accompanied the 'bank wars' and when this failed acted on the advice of

Chubais and Nemtsov to remove Berezovsky from the Security Council. This did not caution Berezovsky, but enraged him. Materials were released that implicated Chubais and some of his closest aides in corrupt practices (they had taken a huge advance for a book on privatization from a company owned by Oneksimbank). Yeltsin was forced to discipline Chubais and fire his aides. Chubais was fortunate to stay in office, and was saved in part because of the growing financial crisis in Asia that was beginning to impact on Russia and which would be one of the causes of Russia's financial collapse in August 1998 (see Chapter 4). However, Chubais's and Nemtsov's fortunes waned further in January 1998, when Chernomyrdin took responsibility for overseeing the Ministries of Finance, Energy, and Foreign Affairs and of defence and security. This, however, was too much for Yeltsin since Chernomyrdin's increased powers made him look too much like a successor to Yeltsin with too long to go before succession had to become fact. Yeltsin therefore faced a loss of authority as both the impetus for reform would be slowed with Chernomyrdin's increased power and as Chernomyrdin became more confident of succeeding Yeltsin and treated as the heir apparent. Yeltsin's reaction was to try to restore the balance in his favour. On 23 March 1998, he removed Chernomyrdin and Chubais, and proposed a relative unknown, Sergei Kiriyenko as the new prime minister.

Kiriyenko's nomination showed that Yeltsin was committed to continuing the reforms started in 1997 as a means of controlling the succession. However, a credible commitment to reform still did not develop. Kiriyenko had to be forced on the Duma, which rejected him twice before approving him when Yeltsin nominated him a third time and signalled he was prepared to dissolve the Duma if it voted a third time against his nominee. However, the Kiriyenko government was doomed to fail economically so that Yeltsin was left to rely solely on the powers of his office to influence the succession. The 'bank wars', January redistribution of government responsibilities and March purge had all taken place against a decline in both Russia's foreign trade earnings and international confidence in its creditworthiness (see Chapter 4). As the economic downturn continued because of the state's inability to increase its tax revenues and because of a fall in oil prices, the ability of the government to rule was increasingly questioned by the Duma, whose co-operation was needed to pass legislation permitting emergency revenue collection. Not surprisingly, this co-operation was not forthcoming: why should the Duma aid a government that had been forced on it, that was dependent on Yeltsin for its tenure and was designed to let him control his succession? The Duma stalled the full passage of the government's anti-crisis package and as a result, the IMF held back some of the extra aid that it had granted Russia to support the rouble. The actions of the Duma and the IMF were precipitating factors of the debt default and rouble devaluation in August 1998 that brought the Kiriyenko government down.

The fall of the Kiriyenko government and the economic shock of devaluation halted any further possibility of Yeltsin trying to control his succession and maintain his influence as President through the promotion of any reform package. Yeltsin tried to put the clock back and nominate Chernomyrdin to be Prime Minister once more, but the Duma rejected him. Yeltsin was forced to find a compromise candidate, the foreign minister Yevgeny Primakov. Primakov began to take on 'presidential' tasks, such as representing Russia overseas as Yeltsin partially withdrew from public life due to a fresh bout of illness. Primakov's cabinet seems to have been formed with less presidential interference than previously and was relatively consensual, containing figures more acceptable to the Duma such as Yurii Maslyukov, the former head of Gosplan, the Soviet central planning agency, and developing links with regional leaders. This effort at creating a kind of a coalition government found favour with the Duma and as a result, but only for a time, the political initiative passed to the government under Primakov and to the Duma. It was even mooted that either Yeltsin might retire, or that he might rule as a figurehead President passing his executive powers to Primakov. Primakov kept the pressure on Yeltsin by attacking Berezovsky as a means of putting pressure on Yeltsin through his daughter and giving more credence to claims that Yeltsin's family had taken bribes.

Yeltsin fought back. In the absence of a credible reform team post-August 1998 and in the economic confusion of 1998–1999, he had to rely solely on the powers of his office to try to place himself and his office back at the centre of political life. The result was a political mess. Primakov, who like Chernomyrdin before him was being touted as a successor to Yeltsin, was censured for his inability to deal with Russia's economic crisis and removed from office by presidential decree. This only improved his reputation and made him an asset to the Fatherland-All Russia bloc that was organized by the mayor of Moscow, Yurii Luzhkov as a vehicle for the 1999 Duma elections and a means of testing the waters for the 2000 presidential elections. Neither Yeltsin nor Primakov's successor, Sergei Stepashin was capable of controlling the development of Fatherland-All Russia, and suggestions that Stepashin take it over and head it failed. Regional leaders rallied around it and its popularity in the polls at the end of the summer was high: as Table 3.4 shows, in October 1999 21 per cent of voters polled said they would vote for it. This meant that Fatherland-All Russia would be the second biggest party in the Duma (after the CPRF) and that Primakov would probably be regarded as the strongest non-communist presidential candidate. Like Yeltsin in 1996, this would mean that he would be the candidate to face Zyuganov in a second round vote and would therefore win as enough of Russia's voters would rally to him to veto a return to communist government.

Yeltsin therefore rolled the dice once more. Stepashin's failure to head off Primakov and the Fatherland-All Russia challenge led to his ouster by another presidential decree. His replacement as Prime Minister, Vladimir Putin, admitted immediately that the change in Prime Ministers 'reflected the desire of the president to alter the arrangement of politics in the country on the eve of the State Duma and presidential elections'.[50] In other words,

Table 3.4 Party list vote in 1995 Duma elections, voting intentions for the 1999 elections, election results for 1999

Party	1995 PR[a] vote	Oct	Nov	Dec	1999 PR vote	Seats from PR vote	Seats from SMC[b] vote	Total 1999 seats	% seats
Communist Party (Zyuganov)	22	26	29	26	24.3	67	47	114	25.3
Fatherland-All Russia (Luzhkov/Primakov)		21	11	10	13.3	37	29	66	14.6
Yabloko (Yavlinsky)	7	11	9	10	5.9	16	4	20	4.4
Medved-Unity		5	8	17	23.3	64	9	73	16.2
Union of Right Forces (Kiriyenko)		4	6	5	8.5	24	5	29	6.4
Liberal Democratic Party (Zhirinovsky)	11	3	4	5	6.0	17	0	17	3.7
Our Home is Russia (Chernomyrdin)	10	2	1	0	1.2		8	8	1.7
Other parties (20)		10	8	2	14.1		9	9	2.0
Independents							105	105	23.3
None of them/against all		3	5	3	3.3				
Don't know		15	19	16					

Source: reports of VTsIOM polls and results from www.russiavotes.org.

Notes
[a] PR vote = party list vote.
[b] SMC = single member constituency.

Yeltsin's chosen heir acknowledged that Yeltsin was using his office to hand-pick a successor and try to change the outcome of the parliamentary elections: he was using his office proprietarily.

At the time of his appointment, and despite Yeltsin's naming him as his heir, Putin looked no more likely to facilitate an orderly transition than his predecessors had. However, Putin had luck on his side. The economy began to improve over the course of 1999, not because of any government action but because rising oil prices raised government revenues. Things did not drama-tically improve for the average citizen but they did not get worse and the general drift of economic news was good. More importantly, Chechen rebels tried to take advantage of Moscow's troubles to launch raids into neighbour-ing Dagestan. At first, Russian troops barely contained these incursions and it looked as if even this limited border skirmish would be an embarrassing demonstration of Russian military limitations. Then, in the autumn of 1999 a series of bomb attacks on apartment buildings in Moscow occurred causing great loss of life and popular anger. These attacks were naturally blamed on the Chechens, although claims were also made against the Russian security services, which, it has been argued, planted or encouraged the planting of the bombs, so that the conflict in Chechnya could be restarted. Whoever was responsible for the apartment block bombings, the war did duly escalate. Russian troops crossed the border once more into Chechnya and gradually extended operations – if not control – to the rest of the breakaway republic.

The 1999 Chechnya campaign was a boon for Putin. The attacks on Russian civilians made it popular and as the campaign was not as badly handled as the 1994–1996 campaigns, Putin was seen as competent. His relative youth and emergence from obscurity to take the post of Prime Minister also probably helped: he bore less responsibility for the political mistakes and fudges of the Yeltsin years. The rise in Putin's approval ratings at the end of 1999 was astounding and had a knock-on effect on Fatherland-All Russia. Its poll rating fell by nearly half in the run-up to the election (see Table 3.4). Medved-Unity, the party set up to counter Fatherland by the government and now perceived to be Putin's party, enjoyed a commensurate increase in popularity, and the broadly pro-Putin Union of Right Forces, headed by former Prime Minister Kiriyenko also began to pick up some support. In the December elections, the CPRF took first place in the PR vote as usual because of the loyalty of its core supporters, the elderly and the impoverished. The Fatherland-All Russia electoral challenge faded as it captured only 13 per cent of the vote and with it went Primakov and Luzhkov's hopes of being strong presidential contenders. Other presidential hopefuls like Chernomyrdin, Zhirinovsky and Grigory Yavlinsky from Yabloko saw their party's vote share decline from 1995. Putin, buoyed by the success of Medved-Unity at the polls, was the leading contender for the presidency. Yeltsin – perhaps willingly, perhaps not – recognized him as his heir and increased his chances of winning by stepping down as President on New Year's Eve 1999. As Prime Minister, Putin took over as acting President and elections were brought forward to March 2000. One of Putin's first acts was to grant Yeltsin immunity from any prosecution for himself and his family for any misdeeds that occurred during his rule. Yeltsin had thus won his last political battle in the same way that he had won so many others. He had used his office and its powers to secure a short-term political outcome favourable to him.

Conclusion

Reforming Russia after the collapse of communism was always going to be a difficult, long and contested process. The state was too fragmented, the economy too weak, and the range of self-interested parties too great for it to be otherwise. Yeltsin was also unfortunate in that the USSR collapsed before certain administrative issues were clarified in the Russian government. However, it is difficult to see that Yeltsin was a positive influence on Russian political development even if we bear these problems and unfortunate contingencies in mind. His personality was an important factor shaping developments. He appointed ministers and presidential staff who were politically incompatible with one another from the onset, never established clear lines of authority in the government and Presidential Administration, and between them, preferring to add institutions rather than create effective ones and to stand above the competition for his attention as it suited him and his interests. The presidency went from being a vehicle for the promotion of radical political change to being an amorphous institution that gathered around it political forces that could ensure the political survival of Yeltsin.

The new 'presidential' Constitution of 1993 did not change this situation very much. With the adoption of the new Constitution, Yeltsin created the formal constitutional shell of a strong executive but operated within it in such a way that it was an empty structure into which content came from the struggle between the rival factions that sought Yeltsin's ear. Although there was an attempt at promoting reform again in 1996 and 1997, it was really a case of too little too late. The government struggled to show it was capable of keeping to a reform policy under assault from its former supporters, the banks. State officials could argue that they were not the servants of any particular interests, but they had difficulty in making such arguments convincingly and the prestige of political authorities dipped. The authority of politicians was not helped by the weak development of representative institutions. Politicians from government only looked to political parties as vehicles for office in the run-up to elections, or when they were ejected from office. They spent little time promoting parties and developing them as channels of popular representation at other times. They did not need to. The 1993 Constitution only gave the Duma limited powers and it was more effective to access power through the executive and by lobbying than to work through the Duma. Moreover, although the CPRF was successful in mobilizing the economically disenfranchised to vote for it, it never looked like it would be able to overthrow the new political order. Defending the 1993 Constitution and the Yeltsin regime by creating a credible party alternative was thus not necessary.[51]

The basic problem of post-communism that we began this chapter with thus remained at the end of the Yeltsin era: political power remained to be reconstructed so that economic reform could be carried out and democracy consolidated. The changes that occurred under Yeltsin were great, but they had not produced a state that was capable of working with society and the economy to renew them and it, and avoid crisis. The Russian state was as weak at the end of Yeltsin's rule as it was at the start no matter that the post of President possessed extensive powers. Russia's degraded democracy did not revert to some form of absolutism in that control of legislative activity and decision-making did not become the sole preserve of Yeltsin. But at the same time, the constitutional order was devalued. Yeltsin was able to intervene in government to suit his own ends and the administrative confusion at the heart of government and the continuity in power of many regional elites placed patronage and personal interest above impersonal service for the good of society as a whole. Constitutionalism and patrimonialism thus sat uneasily with one another at the end of Yeltsin's period of office and he used the powers granted to him by the Constitution to choose a successor from among Russia's competing politicians like a monarch nominating his heir.

Notes

1 On some of these issues and on some of the common problems of post-communist states see S. Holmes (1996) 'Cultural legacies or state collapse? Probing the post-communist dilemma', in M. Mandelbaum (ed.) *Postcommunism: four perspectives*, New York: Council for Foreign Relations; J. Elster, C. Offe and U. Preuss with F. Boenker, U. Goetting and F. Rueb (1998) *Institutional design in post-communist societies. Rebuilding the ship at sea*, Cambridge: Cambridge University Press. The arguments that follow are largely drawn from N. Robinson (2000) 'The presidency: the politics of institutional chaos', in N. Robinson (ed.) *Institutions and political change in Russia*, Basingstoke: Macmillan, and (2000) 'Constructing the crisis of the Russian state', paper presented to the VI International Council for Central and East European Studies World Congress, Tampere, Finland, July–August 2000.

2 A. Przeworski (1988) 'Democracy as the contingent outcome of conflicts', in J. Elster and R. Slagsted (eds) *Constitutionalism and democracy*, Cambridge: Cambridge University Press, and (1991) *Democracy and the market. Political and economic reforms in Eastern Europe and Latin America*, Cambridge: Cambridge University Press.

3 J. Linz (1990) 'The perils of presidentialism', *Journal of Democracy*, 1(1): 61. See also, J. Linz and A. Valenzuela (eds) (1994) *The failure of presidential democracy?*, Baltimore: Johns Hopkins University Press; A. Stepan and C. Skach (1996) 'Constitutional frameworks and democratic consolidation: parliamentarism versus presidentialism', *World Politics*, 46(1): 1–22; S. Mainwaring (1993) 'Presidentialism, multipartism and democracy: the difficult combination', *Comparative Political Studies*, 26 (2): 198–228. The issue of presidentialism and post-communist political development is simply discussed in K. Henderson and N. Robinson (1997) *Post-communist politics*, London: Prentice Hall, pp. 168–70,

and in more detail in R. Taras (ed.) (1997) *Post-communist presidencies*, Cambridge: Cambridge University Press; S. Holmes (1994) 'The postcommunist presidency', *East European Constitutional Review*, 2/3 (4/1): 36–39, G. Easter (1997) 'Preference for presidentialism. Postcommunist regime change in Russia and the NIS', *World Politics*, 49(2): 184–211, and T. Frye (1997) 'The politics of institutional change: post-communist presidencies', *Comparative Political Studies*, 30(5): 523–552.

4 On the Russian presidency in general see E. Huskey (1999) *Presidential power in Russia*, Armonk, NY: M.E. Sharpe. Huskey discusses the foundation of the presidency on pp. 12–43.

5 Subsequent to March 1990, Democratic Russia did develop some of the traits of a party, but it was never to be a strong political actor in its own right, its parliamentary base shrank as deputies joined new factions, and after August 1991 it faded from the political scene. See Y. Brudny (1993) 'The dynamics of "Democratic Russia", 1990–1993', *Post-Soviet Affairs*, 9(2): 141–70.

6 S. White (1997) 'Russia: presidential leadership under Yeltsin', in R. Taras, *Postcommunist Presidencies*, Cambridge: Cambridge University Press, pp. 44–45.

7 *Izvestiya*, 10 July 1991.

8 *Izvestiya*, 28 October 1991.

9 *Rossiiskaya gazeta*, 8 April 1992.

10 G. Smith (1996) *Reforming the Russian Legal System*, Cambridge: Cambridge University Press, p. 134.

11 The thoughts of Yeltsin's successor as Chair of the Supreme Soviet can be found in R. Khasbulatov (1993) *The Struggle for Russia. Power and change in the democratic revolution*, London: Routledge. Parliamentary opinion is reviewed in L. Shevtsova, L. (1996) 'Parliament and the political crisis in Russia, 1991–1993', in J. Hahn (ed.) *Democratization in Russia. The development of legislative institutions*, Armonk, NY: M.E. Sharpe.

12 For lengthier discussions of the conflict see *inter alia*, T. Colton (1995) 'Boris Yeltsin, Russia's all-thumbs democrat', and Y. Brudny (1995) 'Ruslan Khasbulatov, Aleksandr Rutskoi, and intraelite conflict in postcommunist Russia, 1991–1994', both in T. Colton and R.C. Tucker (eds) *Patterns in Post-Soviet Leadership*, Boulder: Westview; J. Löwenhardt (1995) *The Reincarnation of Russia. Struggling with the legacy of communism, 1990–1994*, Harlow: Longman; J. Steele (1995) *Eternal Russia*, London: Faber and Faber; R. Sakwa (1996) *Russian politics and society*, second edition, London: Routledge, pp. 117–30; Henderson and Robinson, *Post-Communist Politics*, pp. 183–98; B. Yeltsin (1994) *The view from the Kremlin*, London: Harper Collins; L. Shevtsova (1999) *Yeltsin's Russia. Myths and reality*, Washington, DC: Carnegie Endowment for International Peace; S. White (2000) *Russia's new politics. The management of a postcommunist society*, Cambridge: Cambridge University Press.

13 Yeltsin implies this in his memoirs. See B. Yeltsin (1994) *Zapiski prezidenta*, Moscow: Ogonyok, pp. 240–49.

14 Gaidar was brought to Yeltsin by Burbulis and was 'as they say in such situations "his man"'. Yeltsin, *Zapiski . . .*, pp. 163–64. Cf. Y. Gaidar (1999) *Days of defeat and victory*, Seattle: University of Washington Press, pp. 61–2.

15 Huskey, *Presidential power . . .*, p. 28.

16 W. Clark (1998) 'Presidential prefects in the Russian provinces: Yeltsin's regional cadres policy', in G. Gill (ed.) *Elites and Leadership in Russian politics*, Basingstoke: Macmillan, 30–1, 37.

17 Yeltsin, *Zapiski . . .*, p. 258.

18 *Ibid.*

19 See E. Lohr (1993) 'Arkadii Volsky's power base', *Europe-Asia Studies*, 45(5): 811–829.

20 T. Colton (1995) 'Superpresidentialism and Russia's backward state', *Post-Soviet Affairs*, 11(2): pp. 144–48.

21 E. Huskey (1995) 'The State-Legal Administration and the politics of redundancy', *Post-Soviet Affairs*, 11(2): pp. 115–43; Huskey, *Presidential power* ..., p. 8, *passim*.

22 Husky, *Presidential power* ..., p. 61.

23 See Colton, 'Superpresidentialism ...'.

24 Huskey, *Presidential power* ...

25 J. Willerton (1998) 'Post-Soviet clientelist norms at the Russian federal level', in Gill (ed.) *Elites and Leadership* ...

26 S. White and I. McAllister (1996) 'The CPSU and its members: between communism and postcommunism', *British Journal of Political Science*, 26(1), p. 107.

27 D. Slider (1994) 'Federalism, discord and accommodation: intergovernmental relations in post-Soviet Russia', in T. Friedgut and J. Hahn (eds) *Local power and post-Soviet politics*, Armonk, NY: M.E. Sharpe, pp. 256–57.

28 P. Hanson (1993) 'Local power and market reform in Russia', *Communist Economies and Economic Transformation*, 5(1), pp. 45–60.

29 Henderson and Robinson, *Post-communist politics* ..., p. 193.

30 On popular opinion of parliament and the president see M. Wyman (1997) *Public opinion in postcommunist Russia*, Basingstoke: Macmillan, pp. 92–6. Descriptions of the events of October 1993 can be found in Yeltsin, *The view from the Kremlin* ...; Steele, *Eternal Russia* ...; Henderson and Robinson, *Post-communist politics*..., pp. 195–6; B. Clark (1995) *An empire's new clothes. The end of Russia's liberal dream*, London: Vintage, pp. 239–64.

31 Colton, 'Superpresidentialism...'; J. Willerton and A. Shulus (1995) 'Constructing a new political process: the hegemonic presidency and the legislature', *The John Marshall Law Review*, 28(4), p. 804. In the language of comparative politics, the Russian political system under the 1993 Constitution is 'semi-presidential'. However, where most presidents in semi-presidential systems are constrained by political parties working through legislatures to construct governments, Yeltsin, and perhaps Putin too, have been constrained only weakly by parliamentary parties which have only briefly been able to influence the composition of the government (after the August 1998 financial crash). More generally, constraints have been extra-parliamentary and it is thus a moot point what advantage can be gained by thinking about the Russian presidency as semi-presidentialism.

32 There have been persistent, and unproven, allegations that Zhirinovsky's vote was inflated so that the turnout figures in the election and in the referendum on the Constitution matched. Analysis of the election can be found in R. Sakwa (1995) 'The Russian elections of December 1993', *Europe-Asia Studies*, 47(2), pp. 195–227; P. Lentini (ed.) (1998) *Elections and political order in Russia. The implications of the 1993 elections to the Federal Assembly*, Budapest: Central European University Press; M.E. Urban (1994) 'December 1993 as a replication of late-Soviet electoral practices', *Post-Soviet Affairs*, 10(2), pp. 127–58; S. Whitefield and G. Evans (1994) 'The Russian election of 1993: public opinion and the transition experience', *Post-Soviet Affairs*, 10(1), pp. 38–60; S. White, R. Rose and I. McAllister (1997) *How Russia votes*, Chatham, NJ: Chatham House Publishers, pp. 107–29.

33 J. Ostrow (1998) 'Procedural breakdown and deadlock in the Russian State Duma: the problems of an unlinked, dual-channel institutional design', *Europe-Asia Studies*, 50(5): pp. 793–816.

34 On compromises between the Duma and the executive see T.F. Remington (2000) 'The evolution of executive-legislative relations', *Slavic Review*, 59(3): pp. 499–520.

35 V. Kostikov (1997) *Roman's prezidentom. Zapiski press-sekretarya*, Moscow: Vagrius, p. 347.

36 E. Huskey (1996) 'The making of economic policy in Russia: changing relations between presidency and government', *Review of Central and East European Law*, 22 (4): pp. 365–87.
37 E. Bacon (2000) 'The power ministries', in N. Robinson (ed.) *Institutions and political change in Russia*, Basingstoke: Macmillan.
38 On the war, see C. Gall and T. de Waal (1997) *Chechnya. A small victorious war*, London: Pan; J. Dunlop (1998) *Russia confronts Chechnya. Roots of a separatist conflict*, Cambridge: Cambridge University Press; A. Lieven (1998) *Chechnya. Tombstone of Russian power*, New Haven: Yale University Press.
39 *Kommersant-Daily*, 31 March 1995.
40 See White *et al.*, *How Russia votes* ..., pp. 197–239.
41 Y. Brudny (1997) 'In pursuit of the Russian presidency: why and how Yeltsin won the 1996 presidential election', *Communist and Post-Communist Studies*, 30(3), pp. 255–75; M. McFaul (1997) *Russia's 1996 presidential election. The end of polarized politics*, Stanford: Hoover Institute Press.
42 See *ibid*, and White *et al.*, *How Russia votes* ..., pp. 241–70.
43 V. Gel'man and O. Senatova (1995) 'Sub-national politics in Russia in the post-communist period: a view from Moscow', *Regional Politics and Policy*, 5(2), pp. 211–23.
44 V. Gel'man (2000) 'Subnational institutions in contemporary Russia', in Robinson (ed.) *Institutions* ...
45 A. Shleifer and D. Treisman (2000) *Without a map. Political tactics and economic reform in Russia*, Cambridge, MA: The MIT Press, chapter 6.
46 Gel'man (2000) 'Subnational institutions ...', p. 101.
47 Shleifer and Treisman, *Without a map...*, p. 113, *passim*.
48 Shevtsova, *Yeltsin's Russia...*, p. 211.
49 The 'bank wars' pitted the Berezovsky-Gusinsky group 'which had developed a close relationship with Chernomyrdin' against Chubais/Potanin and his Oneksimbank group. See *ibid*, pp. 218–19.
50 *Rossiiskaya gazeta*, 10 August 1999.
51 N. Robinson (1998) 'Classifying Russia's party system: the problem of relevance in a time of uncertainty', in J. Löwenhardt (ed.) *Party politics in post-communist Russia*, London: Cass.

4   From planned economy to 'virtual economy'

The failure of economic transformation

Economics lay at the heart of post-Soviet Russian state building because it was the Russian leadership's main response to the legacies of Soviet power. Radical economic reform – popularly known as 'shock therapy' – promised both to deal with the economic collapse of the late Soviet years and to secure democracy by destroying the remnants of the Soviet elite, the *nomenklatura*, and creating new sources of support for Yeltsin and for a democratic state.[1]

Regrettably, just as democratic consolidation was imperfectly carried through under Yeltsin so that the Russian polity became riddled with corruption and private interests prevailed over public ones, so economic reform lead to the creation of a hybrid economy rather than a market economy. The promised public goods of economic reform – the freedom from economic uncertainty created by low inflation, a stable currency, greater access to consumer goods, more economic opportunities and protected freedoms such as the right to own property – were not delivered to the bulk of the population. Elite economic interests from the Soviet period mostly survived the reformist push of 1992 and consolidated their hold over property in 1993 and 1994. Thereafter, economic policy was concerned with dealing with the hybrid nature of the economy to provide the state with a minimum of resources to survive. At times, it was only barely successful. The failure of reform in 1992 meant that the power of the state remained low; it did not have the resources, or its leaders the political will, to force reformist policies on the economy through the use of despotic power, nor did it have the infrastructural power to steer the economy towards a stable market. Economic transformation became stalemated. Those sections of the *nomenklatura* that had consolidated their hold on economic resources could not create what has been called a 'partial reform equilibrium', a stable situation where the 'winners' in an economic reform process use the resources that they control to create oligarchic control over government.[2]

The former *nomenklatura* that managed to survive the first round of reform could not provide the state with the resources that it needed to fund the most minimal of state activities. The government therefore turned to a few commercial banks to fund it and built up a political relationship with them. The relationship between the government and the banks and their heads, the 'oligarchs' proved to be profitable for both in the short-term, but it could not last because of the strains that it eventually put on the state budget. In late 1996 and 1997, the government tried to improve tax collection. This created a conflict between the 'oligarchs', and the government. Just like the survivors of the *nomenklatura* before them, and despite their popular appellation, the 'oligarchs' did not have the resources to create a 'partial reform equilibrium'. Yeltsin had personal reasons to continue support reform and the state needed new streams of income. What the 'oligarchs' could do, however, was to stimulate a rolling crisis of government, that, together with a fall in world oil prices and declining international confidence in emerging economies, would bankrupt Russia in August 1998 when the rouble collapsed and Russia was forced to declare a moratorium on debt repayments (the political aspects of this are covered in Chapter 3).

It was widely expected that this crash would herald a final and complete collapse of the Russian economy. This crash did not occur. The Russian government was lucky. Oil prices rose and it was able to improve its revenue position. The low value of the rouble also meant that imports were so expensive that people had to buy Russian produced goods. Moreover, there was little economic system – in the sense of a national market united by the use of a common currency to measure the worth of goods and economic activity – left to collapse. Many Russians worked in what has been called a 'virtual economy' in which economic exchange is conducted through barter rather than through the acceptance that goods and labour have a common monetary value across the whole of the Russian Federation. Investment in productive activity in the economy had already all but collapsed before August 1998, industrial output had slumped and capital had fled Russia.[3] Ironically, the fact that so many productive structures had survived as a part of the 'virtual economy' meant that as the rouble collapsed and internal demand for imported goods fell, there were industrial structures able to produce for a revived market for Russian goods. Russia thus ended the Yeltsin years on a positive economic note, but its recovery was based not on the consolidation of the market and change in the Russian economy. Underneath the positive economic figures of 1999, many structural economic problems remained for the new Putin government to tackle.

Problems and promises: Soviet legacies and the grand designs of 'shock therapy'

The end of the Soviet Union was marked by the collapse of the planned economy as a productive system and as an economic mechanism for distributing goods and organizing production. The Soviet economy as a productive system collapsed as industrial output slumped and prices rose (see Table 2.3 on p. 61). Food and consumer goods shortages that had plagued the Soviet economy for years because of the inefficiencies of the planned economy reached new levels as shop counters emptied; as new supplies failed to appear people were thrown back on their own resources. Talk of total economic collapse and famine became common. The ability of the Soviet government to deal with this supply crisis was hampered by the collapse of the Soviet economic system as an economic mechanism. This was caused by the fragmentation of the Soviet state into fifteen semi-independent states in the run-up to August 1991 and the final collapse of the USSR in its wake. As the levers of government disintegrated under pressure from nationalists and democrats, the resources that planners had previously been able to command and deploy to ease economic crises were 'spontaneously privatized' (see Chapter 2 and p. 107), and put beyond the reach and employ of what remained of the party-state administrative machine.

The collapse of the Soviet economy meant that the Russian government could not rely on the old administrative system to restore the supply of foodstuffs and goods to its population. Averting the threat of economic collapse meant constructing a new mechanism of economic regulation and distributing goods and services. The first argument for comprehensive economic reform to construct a market was thus that it was necessary as a response to an emergency situation in late 1991. However, there were other aspects that attracted Boris Yeltsin to the economic reform package presented to him by Gennadii Burbulis and Yegor Gaidar. 'Shock therapy' brought some immediate political advantages for Yeltsin, as were described in Chapter 3. Equally importantly, it promised that in creating a new system of economic regulation it would deliver socio-economic transformation to match, and underpin, the political transformation that Yeltsin had helped bring about against the CPSU and the Soviet state since 1989–1990. This economic transformation would change the relationship of state to society by creating new means of socioeconomic regulation, building up support for state regulation and developing a resource base for the state to use to regulate social and economic activity. This promise resonated with the Russian leadership at the end of 1991 because Yeltsin occupied a position at the apex of a state that barely existed. Although the Russian government began to appropriate the functions and resources of some parts of the old Soviet state after August 1991 and Yeltsin had moved to create a 'presidential vertical' (see Chapter 3), the state had little capacity, few resources and small means to collect them. The new regime was committed to democracy and could not appropriate resources from society by force, but since it inherited a collapsed economy and an administrative machine used to enforcing policy by coercion, or threat of it, it had little infrastructural power that could be relied on to deliver resources to it. Potential opponents of both Yeltsin and of political and economic reform from the old Soviet *nomenklatura*, on the other hand, had considerable resources because of 'spontaneous privatization'. 'Shock therapy' promised to alter how these semi-legally held resources could be used and hence to regulate the power granted by their possession.

To understand how this was to happen, and why Yeltsin and the reformers desired it, requires us to understand a few simple things about money, exchange and value in national, capitalist markets and in the Soviet system. National, capitalist markets largely set the value of goods impersonally; both buyers and sellers of goods have choices as to where they trade; the price of goods is largely determined by overall levels of supply and demand, and takes account of costs of production, of the labour, raw materials, that went into their production; finally, the value of a good is expressed in a common, generally accepted unit of exchange, money. An act of economic exchange in a market thus has a *common* or *universal* character with all other exchanges in a national economy. Goods of a similar type can be purchased for roughly the same price across a national market and for the same, commonly accepted unit of exchange, money. One type of good can be compared to another because it is possible to judge their relative worth in monetary terms; market exchange and the value of goods and property are thus fairly transparent. The resources – land, raw materials, labour power, factories, shops – possessed by a person or group can be valued in terms of money, the income that they generate from them can be compared and evenly taxed by the state across the whole national economy. The ability to develop economic power depends on the possession of money since this is necessary to purchase more property, modernize a factory, invest etc. Economic activity that does not take account of costs (measured in money) and demand (the estimation of which creates an idea of what monetary return can be expected of producing and supplying a good) cannot break even or be profitable; any one engaging in such activity may expect to go bankrupt.

The Soviet system was very different to this in both its usual operation from the 1920s onwards and in its legacy.[4] Goods in the Soviet economy had a monetary value assigned by the state. Prices were arbitrarily determined by central planners without regard to the costs of supply, what a product might cost in terms of raw material, labour etc., and without regard to demand. Political priorities mattered more than economic costs. Production was thus subsidized, prices were economically meaningless, and the monetary value of goods was nominal. Since prices were set arbitrarily, no accurate profit and loss calculations could be made of economic activity. If a firm made a 'loss' and had a deficit of roubles due to overspending or poor efficiency, the result was not bankruptcy. Credit did not come from a commercial lending organization concerned to make a profit, but from the state, which only cared about fulfilment of the plan. For this reason, it was often asserted that Soviet enterprises only had 'soft budget constraints'.[5] If an enterprise spent more than its budget allowed, it did not face the hard constraint of not having any more money to spend, a situation in a market economy that would mean an end to economic activity (bankruptcy). More 'soft' credit would be made available to the 'bankrupt' firm so that it could trade from the state in the form of increased subsidy, investment would continue through the mechanism of the plan, tax obligations to the state could be waived, etc. This soft credit would generally not have to be returned to the state and did not incur interest payments. Money did not, therefore, fully play an effective accounting function as it might in a market; success and failure were not measured in monetary terms. There were also strict political limits to what could be done with money. The state owned or controlled all significant property and resources; development priorities and investment were determined and controlled through the planning system. Money earned either by a firm or an individual could not be used to consolidate control over economic activity by the purchase of more land, machinery or business outlets, and shortages meant that money could not, by and large, be used to buy up consumer goods.

Money was thus largely detached from economic activity in the Soviet system. Along with shortages and planning inefficiencies, this helped to create one other difference between the Soviet and a market economy. Most distribution of goods and services took place in the USSR through plan allocations, but there was also an alternative system of exchange in the Soviet system parallel to the planning system with its nominal assignments of monetary value to goods. In economic exchanges outside of the planning system (such as black market deals), or to supplement it (the unofficial exchanges arranged by party-state officials and economic managers to compensate for breakdowns in the plan), value was assigned to goods and services by the actors involved in an exchange. As a result, these transactions, which were widespread given the failings of the planning system and often occurred within the networks and family circles mentioned in Chapter 2, were *particularistic*; each exchange and the value of goods exchanged were, unlike exchanges in a national market economy, unique to that exchange. Again, and as in the official system, these transactions took place without reference to what goods had cost to make, what someone else might pay for them, or what price the state had formally attached to them. Particularistic exchanges were highly personal, based on acquaintance, mutual affinity and trust, rather than on a desire to make profit and avoid loss as in monetized exchanges in capitalist economies.[6] The value of goods was secondary to the value assigned to them through personal relations and such things as considerations of the political power of traders – bureaucrats, party officials and economic managers – the value of being connected to them and the favours that such connections might bring in the future. It was thus the economic underpinning of proprietary officeholding. Soft budget constraints enabled officials to get away with circumventing the plan to fulfil it or enrich themselves (often at the same time) since they did not have to account for their diversion of funds to banks or shareholders, only to their biddable superiors.

As the Soviet system fell apart, particularistic exchange and soft budget constraints changed character and developed. From being an important, if unofficial, mechanism helped to keep the Soviet system functioning when the plan failed, particularistic exchange increasingly became a mechanism that allowed the maintenance of soft budget constraints. As the planning system began to fragment, the flow of goods to enterprises did not become commercialized – based on monetary, market exchange – but took place in the form of barter through the networks of particularistic exchange that had always supplemented the plan. The importance of this development was not only that it kept factories going in a time of crisis. It was also a means of safe-guarding the semi-legal ownership of property acquired through 'sponta-neous privatization'. Trading through barter and/or without regard to the monetary value of goods traded meant that production that was not profit-able was still possible; since they were able to maintain production, enterprise directors were able to keep their positions and prestige, and continue to control the resources that a factory had.

Particularistic exchange was thus necessary for much of Russian industry to keep up at least a semblance of economic activity and a means by which the sections of the *nomenklatura* could protect the resources, and hence the power, that they controlled through spontaneous privatization. This meant that managers kept personal status and position, and also that they could derive personal economic gain even as the rest of the economy declined. Goods and resources could be transferred between elite members at low, fictitious prices, and the state could be deceived and not paid its due in the form of taxes. This form of economic activity and the wealth derived from it was not profit seeking as in capitalist economies, where profit is produced through produ-cing to meet demand and maximized by being efficient in the use of labour and resources. It was rent seeking, taking wealth from economic activity by extracting it from the public purse or by manipulating distortions in the economy caused by policy. Moreover, the personal ties that underpinned particularistic exchange could be used as a barrier to the acquisition of power by those outside of elite networks left over from the communist system. Particularistic exchange devalues resources not held by members of networks since they cannot be converted into other goods or services. In Russia, this meant that the resources held by the mass of the population and the state were devalued. The chief resource held by the population at large was cash money and the chief means that any state has of accumulating resources is through taxation and the gathering of money. However, money had no great power whilst particularistic exchange prevailed since access to economic resources did not flow from the possession of money, but from connections.

At the end of 1991, the new Russian state did not have the personnel or the means (that is the capacity or the resources) to tackle the legacies of the Soviet system head on. But economic reformers argued it did not need to. 'Shock therapy' promised that the legacies of the Soviet era could be tackled through economic policy without building up a new administrative system to implement economic reform. It was thus administratively 'cheap' in that it did not require great bureaucratic capacity to implement it, but political will. Compliance with government policy depended on persuading people that the government had a 'credible commitment' to reform, that it was dedicated to reform and would pursue it no matter what, that evading the implementation of reform would only lead to the pursuit of more reformist policies to keep reform on track. Once people were convinced of the credibility of reform,

Soviet legacies would be diluted as reform provided incentives to act differently and empowered the state and new economic groups relative to the old *nomenklatura*. Reform, as conceived by Gaidar and his team, would take place in two stages.[7] Stage one, which was supposed to last from January 1992 into early 1993, was concerned with macro-economic stabilization, that is financial and monetary stabilization: it would involve controlling inflation and stabilizing the rouble and the budget deficit by liberalizing prices and commercializing economic activity as subsidies were cut and state spending reduced. Stage two, which was to last from early 1993 through to 1995, would consolidate the financial and monetary stabilization and see the restructuring of property rights as mass privatization would pass the bulk of industry and commercial activity into private hands.

The key to success was the successful completion of stage one, when policies to effect price liberalization and financial stabilization were supposed to be mutually reinforcing. The reasoning behind policy went as follows. Central government would end subsidies to industry and consumption by liberalizing prices. Without subsidies, enterprises would be dependent on private investment and credit to cover their economic activity. Acquiring private investment would require transparency in corporate governance, which would be detrimental to the semi-legal control of enterprises by the *nomenklatura*, and a commercial response to market opportunities. Where managers did not respond to the market or open up their books to outsiders they would push their enterprises to the brink of bankruptcy and would be pushed out of office by workers whose livelihoods would be threatened. The ending of subsidies and price liberalization would create accurate information about costs and demands so that there would be ample information about how to commercialize economic activity for managers. It would also create the incentive of profit. Money as a means of accounting and measuring success, and as a common unit of exchange, would thus be recreated across Russia. The need to commercialize and ability to make profit would also ensure a flow of goods to consumers. As demand would be satisfied, prices would be brought down after an initial rise in prices caused by too much money pursuing a few goods. Inflation would thus be controlled and money would become a stable store of value.

Cutting subsidies and freeing prices would thus create a virtuous circle. They would create an incentive – profit – to change behaviour and a threat – loss of control over enterprises – to those who might ignore this incentive. As this circle was completed and behaviour, or management, changed, particularistic exchange would be broken down and replaced by common, monetized exchange which the state could tax and regulate through its control of credit emissions from the Central Bank and taxation policy. The completion of the virtuous circle would be helped by the entry of Russia into global markets. Controlling inflation by cutting the state budget and liberalizing prices would help to facilitate the introduction of foreign capital into Russia and the expansion of trade by expediting the creation of a convertible and stable rouble. Trade, in the form of imports to Russia, would help break down particularistic exchange by introducing market prices to Russia in the form of a ready-made price system used to trade goods in the rest of the world. Competition with importers would force the restructuring of production to ensure competitiveness and prevent monopolies from raising prices once they were freed by providing more consumer choice. Without major restructuring effort and commercialization to facilitate access to resources for modernization, Russian industry could not compete with foreign industries that might enter Russia or sell their products to it. Russian industry at the end of the Soviet period was outdated technologically and made goods of low quality that were unsaleable on world markets, and concentrated in monopolies. For example, only about 16 per cent of plant in Russian factories was of a world standard at the start of the 1990s and the share of industrial production that could be sold on the world market fell between 1985 and 1991 from 65 per cent to 26 per cent. Many goods produced by Russian industry were 'negative value added', that is the value of goods produced by industry was worth less than could have been achieved by selling the raw materials used to make them on the world economy.[8] Trade would thus support the commercialization of economic activity by setting Russian market prices at levels comparable to those on world markets and forcing competition on to Russian industry, and any enterprise that might hope to access foreign capital would have to restructure and open up its management to the detriment of elite power.[9]

'Shock therapy' thus sought to destroy particularistic exchange, remove 'soft budget constraints' and restore value to money in the first stage of reform before the semi-legal control over enterprises enjoyed by the *nomenklatura* could be legalized through privatization. It would balance out the power of the *nomenklatura* by destroying part of it and by creating new economic actors who would have an interest in promoting and supporting the market rather than the Soviet old-boy network. Finally, and in some ways most importantly, it would help secure both the Yeltsin regime and a democratic state with infrastructural power. Yeltsin would have the support of new actors in the economy and of a population able to purchase goods and with greater economic freedoms. The state – with Yeltsin at its head – would be empowered over old elites since it would be able to raise resources by taxing economic activity that would now be transparent. This would give it the financial means to develop its capacity. It would further be empowered by its control of money. This would enable the state to shape economic activity, and hence the balance of power in society, through its control of fiscal policy. The state, by setting interest rates to control access to credit, by controlling the amount of money going into the economy from state-controlled printing presses, and by setting tax rates and customs tariffs, would control the amount of money people and firms could spend and on what. Since money and market exchange would be national, it would be able to do this across the whole of Russia; new economic agents and an economically liberated population enjoying the public goods of reform would support the state so that the exercise of state power would be supported socially and enforced by social demand. New groups would support the state and its activities so as to safeguard property rights, enjoy public goods such as protection from criminality and stable money, and facilitate profit-maximization rather than rent seeking. Making money sound and making all economic transactions monetary were thus central components of the building of infrastructural state power.[10]

The failure of economic reform, 1992–1994: opposition versus credible commitment

The cards were loaded against the reformers from the start. Opposition from parliamentary leaders to the strengthening of presidential power provided a source of support for economic opposition to Gaidar, and as we saw in Chapter 3, the government and presidential administration were divided over policy. Opposition forces therefore had plenty of scope to divide the government and lobby Yeltsin to grant concessions. A powerful economic constituency soon appeared to have mobilized against reform. The organized economic opposition to reform was centred on the Union of Industrialists and Entrepreneurs (UIE) headed by Arkadii Volsky. The UIE claimed to represent directors responsible for up to 65 per cent of production in 1992.[11] This was largely a rhetorical claim. The UIE's influence in 1992 came from a series of alliances and shadow organizations that were formed around it and which made it appear to be at the centre of social opposition to reform, and the fact that industrial managers were taking action that was weakening the government by undermining macro-economic stabilization (see p. 78). The alliances and shadow organizations around the UIE included Civic Union (formed in June 1992) which linked the UIE first with two of Russia's best organized and largest political parties, including vice-president Aleksandr Rutskoi's Free People's Party of Russia, and the *Smena* parliamentary faction, and later with the former official trade union movement.

Even more serious to the reformers' cause was that it proved to be impossible to maintain a credible commitment to reform because the task of reform was too big. Government efforts to end soft budget constraints and change managerial behaviour could not defeat ingrained managerial practices such as the low propensity to innovate that had been ingrained by planning and a lack of concern with profit.[12] Domestic demand slumped as the government cut its spending and stopped being a major customer for industrial production. This lead to a fall in industrial production in 1992 (see Table 4.1 on p. 115), but managers frequently did not respond to pressure to commercialize by changing production practices and manufacturing to meet demand. Instead, they recreated soft budget constraints and devalued money. They did this not in concert with one another, or as part of an organized movement against reform, but within the closed networks of affinity and trade of which they had been a part in the Soviet period. Managers maintained production where possible by continuing to supply their traditional trading partners on credit. This led to massive build-up of inter-enterprise debt. The build-up of inter-enterprise debt enabled enterprises to continue trading and producing (although at ever lower levels as production shrank rapidly) no matter whether or not there was demand for their goods and their production was profitable, and created a tangled web of mutual debts that complicated any attempt to shut down bankrupt factories.[13] Money was devalued as the build-up of inter-enterprise debt in 1992 provided the Russian parliaments with an excuse to authorize the Central Bank of Russia (CBR), which was under parliamentary jurisdiction, to issue credits to industry to cover debts and restore some liquidity to industry. This brought down the level of inter-enterprise debt, but did nothing to help lower inflation or force financial stringency on enterprises. Instead, it boosted the state budget deficit throughout the autumn of 1992 and, along with the wage rises made by enterprises to workers in September and October 1992, pushed inflation up.

The build-up of inter-enterprise debt and the failure to commercialize economic activity were facilitated by the failure of the global economy to act as an agent of change in Russia and the actions of regional authorities. Russian companies could not sell their goods abroad since no one really wanted the poor quality goods produced by Russian industry, only raw materials. Russian firms were therefore unable to fund their restructuring by selling their goods abroad. The uncertainty of making a profit, as well as the lack of a pricing system and stable currency, meant that foreign investment in Russia was low and limited to a few sectors, such as energy, and a few cities and regions, such as Moscow. As a result, foreign trade did not introduce a new price structure to Russia or the norms of competition. The low levels of foreign investment meant less investment capital in Russia and little by way of technology inflows and imported managerial practices.[14] Regional leaders helped to block the development of a national market by preventing the flow of goods between regions, issuing local subsidies, adding their political weight to lobbying for local exemptions to subsidy cutting, issuing economic orders and regulations that ran counter to central attempts at marketization. They were also less than diligent in the collection of taxes due to the centre, and accepted the payment of taxes in kind from local industries (itself a form of particularistic exchange since the goods used to pay taxes are valued not by the market but as a part of a bargain between tax collector and debtor). This also devalued money as a means of exchange and central control and weakened the central state apparatus by denying it its full share of tax revenues.[15]

Finally, the growth of inter-enterprise debt highlighted the absence of supporting institutions needed to make market exchange possible. In particular, the banking system in Russia was either not able, or not willing, to act as a source of commercial credit and investment resources for the productive economy. A large number of banks emerged in Russia at this time – there were 1700 private banks by the start of 1993 – but they were able to make easy profit by using cheap credits from the CBR to fund import deals and energy sales abroad and speculate in foreign exchange against the rouble.[16] The unwillingness of the banks to fund production by providing money with which to trade or investment resources meant that there has been an almost permanent 'credit crunch' in Russia.[17] Investment in industry fell consistently after 1991 so that by 1998, capital investment in Russia was at 22 per cent of the 1990 level (see Table 4.1 on p. 115).[18]

The sheer scale of the problems facing reformers and their inability to control managers and regional elites thus both defeated the macro-economic aims of controlling inflation and creating stable money, showed the limited power of the state to transform the economy and the over ambition of reformers. Compromise over reform began in April 1992 when Yeltsin bowed to parliamentary pressure and introduced some industrialists into the government (see Chapter 3). Further compromises were made in the summer of 1992 over privatization. Under pressure from industrialists, a way of privatizing firms that enabled insider takeovers was included in the privatization legislation adopted in June 1992: an enterprises' workforce was permitted to buy a full 51 per cent of voting shares in an enterprise, with the remaining stock allocated by the privatization vouchers given out to all Russian citizens or sold.[19] All Russian citizens received a voucher with a face-value of 10,000 roubles that could be used to purchase stock in enterprises to be privatized between 1992 and the summer of 1994 (enterprises deemed to be of strategic value to the economy, such as energy companies and telecommunications firms, were to be privatized later). This was designed to co-opt public support for the reform process by making millions of Russians feel themselves to be 'owners' of industry.

It was always debatable whether or not the voucher scheme would actually produce some form of 'popular capitalism'. But after it became possible to organize insider buy-outs it was impossible for this to happen. Economic managers used worker buy-outs to perpetuate their control over factories by manipulating their workforces. The reformers were not concerned about making this concession to managers since they believed that if macro-economic stabilization occurred and market exchange became dominant it did not matter who owned industry in the short-run: the market would force inefficient managers out of business. The distribution of property rights could therefore be arranged for political advantage rather than economic utility since the market would subsequently amend the compromise. The majority of enterprises privatized in the first wave of privatization that ended in July 1994 duly took place through insider buy-outs and most factory directors stayed in place. They did this by manipulating share registers so that it was unclear who owned factories and engaging in shady deals that saw stock transferred to holding companies that they or their associates owned. As a result, privatization 'in Russia created a higher proportion of insider-owned and controlled enterprises than in any other economy' with highly entrenched managers resistant to outside ownership and control.[20] The ownership rights of ordinary citizens were trampled on and did not translate to a check on managerial power. The negative features of management were often amplified as their control over enterprises became more secure. And once their control of enterprises was legalized through privatization, soft budget constraints were needed by managers to maintain the value of the property that they now owned as well as controlled.

The compromise on privatization reinforced the impression that pressure might bring concessions on government policy at a crucial moment in the middle of the reform programme's first year. More opportunity to pressure the government came as the cumulative effect of compromises over the composition of government, industrialist opposition and the issuing of CBR credits to industry imperilled efforts to stabilize inflation and create sound money. Monthly inflation that had fallen from a peak of 240 per cent in January at the initial liberalization of prices to 9 per cent in August was back up to 26 per cent a month in November 1992. This undermined Gaidar's authority and his political usefulness to Yeltsin, who began to court the industrialist opposition in the autumn of 1992 (see Chapter 3). Gaidar was sacrificed in December 1992, losing his post as (acting) Prime Minister to Viktor Chernomyrdin. Chernomyrdin's attitude to economic reform was more in line with the thinking of groups like Civic Union so that the credibility of reform was weakened irrevocably from December 1992 onwards.

Chernomyrdin's accession to the office of Prime Minister did not see the victory of the *nomenklatura*. Although united in opposition to the threat posed to their control of property by economic reform, industrialists were not united as a group that could take power. Managerial resistance to reform was not collective action by a social group aware of its interests, but the continuation of traditional behaviour that benefited managers more than the uncertain gains that could have been made through commercialization. The lack of unity amongst managers meant that Civic Union waned in 1993 as the economic interests and political factions that made it up split over opposition to Yeltsin. Managers concentrated on securing control over the enterprises rather than supporting the UIE and the rump of the Civic Union performed poorly in the 1993 Duma elections.[21] Chernomyrdin's replacement of Gaidar and privatization between them thus saw the victory of the economic *nomenklatura* over reform, rather than their capture of the new Russian state.

As it was to turn out, such a capture would not have been sustainable over the longer term anyway. Inter-enterprise debt and barter continued to grow over the course of 1993. By the end of the year, enterprises owed their suppliers over US\$3 billion and total overdue payments (including delayed wage payments and taxes) were equivalent to over 15 per cent of GDP.[22] Again, regional governments colluded in this by allowing the payment of taxes in kind and pressuring energy companies to take payment in kind, by barter.[23] This was the point at which the 'virtual economy' began to take off as a system of non-monetized exchange in which resources are transferred from sectors that could make a profit – such as the energy sector – to sectors producing goods of low, or negative value so that they appeared economically viable. Accepting taxes in kind gave particularistic exchange an official sanction; pressuring energy companies to supply to firms that either would not pay, or could only pay in kind, was an explicit subsidy to production. Accepting payment in kind began to encourage firms that were producing 'negative value added goods' (goods worth less than the materials used in their manufacture) to claim that they were producing goods of greater monetary value than they were. This allowed them to pay taxes and energy bills in kind with only small transfers of low value goods to regional authorities and the state. Firms that were making goods that could be sold at a profit had an incentive to join in this behaviour too since paying taxes and bills in kind at inflated barter prices meant that they could divert any money they made to other, more profitable activities such as buying government stocks (GKOs, see p. 117).

A loser in this process was the state. It was unable to use fiscal mechanisms to control economic activity since much of the economy was becoming demonetized, it could not gather the money it needed to fund its commitments because money was not available to be taxed, or because it could not get the full worth of taxes paid in kind and accepted by regional governments and local tax offices. These did not lose by accepting such payments because they did not pay interest on any debt that they owed by failing to transfer tax owed to the centre. The pressure that these problems placed on the central budget became acute in 1994 as the government's financial discipline broke down. The Chernomyrdin government paid out credits to alleviate some of the debt problems and to ease the burden on energy companies. The strains on the budget caused by the lack of reform and the issuing of credit caused a rouble crash in October 1994 as its value plummeted against the US dollar. The crash threw into relief the vacuity of Chernomyrdin's claims to be able to better manage the economy than the reformers. More importantly, it showed that although the state did not have the means to force the commercialization and monetization of the economy, it had to develop relations with groups in the economy other than the industrial managerial stratum that it had inherited from the USSR if it was to raise revenue and maintain even minimal government functions.

Banks, bonds and state bankruptcy: from the crash of 1994 to the crash of 1998

The compromising of reform meant that serious effort to replace particularistic exchange with market exchange was derailed and a hybrid economy balanced between the old economic order and the market emerged. Stuck between economic systems, the Russian economy went into decline, the basic facts of which are shown in Table 4.1. Gross Domestic Product (GDP) and industrial production fell year on year throughout the 1990s, with only small respites in 1997. Domestic investment also fell year on year and was not

Table 4.1 Selected economic indicators, 1992–1998

	1992	1993	1994	1995	1996	1997	1998
GDP, %	-14.5	-8.7	-12.6	-4.2	-3.5	0.8	-4.6
Industrial production, %	-18.2	-14.2	-20.9	-3.0	-4.0	1.9	-5.2
Fixed investments, %	-40.0	-12.0	-27.0	-13.0	-18.0	-5.0	-6.7
Inflation (consumer prices, year end % change)	2,506.1	840.0	204.4	128.6	21.8	10.9	84.4
Exports, US$ billions	53.6	59.7	68.1	81.3	88.4	86.7	73.9
Imports, US$ billions	43.0	44.3	50.5	60.9	61.5	66.9	59.5
Metals, metal products, fuels and precious stones as a % of total exports	68.5	69.9	71.6	68.0	71.1	71.8	69.7
Machinery and equipment as a % of total imports	37.7	33.8	35.2	33.7	31.7	35.3	35.9
Unemployment, % (end of period)	4.9	5.5	7.5	8.2	9.3	9.0	11.8
Wage arrears (US$ millions, end of year)	69.0	614.0	1,183.0	2,884.0	6,221.0	6,657.0	8,240.0
Earnings inequality (Gini coefficient)	37.1	46.1	44.6	47.1	48.3		

Sources: Bank of Finland Institute for Economies in Transition (2000) *Russian Economy – the month in review*, (6): pp. 1, 3; EBRD (1999) *Transition Report 1999. Ten years of transition*, London: European Bank for Reconstruction and Development, pp. 260–1; OECD (1997) *Russian Federation*, Paris: Organization for Economic Co-operation and Development, p. 257; V. Tikhomirov (2000) *The political economy of post-Soviet Russia*, Basingstoke: Macmillan, p. 23; Goskomstat (2000) *Rossiiskii statisticheskii ezhegodnik*, Moscow: Goskomstat Rossii, pp. 582–83.

replaced by an influx of foreign monies. Rather, capital fled Russia in massive quantities (reasonable estimates put capital flight at about US$15 billion a year).[24] The source of this capital flight was often the revenue earned by exporters of raw materials. As can be seen in Table 4.1 the value of Russia's exports was consistently above the value of its imports. This was partly because domestic economic collapse suppressed demand, but also caused by the high volumes of raw materials and fuels, particularly oil, exported from Russia. As can be seen in Table 4.1, exports of metals, metal products, fuels and precious stones accounted for about 70 per cent of Russia's exports year on year. Much of the money earned from these sales stayed abroad, robbing the Russian state of taxation revenue and the Russian economy of potential investment. The structure of Russian trade in the 1990s resembled that of an underdeveloped country with low value raw materials exported in bulk and high value machinery and equipment imported.

Unemployment rose throughout the 1990s, but given the contraction in industrial production, investment and GDP, was actually still quite low. This was a sign of the lack of restructuring in Russian industry. With little threat of bankruptcy and the ability to trade and pay taxes through barter and on credit, enterprises did not lay workers off, but put them on short working weeks, paid them in kind rather than with money, or delayed wage payments. As Table 4.1 shows, wage arrears rose dramatically over the course of the 1990s, with a particular sharp increase in 1996, to reach US$8 billion by the end of 1998. Unemployment was thus kept down, but underemployment was rife and the mass of the population saw a decline in living standards. One aspect of this was a dramatic increase in inequality. This is shown in the last row of Table 4.1, which shows the rise in a standardized measure of wage inequality, a Gini coefficient. The larger the number of a Gini coefficient, the greater the degree of wage inequality. Russia shows a high figure relative to other post-communist states and also a growing one. The gap between the richest and poorest sections of the population in the 1990s grew at a greater pace than even these figures show. In 1990 and 1991, the last years of Soviet power, the total incomes of the 10 per cent of the population with the highest incomes were about four times larger than the total incomes of the 10 per cent of the population with the lowest incomes; by 1995, the difference was fifteen times.[25] Russia was thus marked in the 1990s by a growth in both total and gross inequality.[26] This also had an effect on the quality of life for the mass of people and on their health and well-being. Life expectancy at birth for Russian males and females in 1991, for example, was respectively 63.5 and 74.3 years; by 2000 it had dropped to 59.9 years for men and 72.4 years for women. Consequently, Russia developed what some analysts and politicians have called a demographic crisis; the population of the Federation fell from 148.7 million people in 1992 to 145.9 million in 2000.[27]

The slump in the Russian economy is in part an explanation for why decline was not arrested. As the economy shrank so did confidence in the future and the resources available to the government to take action to reverse decline. The government was also blocked by its own weakness. The Russian state had no more capacity to undertake reform than it had possessed in 1992. It had no better control over monetary policy after 1992 than it had had at the start of 'shock therapy' thanks to inter-enterprise debt and barter, which undermined its attempts at financial control and demonetized the economy. Indeed, thanks to Yeltsin's divide and rule policies and the politics of institutional redundancy described in Chapter 3, the capacity of the state to transform the economy was possibly worse by 1994 than it had been at the start of 1992. Yeltsin's compromise on the composition of government in 1992 meant that the autonomy of the central executive, the ability of government ministers to act independently of social interests, was compromised. Radical reform was not a political option from such a position of weakness, especially as the government's commitment to it could not be presented as credible after the compromises of the last two years. But the October 1994 crash showed that without some policy innovation, the economy would be thrown into recurrent and ever deeper crisis by the draining away of resources to the unreformed productive sector now run by the survivors of the economic *nomenklatura*. Since the state possessed no more effective policy tools or powers available to enforce tax collection or control its finances than before the crisis, ways had to be found of raising revenue that could be used to fund the state's activities that did not require much complex administration from the enfeebled state.[28] It was also politically expedient for the reformers led by Anatolii Chubais, who was promoted after the 1994 crash, to develop their relations with new economic actors that might support them and balance out the influence of other lobbies and their representatives in the executive. To this end, and to gather resources to fund the state's budget deficit, they began to develop a relationship with Russia's commercial banks.

The banks came to the aid of the government in two contradictory ways after the 1994 rouble crisis. On the one hand, the banks began to fund the budget deficit as the market in government stock (GKOs, short-term government discount bills, and OFZs, government fixed coupon bonds) set up in 1994 began to take off. The market soon reached a point where treasury bills could be used to replace CBR credits as a source of deficit financing. This method of deficit financing was justifiable in reformist eyes in that it was not inflationary; very simply, it financed the state by shifting money around rather than printing more money, which would then chase goods and push up their price. Like 'shock therapy' before it, therefore, it might serve to stabilize the rouble and this could encourage inward investment and change the configuration of economic power. The boom in treasury bills, as Treisman has noted, not only funded the budget deficit, it also allowed the banks to secure an alternative source of profit to the inflationary speculation that had fuelled the growth of the banking sector in 1992–1994. Commercial bank investments in government securities rose eightfold between the rouble crisis and mid-1996 and were equal to 7.1 per cent of GDP in 1996, rising to 12 per cent by May 1997.[29] On the other hand, the commercial banks came to the aid of the government by proposing a 'shares for loans' programme in the spring of 1995. The stock that the banks had in view was in major and strategic industries not privatized in 1993 and that promised a profit through the production of goods for export or in near monopoly conditions (oil, tele-communications, certain metals etc.). The government accepted the scheme and an auctioning system that was supposed to pit the major banks against one another and secure the best possible deal for the government was intro-duced.[30] Again, this had attractions for reformists in that it appeared to link industries to sources of finance, could be justified as a means of changing corporate governance in major strategic industries, and was supposed to create new revenue sources for the state budget. State income from the first round of privatization had been very low since privatization had been voucher, rather than monetary, privatization.

The contradiction between these two means of assistance to the state from the banks lay in the fact that they led to different demands from the banks to maintain profitability. Profits from 'shares for loans' were based, first, on making sure that the government did not get a good price for the assets that it was disposing of, and, second, on avoiding paying tax on either the limited amounts of money that could be squeezed out of domestic customers, or on foreign currency earnings. Like other industries, enterprises controlled by banks through the 'shares for loans' scheme frequently paid taxes in kind at inflated prices and kept their money to invest at a great return in GKOs and other financial schemes. Profits from GKOs on the other hand, required, first, that the government's revenues were maintained so that there was con-fidence in its ability to meet debt repayments, and second, that inflation be kept low so that investors could be confident of a good return on the bonds that they purchased.[31] This meant that taxes had to be paid so that the government had money to pay off investors if they did not wish to roll their investment over and buy more bonds, and that inflationary trends in the rest of the economy had to be suppressed.

In the short-run, this tension was not apparent. The government main-tained the profitability of securities and hence commercial banks' commit-ment to investment, and allowed the banks to get stock very cheaply through the 'shares for loans' programme. The profitability of bonds was achieved not by improving tax collection, which would have required economic activity to be commercialized and the centre to have the power to stop the collection taxes in kind, but by securing a low inflation rate and providing the banks with concessions. The government kept inflation low by not paying some of its bills (such as wages) and pressured energy firms to provide industry and local authorities with non-monetary subsidies in the form of fuel supplies, and by cutting expenditure. In 1995, state spending was cut back by 20 per cent. By mid-1996, Gazprom (the gas monopoly) had 'practically replaced the CBR as the source of centralized credit' and was owed 57 trillion roubles by its customers (US$10 billion).[32] In return for making these fuel deliveries, oil companies and Gazprom received tax and exporting concessions.[33]

Cumulatively, these actions helped bring yearly inflation down from over 837 per cent in 1993 to 10.9 per cent by the end of 1997 (see Table 4.1). The concessions to banks were that they were allowed to have the GKO market to themselves because foreign purchase of government stock was at first banned, and that certain 'authorized' banks were licensed to trade in GKOs as agents of the state to their financial advantage.[34]

The 'shares for loans' scheme consolidated bank power as they expanded their fields of activity and influence. The terms of the scheme called for banks to manage a block of shares won at auction until September 1996 on provision of a loan to the government and to invest in the company whose stock the bank held. Thereafter, if the government did not redeem the loan, the shares could be sold on with the bank taking back its original loan plus 30 per cent of any capital gain, the rest going to the government. The auctions for shares in the enterprises privatized under the 'shares for loans' scheme were basically fixed: they were not really competitive so that the reserve price was generally not exceeded and foreign participation was blocked. The banks thus acquired very valuable resources that could generate revenue for them through exports for give-away prices. Subsequently, when the loans were not redeemed and the shares were sold on, auction winners bought the firms they had managed and did so at bargain prices. Menatep bank, for example, won control of one-third of YuKos (Russia's second largest oil holding company) for a loan of US$159 million (the reserve price was US$150 million). When Menatep sold its share of YuKos on, the sale was to one of its subsidiaries for US$160.1 million; the state's share of the capital gain was only US$770,000. In another sale, Oneksimbank sold another oil firm to one of its subsidiaries for below the original loan price so that the state got nothing.[35] The acquisition of these companies by the banks, together with their often extensive, near monopoly, holdings in the media, turned them into 'financial-industrial groups' (FIGs) and made them the most powerful groups in the Russian economy.[36] Estimates of the extent to which the bank-led FIGs dominated the Russian economy at this time vary. At the end of 1996 Boris Berezovsky (a business-man with wide financial, media and industrial interests centred on the car maker LogoVaz), claimed that they controlled about 50 per cent of economy.[37] This is probably too high a figure, although it tallies with forecasts from the time which predicted that 120 FIGs would soon control half of Russia's industrial structure and 70 per cent of finance.[38] Whatever their actual level of industrial might, the bank-led FIGs through the taxes that they paid (intermittently) and their purchase of GKOs, were, with one or two rich regions of Russia like Moscow City, the major sources of revenue for the state, and their heads, like Berezovsky and Vladimir Potanin became popularly regarded as 'oligarchs' because of their political influence (see also Chapter 3).

'Share for loans' was thus not a great source of revenue for the government. Although it brought it some money in the form of loans, it did not generate much income for the government thereafter. However, sooner or later, the inherent contradiction in the bank–state relationship had to emerge: the government's reliance on the commercial banks to fund the state could not last forever. In the absence of reform and as the government failed to pay some of its bills, the demonetization of the economy through the growth of barter continued. By the middle of 1997, 49 per cent of Russian firms reported that they were loss making; by the end of 1997, overdue payments on company balance sheets were worth 40 per cent of GDP and just over 50 per cent of industrial sales were accounted for by barter.[39] The profits that could be made on GKOs also sucked money out of the economy from banks and other organizations so that the credit crunch in the economy was extended.[40] As the 'virtual economy' expanded, the amount of government revenue that could be raised through taxes fell. In 1992, tax non-payments were 1.86 per cent of planned tax revenues and equal to 0.44 per cent of GDP; in 1996, non-payments were 18.94 per cent of planned tax revenues and equal to 4.9 per cent of GDP.[41] The ability to make up this shortfall through the sale of GKOs was limited as long as the market was reserved for Russian commercial banks. The banks did not have the money to fund the growth of the GKO market over the long term; by the autumn of 1996, the stock of GKOs and OFZs had risen above the total stock of rouble deposits in the banking system.[42] The amount of money needed to service its debt was also becoming a problem as bonds became due and the amount of money needed to service debt grew. By the end of 1996, government debt was roughly 50 per cent of GDP thanks to the expansion of the GKO market.[43] Finally, pressure on the government to improve its financial position came from the International Monetary Fund (IMF), which delayed a US$10.2 billion transfer of budgetary aid because of the shortfalls in state revenue in October 1996.

The inability of the banks to fund the continued expansion of the GKO market meant that the only source of funds to roll domestic debt over was international finance. However, this meant that state revenues had to be secured to ensure investor confidence and that something had to be done about tax defaulters. Reform was thus imperative by late 1996 to deal with state finances, and as we noted in Chapter 3, it had some personal advantages for Yeltsin because it tied the government to him and threatened to weaken regional leaders. However, dealing with the tax defaulters was bound to bring the government and the banks into conflict. Many of the biggest tax defaulters were the energy companies that the banks had a stake in thanks to the 'shares for loans' sales and which they had been squeezing for profit ever since by defaulting on taxes and using the money that should have been paid in tax to buy profitable GKOs.[44] If it was to raise tax revenues, the government had little option but to try to squeeze taxes from bank-led FIGs; it did not have the capacity to collect it from defaulters in the economy as a whole or to pressure regions to increase tax collection in money so that the centre might receive more revenue. It only had the capacity to target a few major enterprises and try to squeeze more tax from them. A side-benefit of this for the government was that when squeezed by tax authorities, the FIGs might insist on payment in cash from their debtors so that barter and tax in kind payments would decline throughout the economy. Finally, the move to open up the GKO market internationally would add an additional source of friction to bank–state relations since it would push down the interest rates on GKOs so that the banks would earn less money than previously from them.

The needs of the state thus had to lead to the relationship that had developed between the banks and the government breaking down. As this relationship broke down, the 'oligarchs' in charge of the banks and FIGs would try to protect their sources of revenue. However, and like the *nomenklatura* before them, their ability to do this, to force political compromise and create a situation where there was a partial reform equilibrium in their favour, was limited. Although they were to resist some of the government demands and create political trouble, international pressure from changes in commodity and financial markets and the state's need for new revenue sources were to keep the drive to improve tax collection going until the collapse of international confidence in Russia created such pressure on the rouble that it had to be devalued and government debt defaulted on in August 1998. The contest with the oligarchs did not help the Russian government cope with this pressure, but neither were they responsible for it.

The first moves to restore state finances began in the autumn of 1996 as parts of the tax service was reorganized and placed under direct presidential control. This was designed to curtail regional autonomy in tax collection (see Chapter 3). Again, and as in 1992, policy relied on people believing that the government was committed to it and that there was no point in resisting it. To this end, the reorganization of the tax service saw the establishment of a special commission on taxation, the acronym for which was the same as for the first Soviet secret police, the Cheka.[45] Yeltsin's commitment to improving state finances was signalled more seriously in the spring of 1997 when Vladimir Potanin was removed in a government reshuffle, and Chubais and Boris Nemtsov were brought into government as first Deputy Prime Ministers with, respectively, responsibility for economic reform and the Ministry of Finance, and for energy monopolies. This was quickly followed by an order requiring companies in debt to the state to hand over 50 per cent plus 1 share of their equity to the government. Pressure was applied in particular by Nemtsov to Gazprom, the gas monopoly, and it paid its back taxes in the summer. Nemtsov further tried to break up the power of the energy lobby by pressing for improved corporate governance and government oversight, and for conditions in which foreign capital could balance the power of the commercial banks in the sector.

The government's efforts to improve state revenue collection found a favourable response from international financiers. The GKO market was opened up to foreigners in 1996, but the major influx of foreign money into GKOs came in the first six months of 1997 and financed 56 per cent of the budget deficit when taxation revenue was still very low.[46] By the end of 1997 foreigners owned 33.9 per cent of the market in GKOs and OFZs to the value of US$19.7 billion: in the space of a year, the value of foreign holdings of short-term government debt had risen threefold and doubled in percentage terms.[47] Foreign money also began to enter the Russian stock exchange in large quantities for the first time on the back of the boom in treasury bills. The value of stock traded on the Moscow exchange rose by 155 per cent in the first half of 1997 to a value of about US$100 billion.[48] In total, an estimated US$44 billion of foreign capital was invested in the Russian economy over the year.[49]

The inflow of foreign capital into the market for treasury bills and the increase in tax collection helped control the government's debt problem. Interest rates on government bonds fell to 9–10 per cent in the summer of 1997 from a high of over 100 per cent in 1996 and the rate of increase of state domestic debt fell to less than 2 per cent a month by the autumn of 1997 (it had tripled in 1996).[50] Unfortunately, this success in attracting foreign money was not mirrored in other areas. Government policy made Russia look more attractive as an investment proposition, but there was no real objective change in the state's financial position, or transformation of the economy outside of the stock exchange and bond markets. The government managed to force up collection of tax payments in cash for a short time in 1997, but it could not increase its revenues in general. Tax collection at the end of 1997 was about 15 per cent higher in cash terms than at the same time in 1996, but the overall level of enterprise tax indebtedness rose over the course of 1997 by 50 per cent and including tax penalties was worth US$93 billion.[51]

The government's commitment to reform was thus not enough to secure mass compliance with its efforts at improving tax collection. Regional authorities continued to collude with enterprises and accepted tax payments in kind that did not reflect the value of the goods used to pay tax bills. Worse, as the year progressed, the government's commitment to reform was attacked and changes in the global economy began to threaten investor confidence. The attack on the government came as the squeeze on FIG profits led to confrontation over the blocks of shares to be allocated by the 1997 of the 'shares for loans'. Control of these shares would have spread the risk of government strategy leading to losses for banks/FIGs because the shares to be allocated were in firms where there was potential for income generation through export earnings (such as Norilsk Nickel and the Rosneft oil group), or linkage with foreign investors (the Svyazinvest telecom network). Control over these firms would have allowed tax losses and the lower profits from GKOs to be offset against new income streams. Competition to control these enterprises intensified over the summer of 1997 and soon became political as access to politicians was seen as a key ingredient to a successful bid. A rolling crisis of government developed from the summer of 1997 as the perception that Oneksimbank was doing better than everyone else in the 'shares for loans' auctions took hold. Oneksimbank won the Norilsk Nickel and Svyazinvest auctions and its rivals accused Chubais of favouring it unfairly. The 'bank wars' erupted and led to Chubais losing control of the Ministry of Finance and the firing of three officials close to him. This kicked off a round of personnel changes in 1998 (see Chapter 3) as Yeltsin tried to keep control over the government.

This turmoil came at precisely the wrong time – just as the crisis in Asian markets began to affect other emerging markets and as Russia began to suffer from balance of payments problems – and it was these pressures rather than 'oligarch' manoeuvrings that ended the drive to stabilize the state's budgetary position by opening up to the global economy and squeezing the FIGs. Russia had run a trade surplus after 1991 by exporting fuels and metals (see Table 4.1). In 1997, the prices of these goods fell on world markets and continued to fall in 1998. This had a major affect on the state budget, which raised a significant sum of income from export taxes and taxing the foreign currency earnings of exporters, and questions began to be asked about the valuation of the rouble. Government income from fuel and metals sales fell, according to Prime Minister Kiriyenko, by 20–40 per cent in the first months of 1998.[52] This, together with the government crisis, magnified the effect of declining investor confidence caused by the crisis in Asian markets in late 1997. Most of the foreign money that had entered the government debt market in 1997 was in short-term debt that matured in under a year. Maintaining investor confidence was therefore very important because as debt matured the government sought to roll it over in new GKO issues. When this confidence began to decline as a result of the Asian crisis and in response to government troubles (international credit rating agencies reduced Russia's credit rating several times after October 1997), money began to leave the government debt market. Foreign investors withdrew US$5 billion from the government debt market in November 1997 alone.[53] To counteract falling confidence, the government raised interest rates. The cost of government borrowing thus rose whilst worries remained about revenue generation because of continued tax collection problems and falling export prices.

The loss of international confidence, the failure to raise tax revenues to fund government debt repayments and the fall in export prices turned Russian financial markets from being an international success story of 1997 into a financial pyramid that was just waiting to collapse.[54] As the amounts of money coming into the economy dried up, the ability of the government to service its debts and defend the rouble as people sold it to move into a currency in which they had confidence crumbled. A whole series of measures were introduced in 1998 to try to avert a crisis. The Kiriyenko government appointed after March 1998 swapped short-term debt for longer term bonds, promised major cuts in the 1998 budget by presidential decree, and appointed 'foreigner-friendly' economists like Boris Fedorov, the former Minister of Finance, to head the State Tax Service. Chubais, who had been removed from government in March 1998, was made Russia's representative to the IMF and World Bank to try to encourage them to prop up the state's finances. These efforts produced only momentary relief. Russia did not have solid enough financial institutions to win back investor confidence. The government did not have the reserves to prop up the rouble over a long time, or broad political support for measures that would restore confidence. The Duma moved slowly in support of the government's anti-crisis package during July 1998. By the time it dissolved for the summer, the Duma had voted through new laws creating only about one-third of the extra tax revenue wanted by the government (although whether the government would have been able to collect this revenue is another matter). As a result, the IMF held back US$800 million of the extra aid that it had granted Russia to support the rouble at the end of July.

In early August 1998, the price of Russian debt plummeted once more and the stock market began to sink to new lows (between October 1997 and August 1998 the market lost 84.9 per cent of its value). Confidence in Russian banks also collapsed. They were exposed by the forward options on the rouble they had taken out with foreign banks and that they could not afford to honour as the rouble's worth was in question, by the size of their GKO holdings and lack of reserves. After some political posturing to try to hold the rouble up, the government faced the inevitable. On 17 August, Kiriyenko announced that the rouble would be allowed to float in a wider band so that it could be devalued by over a third by the end of the year (it soon broke this barrier). A moratorium on payment of foreign commercial debts and a freeze on domestic debt repayment were also announced.

Conclusion: after August 1998 – the crash that never happened and Yeltsin's economic legacy

The underlying theme in the story of the failure of economic transformation in Russia after 1991 is that reform failure and economic decline are explained by state weakness. The Russian state did not have administrative capacity to implement reform or to gather the resources that might have allowed it to develop to a point where it could implement change. As a result, a whole series of policies that did not require much state capacity to implement – that were low cost administrative solutions to economic problems – were tried: 'shock therapy'; financing through 'shares for loans' and bond sales; and finally, improving tax collection by attacking a few rich, but socially irresponsible firms, and opening up to the global financial market. Where they offered a solution to Russia's problems, rather than a palliative to the state's budgetary troubles, these relied either on the ability to maintain the idea that the government was committed to reform so that people complied willingly. Such commitment was impossible to maintain because Yeltsin compromised reform to ensure his political survival, the Soviet legacy was too great to be overcome by projecting 'credible commitment', supporting institutions were missing or did not behave as reformers expected, and because opposition, first from the remnants of the economic *nomenklatura* and later from the banks and FIGs, chipped away at the government and policy.

A major economic legacy of the Yeltsin era has thus been a realization that the role of the state needs to change, that economic policy cannot on its own create a new state, but itself needs to be supported by state institutions capable of implementing it. The crisis of August 1998 weakened the influence of pro-market ideology in the Russian government because the most recent efforts at improving the revenue position of the state and the crash were associated with liberals like Chubais, Nemtsov and Kiriyenko. Consequently, the idea of state intervention to direct the economy became more respectable in the wake of August 1998. The Primakov government, which included Yurii Maslyukov, a former chair of Gosplan, was ideologically more committed to state action than its predecessor was. Primakov argued that 'the market is not capable of putting all things in their correct place and so the government has to take on the function of supporting and regulating domestic producers'.[55] However, the ability of the Primakov government to intervene in the economy was too slight to move Russia away from its hybrid economic system and actions that might have been taken to increase the state's role were halted by the need to negotiate with the IMF and Western debtors. A consolidated vision of the role of the state in the economy never developed in the Primakov government's economic programmes. Indeed, an economic plan never emerged from the government, just a 'system of measures' that might be pursued.[56] Consequently, some measures were taken to increase state control, but more were announced and not acted on.[57]

The ousting of Primakov did not end the possibility of greater state intervention in the economy, but nor did it create the conditions for it. His immediate successor, Sergei Stepashin did not depart from many of the initiatives announced under Primakov (for example, the possibility of regulating agricultural prices, plans for a national development budget), but had neither the time nor the resources to pursue a programme for economic change.[58] In turn, Stepashin's successor, Vladimir Putin, whilst eschewing any 'return to a system of planning and managing the economy by directives where an omnipresent state regulates every aspect of every factory's work from above', also called for a greater state role. Putin argued that Russia will not be 'like the USA or Britain, where liberal values have deep historical roots ... For Russians, a strong state is not an anomaly against which one struggles; on the contrary, it is the source and guarantee of order, the initiator and main moving force of all changes.'[59] The economic policy ramifications of this were not clear before the election in March 2000 and have only become slightly clearer since then, as we will discuss in Chapter 6. The Putin administration did not want to launch any major economic initiatives, or take any significant steps towards improving public administration before the presidential election.

Perhaps even more importantly, the Putin government was able to avoid even minimal economic decisions because it was able to take advantage of the post-crisis 'strength' of the Russian economy. (Strength that is, in comparison to the almost unbroken run of decline over most of the previous decade.) Russia's relative recovery, it should be remembered, is from a rock-bottom position. Forecasts of economic collapse were widespread after August 1998. It was expected that economic production – already in a state of parlous slump – would collapse further and that inflation would rocket as the government pumped money into the economy. Instead, as Table 4.2 shows, the economy showed stronger signs of recovery than at any time previously. Industrial output and GDP both rose as the weakness of the rouble meant that consumers turned back to Russian producers because they could no longer afford foreign made goods: the value of imports fell by US$18 billion in 1999 and continued to be low in the first months of 2000. A (greater) social disaster was avoided as the unemployment rate remained constant. Inflation fell as domestic demand was dampened by the rouble crash and as the government avoided pumping money into the economy. It did not reach the lows of 1996–1997, but then the fall in inflation was not based so much on the demonetization of the economy. The amount of barter in industrial sales fell from 46 per cent to 33 per cent between January 1999 and January 2000.[60] Investment picked up only slowly in 1999 in comparison to the growth in GDP and industrial production, but began to grow in 2000. At the same time, the value of exports held as world oil prices rose to levels not seen since the Gulf War of 1991. In these circumstances, tax payments on foreign economic activity rose due to the weakness of the rouble and improved world oil prices. Tax payments may also have improved as barter has declined in industrial sales. The crash made paying taxes in cash cheaper than before: the rouble was so weak that there was little point in converting earnings into dollars and paying taxes in kind rather than in cash; the collapse of the GKO market

Table 4.2 After the crash: selected economic indicators, 1998–2000

	1998	*1999*	*2000*
GDP, %	−4.6	3.2	7.5[a]
Industrial production, %	−5.2	8.1	10.0[b]
Fixed investments, %	−6.7	1.0	17.6[b]
Inflation (consumer prices, year end % change)	84.4	36.5	18.7[b]
Exports, US$ billions	73.9	74.3	57.7[c]
Imports, US$ billions	59.5	41.1	24.4[c]
Current account (US$ billions)	2.1	25.0	11.2[d]
Unemployment, %	11.8	11.7	9.8[b]

Source: Bank of Finland Institute for Economies in Transition (2000) *Russian Economy – the month in review*, (9): pp. 1, 3.

Notes
a First half of 2000.
b As of 1 August 2000.
c As of 1 July 2000.
d First quarter of 2000.

meant that it was no longer possible or attractive to divert money that should have been earmarked for tax payments into the government securities market. The strength of Russian trade also helped to stabilize Russia's current account surplus, taking some pressure off the rouble and allowing it to stabilize in relation to other currencies.

The 'strength' of the post-1998 economy meant that the Russian government has been able to post a budget surplus without major policy effort. But although the economy looked healthier at the end of the Yeltsin period in December 1999 in statistical terms than might have been expected a year earlier, the Yeltsin legacy in the economy was ambiguous. The government's fiscal position is based on good fortune, rather than a growth of its power to extract resources from society. The boom in oil prices will in all probability evaporate as quickly as it emerged. Tax collection systems still needed to be developed by the new Putin administration. Massive state debts remained to be dealt with. Russia was allowed to default on several debt payments in 1999 by the international community that did not wish to complicate the government's economic position in 1999, and some debt rescheduling was renegotiated just before the March 2000 presidential election. However, foreign debt servicing will rise in the future and without further rescheduling it will claim a major part of government revenue. Moreover, the improvements in the economy did not necessarily signal that the interests of the economic forces that had helped shape Russia's 'virtual economy' had changed. The commercial banks suffered major losses in the August crash since they owed large foreign currency debts to international lenders. Bankruptcy, however, remained rare. Bankers transferred valuable assets from banks that were technically bankrupt to new holding companies so as to put them beyond the reach of creditors. FIGs made massive profits on the sale of oil from the companies that they owned thanks to the 'shares for loans' scheme. The hold of FIGs over these enterprises was also consolidated as dubious business practices devalued the share holdings of other investors in oil companies, and as FIGs transferred their share holdings to dummy companies abroad. Such practices helped to ensure that foreign investment in Russia remained low. Yeltsin thus left Putin a 'plutocrat problem' despite the bankers' losses in 1998.[61] The 'oligarchs' might not have been able on their own to deflect the attacks on them by the government in 1997 and 1998 and establish their own version of a 'partial reform equilibrium', but they remained a potent force and a wealthy group. As we shall see, Putin soon turned his attention to them.

Finally, although industrial production rose in 1999 and was gradually followed by a rise in investment in 2000, it was too soon to say that the Russian economy had moved beyond barter to a monetized system in which corporate governance was transparent and profit seeking had replaced rent-seeking. Trade may be more monetized, but this is because some money flows to industry from consumers whilst imports remain too expensive and because it is cheaper to use the rouble than to pay taxes in kind and barter with trading partners. Moreover, barter still accounts for a considerable proportion of industrial sales. Barter and particularistic exchange between business and regional authorities, and between enterprises, may once more reach the levels of 1996–1997 when they helped to create a crisis of the state budget. They have served well as survival strategies in the past, even though they impose great general costs to the Russian public, and may do so again if money becomes short, or there are alternatives to using it for trade and tax payments. A key task before the economic reformers of the new Putin administration is to ensure that monetary stabilization continues and monetary exchange thrives. And this, of course, is where all their predecessors have failed because of the weakness of the Russian state.

Notes

1 Accounts of the economic reform programmes of the 1990s and their fate written with the participation of members of both the Russian reform team and Western advisers can be found in Ye. Gaidar (1999) *Days of defeat and victory*, Seattle: University of Washington Press; J. Sachs (1993) 'Western financial assistance and Russia's reforms', in S. Islam and M. Mandelbaum (eds) *Making markets*, New York: Council on Foreign Relations Press; A. Åslund (ed.) (1994) *Economic transformation in Russia*, London: Pinter and (1995) *How Russia became a market economy*, Washington, DC: Brookings Institute Press; A. Åslund and R. Layard (eds) (1993) *Changing the economic system in Russia*, London: Pinter; M. Boycko A. Shleifer and R. Vishny (1995) *Privatizing Russia*, Cambridge, MA: The MIT Press; A. Shleifer and D. Treisman (2000) *Without a map. Political tactics and economic reform in Russia*, Cambridge, MA: The MIT Press. Other general accounts include T. Gustafson (1999) *Capitalism Russian-style*, Cambridge: Cambridge University Press; R. Brady (1999) *Kapitalizm. Russia's struggle to free its economy*, New Haven: Yale University Press; V. Tikhomirov (2000) *The political economy of post-Soviet Russia*, Basingstoke: Macmillan.

2 J. Hellman (1998) 'Winners take all: the politics of partial reform in postcommunist transitions', *World Politics*, 50(2): pp. 202–34.

3 The term 'virtual economy' was coined by C. Gaddy and B. Ickes (1998) 'Russia's virtual economy', *Foreign Affairs*, 77(5): pp. 53–67. A formal description of the 'virtual economy model' can be found in R.E. Ericson and B.W Ickes (2000) 'A model of Russia's "virtual economy"' *BOFIT Discussion Papers*, no. 10, Helsinki: Bank of Finland Institute for Economies in Transition. For a critical comment on the idea of 'virtual economy' see D. Woodruff (1999) 'It's value that's virtual: bartles, rubles, and the place of Gazprom in the Russian economy', *Post-Soviet Affairs*, 15(2): pp. 130–48.

4 A longer discussion of these issues can be found in D. Woodward (1999) *Money unmade. Barter and the fate of Russian capitalism*, Ithaca, NY: Cornell University Press.

5 J. Kornai (1986) 'The soft budget constraint', *Kyklos*, 39(1): pp. 3–30 and (1992) *The socialist system. The political economy of communism*, Oxford: Clarendon Press, pp. 140–44.

6 On the sources of particularistic exchange in the USSR see M. Urban (1985) 'Conceptualizing political power in the USSR: patterns of binding and bonding', *Studies in Comparative Communism*, 18(4): pp. 207–26.

7 A simple description of the logic of the stages can be found in K. Henderson and N. Robinson (1997) *Post-communist politics*, London: Prentice Hall, pp. 176–79. A lengthier, but very accessible description of the reform options before post-communist states can be found in W. Adams and J.W. Brock (1993) *Adam Smith Goes to*

Moscow, Princeton: Princeton University Press. The basic reform strategy adopted in Russia was laid out in speeches made by Yeltsin in October 1991 and January 1992 (*Sovetskaya Rossiya*, 29 October 1991, *Rossiiskaya gazeta*, 17 January 1992), in the memorandum on economic reform written by Gaidar and Georgii Matyukhin (then head of the Russian Central Bank) in *Nezavisimaya gazeta*, 3 March 1992, and in the 1992 'Medium-term programme of the economic reforms of the Russian Government', *Russian Economic Trends*, 1(3): pp. 43–69.

8 On the technical level of Russian industry, its competitiveness and monopoly levels see: A.P Abelin (1996) 'Long-term Economic Growth Strategy' Working paper no. 47, Tokyo: Economic Planning Agency, pp. 4–5; D.V. Kuzin (1993) 'Rossiiskaya ekonomika na mirovom rynke: problema konkurentosposobnosti', *Obshchestvo i ekonomika*, (3): pp. 32–44; Åslund, *How Russia became a market economy*, pp. 153–4. On 'negative value added' production see Gaddy and Ickes, 'Russia's virtual economy'; R.I. McKinnon (1993) *The order of economic liberalization. Financial control in the transition to a market economy*, second edition, Baltimore: Johns Hopkins University Press, chapter 12; C. Senik-Leygonie and G. Hughes (1992) 'Industrial profitability and trade among the former Soviet republics', *Economic Policy*, 15: pp. 353–86.

9 On the hopes for foreign involvement in support of reform see N. Robinson (1999) 'The global economy, reform and crisis in Russia', *Review of International Political Economy*, 1999, 6(4): pp. 531–64.

10 On the importance of monetary control to state building, see Woodruff, *Money unmade ...*, pp. 12–13.

11 For fuller discussions of the organization see E. Lohr (1993) 'Arkadii Volsky's power base', *Europe-Asia Studies*, 45(5): pp. 811–29; M. McFaul (1993) 'Russian centrism and revolutionary transitions', *Post-Soviet Affairs*, 9(3): pp. 196–222; N. Robinson (1998) 'Corporate interests and the politics of transition in Russia, 1991–1994', in J. Gary Hopps and D. Iatridis (eds) *Privatization in Central and Eastern Europe*, Westport, CT: Praeger.

12 A. Kuznetsov (1994) 'Economic reforms in Russia: enterprise behaviour as an impediment to change', *Europe-Asia Studies*, 46(6): pp. 955–70.

13 B.W. Ickes and R. Ryterman (1993) 'Roadblock to economic reform: inter-enterprise debt and the transitions to markets', *Post-Soviet Affairs*, 9(3): pp. 231–52; J. Rostowski (1993) 'The inter-enterprise debt explosion in the former Soviet Union', *Communist Economics and Economic Transformation*, 5(2): pp. 131–59.

14 Robinson, 'The global economy ...'.

15 See P. Hanson (1993) 'Local power and market reform in Russia', *Communist Economies and Economic Transformation*, 5(1): pp. 45–60.

16 D. Treisman (1995) 'The politics of soft credit in Russia', *Europe-Asia Studies*, 47 (6): p. 949; Gustafson, *Capitalism Russian-style*, pp. 84–7.

17 On the shortage of credit as a stimulus to barter see S. Commander and C. Mumssen (1998) 'Understanding barter in Russia', *EBRD Working Paper*, 37.

18 A. Batyaeva (1999) 'Masshtaby neinvestirovaniya v rossiiskoi promyshlennosti', *Voprosy ekonomiki*, (10): p. 85.

19 There is a large literature on privatization, its origins, forms and failures. For accounts written with the participation of members of both the Russian reform team and Western advisers see A. Chubais (ed.) (1999) *Privatizatsiya po-rossiiski*, Moscow: Vagrius; M. Boycko, A. Shleifer and R. Vishny (1995) *Privatizing Russia*, Cambridge, MA: The MIT Press; Shleifer and Treisman, *Without a map ...*, pp. 21–38; Åslund, *How Russia became a market economy*, pp. 223–71. Other, and often more critical accounts can be found in the general literature on reform cited in note 1, and specifically in R. Frydman, A. Rapacynski and J. Earle (1993) *The Privatization Process in Russia, Ukraine and the Baltic States*. Budapest: Central European University Press; S. Clarke (1994) 'Privatisation: the politics of capital

and labour', in S. White, A. Pravda and Z. Gitelman (eds) *Developments in Soviet and Post-Soviet politics*, Basingstoke: Macmillan; P. Rutland (1994) 'Privatisation in Russia: one step forward: two steps back?', *Europe-Asia Studies*, 46(7): pp. 1109–131; S. Fortescue (1995) 'Privatization of large-scale Russian industry', in A. Saikal and W. Maley (eds) *Russia in search of its future*. Cambridge: Cambridge University Press.

20 I. Filatotchev, M. Wright, and M. Bleaney (1999) 'Privatization, insider control and managerial entrenchment in Russia', *Economics of Transition*, 7(2): pp. 491, 494–6. For a fuller review of privatization's impact on management and ownership see J. Blasi, M. Kroumova and D. Kruse (1997) *Kremlin capitalism. Privatizing the Russian economy*, Ithaca, NY: Cornell University Press.

21 L.J. Cook and V.E. Gimpelson (1995) 'Exit and voice in Russian managers' privatization strategies', *Communist Economies and Economic Transformation*, 7(4): pp. 465–83.

22 Tikhomirov, *The political economy of post-Soviet Russia*, pp. 22–4.

23 Woodruff, *Money unmade. . .*, pp. 129 *passim*. For further analysis of the role of barter in the Russian economy see S. Aututsionek (1998) 'Industrial barter in Russia', *Communist Economies and Economic Transformation*, 10(2): pp. 179–88.

24 For a range of estimates of capital flight see V. Tikhomirov (1997) 'Capital flight from post-Soviet Russia', *Europe-Asia Studies*, 49(4): pp. 591–615.

25 Tikhomirov, *The political economy of post-Soviet Russia*, p. 187.

26 See S. White (2000) *Russia's new politics. The management of a postcommunist society*, Cambridge: Cambridge University Press, pp. 145–58 for a description of the different lifestyles of the new rich and the poor.

27 Goskomstat (2000) *Rossiiskii statisticheskii ezhegodnik*, Moscow: Goskomstat Rossii, p. 53. On the causes of the decline in life expectancy see W.C. Cockerman (1997) 'The social determinants of the decline of life expectancy in Russia and Eastern Europe: a lifestyle explanation', *Journal of Health and Social Behaviour*, 38(2): p. 118.

28 The next section draws on Robinson, 'The global economy . . .' and N. Robinson (2000) 'The economy and prospects for anti-democratic development in Russia', *Europe-Asia Studies*, 52(8): pp. 1391–416.

29 D. Treisman (1998) 'Fighting inflation in a transitional regime. Russia's anomalous stabilization', *World Politics*, 50(4): p. 255; EBRD (1997) *Transition report 1997. Enterprise performance and growth*, London: European Bank for Reconstruction and Development, p. 197

30 *Kommersant*, 26 September 1995.

31 For example, a 100 rouble GKO paying 50 per cent interest after a year could be redeemed for 150 roubles. If inflation for the year was less than 50 per cent this would be profitable. If inflation was higher than 50 per cent, it would be unprofitable since the money received from the redeemed bond would be worth less in real terms than the amount originally invested. So, if inflation ran at 100 per cent, for example, an investor would make a loss of 25 per cent in real terms on their original 100 rouble investment: 100 per cent inflation would mean that 100 roubles were worth 50 per cent less than a year previously; a redeemed 100 rouble investment plus the 50 roubles earned in interest could be used to buy just 75 per cent of the goods that could have been purchased a year ago with the original 100 roubles.

32 *Nezavisimaya gazeta*, 4 June 1996.

33 Treisman, 'Fighting inflation . . .', pp. 260–4.

34 J. Johnson (1998) 'Russia's emerging financial groups', *Post-Soviet Affairs*, 13(4): p. 353.

35 *Russian Economic Trends*, 1997, 6(4): pp. 151–2.

36 Johnson, 'Russia's emerging financial groups . . .'

37 *Financial Times*, 1 November 1996. For a critique of this claim, see *Russian Economic Trends*, 1996, 5(3): p. 118.

38 *Ekonomika i zhizn'*, 13 July 1995; *Finansovie izvestiya*, 17 June 1997.
39 EBRD (1998) *Transition Report 1998. Financial sector in transition*, London: European Bank for Reconstruction and Development, p. 16
40 Commander and Mumssen, 'Understanding barter ...'.
41 Tikhomirov, *The political economy of post-Soviet Russia*, p. 66.
42 EBRD, *Transition report 1998...*, p. 13.
43 I. Korhonen (1998) 'The sustainability of Russian fiscal policy', *Review of Economies in Transition*, (1): p. 5.
44 *Russian Economic Trends* (1998) 7(3): p. 36.
45 Woodruff, *Money unmade...*, p. 188.
46 Bank of Finland Institute for Economies in Transition (1997) *Russian and Baltic Economies – the week in review*, (48) and (49) e-mail version (www.bof.fi/bofit).
47 *Russian Economic Trends* (1998) 7(1): p. 58.
48 *Financial Times*, 14 July 1997.
49 *Nezavisimaya gazeta*, 12 August 1998.
50 *Izvestiya*, 15 October 1997.
51 Bank of Finland Institute for Economies in Transition (1997) *Russian and Baltic Economics – the week in review*, (51–52) e-mail version (www.bof.fi/bofit) and (1998) *Russian economy. The month in review*, (2): p. 2
52 *Rossiiskaya gazeta*, 11 April 1998.
53 Bank of Finland Institute for Economies in Transition (1997) *Russian and Baltic Economics – the week in review*, (48) e-mail version (www.bof.fi/bofit).
54 For other accounts of the 1998 crisis see A. Illarionov (1999) 'Mify i uroki Avgustskogo krizisa', *Voprosy ekonomiki*, (10): pp. 4–19 and (11): pp. 24–48; T. Malleret, N. Orlova and V. Romanov, (1999) 'What loaded and triggered the Russian crisis?' *Post-Soviet Affairs*, 15(2): pp. 107–29; J. Sapir (1999) 'Russia's crash of August 1998: diagnosis and prescription, *Post-Soviet Affairs*, 15(1): pp. 1–36; P. Hanson (1999) 'The Russian economic crisis and the future of Russian economic reform', *Europe-Asia Studies*, 51(7) pp. 1141–166.
55 *Nezavisimaya gazeta*, 21 October 1998.
56 *Nezavisimaya gazeta*, 3 November 1998.
57 For example, the government consolidated its remaining holdings in the oil industry into a new company to improve its management of them and to be able to use the firm as a source of subsidy in the absence of budgetary revenues. *Izvestiya*, 27 January 1999. Promises were made to miners to double investment in the coal industry, halt the closure of unprofitable mines, and subsidize transport costs to make coal more competitive nationally and internationally. *Kommersant*, 2 February 1999. Privatization plans for 1999 were scaled back and the formation of a 'Russian Development Bank' to channel government money into industrial restructuring and other investment projects. *Kommersant*, 3 February 1999; *Kommersant*, 8 December 1998. An investigation into agricultural prices was announced as a possible prelude to the reintroduction of state regulation, *Nezavisimaya gazeta*, 26 March 1999.
58 *Kommersant*, 20 May and 2 June 1999.
59 V. Putin (1999) 'Rossiya na rubezhe tysyachiletii', www.pravitelstvo.gov.ru/minister/article-vvp1.html.
60 Bank of Finland Institute for Economies in Transition (2000), *Russian economy – the month in review*, (5): p. 1.
61 L. Wolosky (2000) 'Putin's plutocrat problem', *Foreign Affairs*, 79(2): pp. 18–31.

5   The politics of faded grandeur

Russia's new international relations

The Russian state created at the end of 1991 was heir to a long established tradition of 'great power' politics that stretched back beyond the Soviet period and the conflicts of the Cold War to Tsarist times. Russia emerged as a major player in international politics under Peter the Great in the eighteenth century and for the next 250 years expanded its role in the world almost without end. The Russian state was never a major imperial power with overseas possessions (apart from a brief period of colonial expansion across the Bering Straits into Alaska), but it developed into one of the largest land empires ever seen in the eighteenth and nineteenth centuries and struggled first with the United Kingdom, and subsequently with Japan, for imperial mastery over Asia. Russia also played an ever-greater role in Europe, engaging in a series of wars with France, Turkey, and the United Kingdom, dominated Poland in alliance with Prussia and Austria, controlled Finland, and was a major influence on the conflicts that wracked the Balkans and eventually led to the outbreak of World War I.

The demise of the Tsarist empire due in part to its shortcomings as a great power had the paradoxical effect of increasing Russia's part in world affairs. The Tsarist state had been a regional superpower that dominated its weaker neighbours, but the USSR became a global power. The influence of the USSR was first felt in world affairs through its ideology. The Soviet Union was the first socialist state in the world and was the object of hostile action from all of the other major global powers that objected to the Bolsheviks' socialist vision. In the eyes of Soviet leaders, international relations were a global struggle between social systems. The struggle of the socialist system to survive helped to mobilize the Soviet population in support of the new state and made it an inspiration to revolutionary and anti-imperialist movements throughout the world. Its support for such movements, and the support that many people across the globe gave it in turn, gave the USSR an influence beyond that which the Tsars had enjoyed. Economic and military strength also played a part in the rise to global influence of the USSR. Stalin's policies of rapid industrialization and the party-state's ability to command resources for military development were not sustainable over the long term, but they played a part in enabling the USSR to defeat Nazi Germany and replace it as the hegemonic power in Eastern Europe, to develop a nuclear weapons capability to match that of the USA, and to launch prestige projects such as its space programme that led the world in the 1950s and early 1960s with the launch of Sputnik (1957) and the first manned space flight of Yuri Gagarin (1961). The USSR achieved a rough strategic parity with the USA in nuclear weapons in the 1960s and had allies in the socialist bloc and amongst what it liked to call 'progressive states' around the world, from Cuba to Vietnam, and throughout the Middle East and Africa. Dealing with the USSR and containing its influence was the main foreign policy priority of Western leaders from the 1940s onwards and its opinions and wishes had to be taken account of on most major foreign policy issues.

Hostility between the USSR and its capitalist opponents died down after the accession of Mikhail Gorbachev to the post of CPSU General Secretary in 1985 and as the new leadership realized that the Soviet Union could not bear the financial stresses of military competition with more adaptable and dynamic capitalist economies. However, the USSR remained a major force in the world thanks to negotiations over nuclear and conventional armaments, the need to disentangle the USSR from its involvement in Eastern Europe after 1989, and because of Gorbachev's personality and popular appeal, which won him support from Western leaders and publics. The Soviet Union thus lost some influence in the world under Gorbachev as the socialist states of Eastern Europe broke away from its sphere of influence from after 1989 and began to align with the wider Europe, but its place as a power in the world was not completely questioned. It had a leader of recognized international stature and appeared to be renegotiating its relationship with the rest of the world towards some form of partnership with the USA, Japan and the rest of Europe. The final collapse of the USSR, although it had been forewarned by the declarations of sovereignty in 1990 by republican governments and Baltic agitation for full independence, upset this balance.

As the USSR collapsed, Russia emerged as the largest of the fifteen Soviet successor states, but the diplomatic, military and economic factors that led the USSR to be considered a great power were destroyed. Four of the new states created from with the USSR – Russia, Kazakhstan, Belarus and Ukraine – possessed nuclear weapons and all of the Soviet successor states had to rethink their security relationship with one another. Borders and the rights of mixed ethnic populations had to be agreed and assured since 60 million former Soviet citizens lived outside of their nominal ethnic homelands. Russia, as the former centre of the Tsarist empire and the Soviet federation, had to come to terms with dealing with these new states as equal sovereign powers. Finally, Russia had to come to terms with a huge loss of population, territory, military and economic power. The new Russia comprised 76 per cent of the area and 60 per cent of the population of the old USSR, but about 25 million Russians, or 17 per cent of the Russian population of the former USSR, now lived outside of Russia, and territory (such as Ukraine) had been lost that had been viewed as a part of Russia for centuries.

Over half of Soviet combat aircraft, tanks and armoured vehicles, and over a quarter of its warships and much other military matériel were located outside of Russia's borders. Russia possessed 80 per cent of the USSR's defence industry's potential production, but without co-operation of other newly independent states could produce only 17 per cent of Soviet military production. Russia's economy produced only about a half of the USSR's GDP, or 17 per cent of the USA's GDP.[1] These losses and changes meant not only that Russia could no longer be a global power, but that it also had major tasks before it in adapting to its new regional circumstances.

Russia's loss of great power status and the foreign policy problems that it faced caused concern globally about peace in the former Soviet area and raised the question of whether acclimatizing to its new circumstances would destabilize Russia. Dealing with Russia's new foreign policy problems meant securing a functioning state, a body that was able to make agreements and honour them and provide security to its citizens and allies. However, at the same time, building a state required that Russia solve some of its foreign policy problems since it had to define its territory and the social community that it was responsible for, and establish the military and economic responsibilities that it had in the post-Soviet geographical space. As we have seen in the last two chapters, Russia under Yeltsin was not particularly successful in developing effective governmental machinery, or in establishing the framework for a national market economy that might have provided the resources to fund public administration. In this chapter, we will see that it was only very slowly able to come to terms with its foreign policy problems.

The slow adaptation of Russian foreign policy to its new conditions has had a negative effect on state building but that effect is harder to gauge than the effects of failed economic transformation and domestic political development. Historically, states have been charged with providing security for their peoples and ensuring territorial stability. The need to organize to meet security threats shaped the state by presenting political leaders with challenges – borders to protect, foreign forces to counter – and legitimized state building as necessary to deal with external threats.[2] Where external threats to a society have been simple and unambiguous – an invasion threat for example – the ways in which international factors have stimulated state building have been easy to identify. States have been able to play major roles in social and economic organization during times of war, or when there is a clear threat to national security. In times of peace and when security threats are more oblique, as they are at the present moment in history, the link between international relations and state building is harder to define. There is no unambiguous threat to Russia and Russian politicians, with the exception of extremists whose view of the world is formed by racial and social prejudice, have not plausibly been able to argue that the powers of the state need to be increased to deal with an external menace. The failures of foreign policy adjustment have thus been a backdrop to domestic failure, a reflection of Russia's inability to re-establish a function-ing economy or embed democratic norms in its political system.

In failing to find its place in the world, to achieve co-operation with the West (which here means the states of North America, Western Europe and Japan), or to achieve multi-lateral co-ordination of policy, or integration, with the Soviet successor states of the Commonwealth of Independent States (CIS), Russia has been unable to derive any great positive benefits from foreign policy. Russia remains uncertain of itself as a state in the world and of its relations with other powers. There are no obvious threats to Russia, but there is no obvious role for it either except to be awkward in international councils and remind the world that it exists and that its views have to be considered. The tension that this creates provides extremist politicians with the chance to claim that there are real and direct threats to Russia and voice their desire to show Russia's superiority to other nations through conquest, and blame the West for Russia's failures. Such radical positions have brought their proponents, like Vladimir Zhirinovsky, notoriety, but have not neces-sarily served as the basis for long-term electoral success.[3] Where radical for-eign policy positions have been matched with electoral success over time, as with the CPRF, it is not clear that it is foreign policy that attracts votes.[4] Russian popular opinion in 2000 is overwhelmingly in favour of strengthen-ing ties with the West (74 per cent), only 4 per cent of people think that Russia is very likely to be attacked by another country in the next five years, the majority (75 per cent) think such an event not very, or not at all, likely.[5] Even if members of the political elite think the world hostile and believe that it might be necessary to use force in international affairs, the population does not, although this does not mean that Western actions in places like the former Yugoslavia are approved by Russian citizens or that public opinion is immune to nationalist appeals against the West.[6] Russia's international relations have thus left it caught in the dilemmas that it faced at the start of the 1990s. It still needs to establish how to live as a former global power by stabilizing its relations with the West and what it means to be a post-imperial power by regularizing its relations with the other Soviet successor states.

After globalism: from confrontation to co-operation to divergence with the West

Russia's national interest has been constantly debated since 1991. Russia is not unique in having had a debate about its foreign policy during this period. All states found themselves in a new international environment at the end of the Cold War and have been adjusting ever since. The direction that Russia's foreign policy debate has taken is, however, unique. Most foreign policy discourses have moved towards emphasizing the weakening of traditional security threats from other states (with some exceptions made for so-called rogue states like Iraq and North Korea), the interdependence of states in dealing with economic, social and environmental problems and tackling new security threats such as terrorism, international crime and ethnic conflict, and the need for international institutional development to aid in finding solutions to common problems. This rethinking of security has been most notable in the developed capitalist countries of NATO and Western Europe, but has also taken place in other post-communist states which have sought to 'return to Europe' through joining the European Union and NATO. Russia, however, has moved from emphasizing co-operation and interdependence towards what looks like a more belligerent assertion of national interest. This divergence in the development of a foreign policy occurred as Russia found that it could not maintain its influence in the world, let alone be a great power. Its hopes of influence through participation in international institutions were not matched by change in those institutions to accommodate Russia and because compromises in foreign policy were made as it came under attack from domestic opponents of Yeltsin. In short, Russia's highly liberal foreign policy of 1991–1992 and great faith in the ability of international institutions to solve Russian and global problems proved untenable. When foreign policy changed, as it had to, Russia was left looking belligerent in the eyes of the West and appeared a doubtful potential ally. The roots of this breakdown in relations with the West lie in Russian reactions to both Soviet foreign policy and Gorbachev's reforms. At the end of the Cold War these helped create expectations of Russian behaviour in the West, and of Western behaviour in Russia, which were far too high and could not stand the test that they were put to by such things as the conflicts in Yugoslavia and NATO expansion.[7]

Gorbachev's reforms had been most radical and most effective in the transformation of foreign policy thinking. Prior to Gorbachev's accession as CPSU General Secretary in 1985, the basic understanding of international relations in the USSR was informed by class analysis. Soviet leaders saw the world in terms of class struggle between progressive forces (the working class and its allies) and their capitalist opponents; international relations was a global struggle between capitalism and socialism.[8] This basic view of international relations as conflict led Soviet leaders to distrust anything that was not under their control, including diplomacy and international institutions. This distrust, which was reinforced by the Soviet Union's early struggles to survive and its economic weakness as it first strove to develop an industrial economy and subsequently tried to maintain growth, made it overly reliant on military power to justify its role in the world.[9]

Maintaining military was a constant priority for the Soviet leadership until 1985 because the USSR was drawn into conflict with the West and vice versa. There were attempts to control this conflict and manage it. Most importantly, war between the capitalist and socialist worlds was no longer seen as inevitable from the 1950s onwards thanks to Khrushchev's development of the idea of 'peaceful coexistence'. However, whilst war was deemed to be no longer inevitable, conflict and competition were not avoidable. The USSR's self-image as the leader of 'progressive' forces worldwide meant that it had to help the 'progressive' regimes that emerged as the empires of France, the United Kingdom, Belgium and Portugal collapsed after World War II to validate its claim that it was at the head of a historic transformation of human society. In the eyes of the USA and other Western states, this involvement in the Third World was testimony to Soviet expansionism. The USA and its allies endeavoured to 'contain' and 'roll back' Soviet expansion so that both sides were locked into conflict despite their leaders' occasional realization that this might lead from Cold War to Mutually Assured Destruction.[10] A similar logic dominated Soviet relations with the states of the Warsaw Treaty Organization (the Warsaw Pact). The 'Brezhnev doctrine' enunciated after the invasion of Czechoslovakia in 1968 held that if socialism was imperilled in one of the states of Eastern Europe, members of the Warsaw Pact were obliged to invade it to correct its course back to a correct socialist path.[11] This theory demonstrated that the USSR's hegemony over Eastern Europe rested on force rather than popular acquiescence and further demonstrated to the West that the USSR was a threat to be contained politically and deterred militarily. The USSR's reliance on military power and its ideological imperative to involve itself in conflict in the Third World meant that there was little prospect of the USSR being seen as a state with legitimate interests in managing international politics by its rivals: it was seen as a state to be managed rather than as an ally with which to co-operate. The USSR had a seat on the United Nations (UN) Security Council and was involved in establishing the CSCE (Conference on Security and Co-operation in Europe, known from 1994 as the Organization on Security and Co-operation in Europe, the OSCE). But it played no part in much of the rest of the system of international organizations founded after World War II and large parts of that system – such as the North Atlantic Treaty Organization (NATO) – were designed to contain its military power and political influence.

The isolation of the USSR and its allies from the rest of the world came to a head in 1979 when the 'Brezhnev doctrine', Soviet preference for using military might to solve the foreign policy problems, and expansionism came together in the Soviet invasion of Afghanistan. (Afghanistan was a nominal socialist state and the Soviets invaded to force its ruling communist party to follow its directives and to shore up its crumbling rule.) The invasion pushed the fragile relationship between the USSR and the USA over the edge into a fresh round of arms build-ups, covert warfare in the Third World and paranoia about nuclear attack. Gorbachev realized that this situation and the budgetary strains that it put on the USSR were incompatible with reform of the USSR. Indeed, even before Gorbachev was sure of what the problems of the USSR were and how to solve them, he was convinced of the need to ease international tensions so as to reduce the burden of military competition. To do this he overturned Soviet thinking on international relations. In his 'New Political Thinking', Gorbachev strove to replace 'class' analysis in foreign policy with a concern for 'common human values'.[12] 'Common human values', Gorbachev argued, were those things that human being shared irrespective of social class; they included such things as freedom from fear of nuclear war and military conflict, a desire to share of the wealth produced by economic development, and environmental security. Securing these 'common human values' required an international politics based on co-operation through international institutions and multi-lateral policies. Military power, Gorbachev believed, was no longer a prerequisite for international influence and no longer a priority for development; influence would be better secured by showing the merits of one's political and economic system and taking up a position of moral leadership.[13] The Soviet Union, in Gorbachev's view, would no longer be a great power with global influence because of its military might and ideological vigour, but because it was successful at proposing solutions to global problems through international institutions and because it was able to demonstrate its capacity for renewal as a social system that delivered a good standard of living to its people.

This was a revolutionary change of position. It brought Gorbachev great popularity in the West and helped affect major changes in international politics. Conflict with the USA was reduced. A momentum for arms control was created and Soviet troops withdrew from Afghanistan. In 1987, Gorbachev signalled that the 'Brezhnev doctrine' was defunct and in 1989 allowed the communist regimes of Eastern Europe to collapse. However, Gorbachev's ideas about multi-lateralism and co-operation through international institutions were not taken up by the West, and the increasing political crisis in the USSR meant that there was no chance of its developing global leadership through demonstrating its efficacy as a social system. The West supported Gorbachev's narrow foreign policy agenda of reducing East–West tensions, but did not agree either that there should be a more co-operative management of international problems, or that military power should be less important as a foreign policy instrument. The former was not in the interests of Western governments at the start of the 1990s because economic problems left them more interested in marshalling their economic resources and developing institutions like the European Union or the North American Free Trade Area that would help them cope with economic change. The need for the latter was demonstrated to the West in 1990–1991 by the Iraqi invasion of Kuwait, and by the onset of state breakdown and communal violence in states such as Somalia and Yugoslavia.

The Russian government that took shape after the March 1990 Russian elections and Yeltsin's election as Chair of the Russian Supreme Soviet (see Chapters 2 and 3) shared Gorbachev's basic negative reaction to Soviet foreign policy ideas and went beyond it.[14] Where Gorbachev wanted to develop a new morality in international relations and through international institutions, the Russians wanted to submerge Russia into existing international institutions so as to share the benefits of them in tandem with Western states and become a member of the 'community of civilized states'.[15] Status for Gorbachev would have come from developing a new international morality; status for Russia was to come from being in tune with existing international norms. This was in line with the Russian government's view of itself the only force in Russia that could create democracy and capitalist prosperity comparable to that of the West. There was also a tactical element to its foreign policy stance. The Russian government hoped that by following a pro-Western policy it would win international recognition. This would first strengthen in its struggles with Gorbachev and the Soviet state, and thereafter would support efforts to develop economic and political structures akin to the West.[16] This position was labelled 'Atlanticism' since it looked towards the countries of NATO for support and as Russia's allies, and to contrast it to from 'Eurasianism', which argued that Russia needed to build up its strength and alliances with other Soviet successor states and pursue its interests independently of the USA and its allies, and 'statism', a variant of Eurasianism that argued for policies that put Russian national interests first across the globe.[17] Yeltsin, foreign minister Andrei Kozyrev and politicians such as Burbulis and Gaidar all expressed Atlanticist views in 1992 so that it was easily the dominant view of foreign policy in the Russian government.

Initially, the prospects for an Atlanticist foreign policy looked promising. Western politicians realized that Russia had to be dealt with as an independent power after the August 1991 coup and were relieved to find that the Russian government was willing to honour international agreements that Gorbachev had made. Moreover, they found that Russian politicians shared their concerns over such matters as nuclear proliferation and were willing to work with Western powers to resolve them. Some progress was thus made in coping with the legacies of the Soviet collapse through multi-lateral agreements such as the Lisbon Protocol of May 1992 in which Russia and the USA worked with Belarus, Kazakhstan and Ukraine to amend the START-I treaty to cover the nuclear weapons held by Belarus, Kazakhstan and Ukraine and arrange their transfer to Russia. However, co-operation was not to last. The Russians should have been warier of a pro-Western policy than they were at independence. The West had an agenda of its own before and after independence that was not the same as the Russians. For example, before independence, Russia had concluded a series of inter-state treaties with other Soviet republics that recognized their mutual right to independence and some attributes of statehood such as borders.[18] To Western states hopeful of co-operation on issues such as nuclear disarmament and in trouble spots like the Persian Gulf, and fearful of the foreign policy problems that would be caused by Soviet collapse, this appeared to be undermining Gorbachev and they had therefore ignored the Russian government and failed to recognize its right to have a say in foreign policy. After independence, the West was happy for Russia to join more international institutions, but it did not go out of its way to adapt institutions to facilitate Russia's entry into them, or to take account of its circumstances and preferences. An example of the former is in international economic relations where the West let the IMF and the World Bank set the agenda for giving aid to Russia. The IMF and the World Bank followed their customary practices and charters so that Russia had to fit in with criteria that had been developed for states with some form of market economy, rather than for a socio-political system in extreme crisis.[19]

Russia's circumstances and preferences were further ignored in considering what bodies should be used to develop co-operation. Although Russian politicians made very bold statements at the time of independence about joining NATO and even the EU, Russia's preference was for developing partnership through pan-European structures such as the CSCE/OSCE. The USSR had helped to set the CSCE up and it had not been a weapon in the Cold War against Russia. As a pan-European organization that drew in the USA, it could be used for co-operation with the USA and could encompass all of the successor states of the USSR. However, developing a new security system through CSCE was not a priority for other post-communist states in Eastern Europe, which were more interested in membership of NATO and the emerging EU foreign policy and security agendas. They saw this as their best guarantee of safety from Russia and as a means of supporting their applications for EU membership. Since Western states were also keen to develop the EU and did not want organizations like NATO dismantled because they wanted to maintain US involvement in guaranteeing European security, Russia was soon pushed to one side in discussions about European security. Russia in some ways aided in this process. In 1993, Yeltsin proposed that NATO guarantee security in Eastern Europe in tandem with Russia. This lead to the USA proposing a 'Partnership for Peace' scheme that gave Eastern European states access to NATO training and advise but stopped short of full membership.[20] Once such programmes began it was difficult to stop them from developing further. Although Russia had a voice in deliberative bodies such as the North Atlantic Co-operation Council that were attached to NATO it could not stop 'Partnership for Peace' developing towards NATO expansion, a measure that Russia saw as isolating it in Europe and directed against it (see pp. 143–4).

The requirement that Russia adapt to suit international institutions did not worry Atlanticist politicians. They hoped that connecting Russia to international institutions would help to transfer democratic norms to Russia and guarantee co-operation whilst these norms became embedded in Russian society and capable of guaranteeing peace with the West in the future. To many Russians this looked disdainful of Russian traditions. When Russia was sidetracked by the preferences of other states, the Atlanticists were open to criticism that they were serving foreign interests. This wore away at the Atlanticist position, but the final nail in Atlanticism's coffin was that Russia did not have the strength to make its foreign policy look successful in practice. Its decline in military power, enfeebled economy and lack of allies after the collapse of the Warsaw Pact meant that Russia was unable to make positive contributions to international affairs when it did not have the support of more powerful states such as the USA.

The problems of Russian foreign policy can clearly be seen in the development of Russian policy towards the conflict in Yugoslavia. Russian policy towards the Yugoslav conflict developed from a policy of expecting co-operation and working for it through European bodies and the UN, to a policy of using the conflict in Yugoslavia as a means of being treated as an equal partner with the USA and the major West European powers. As a result, Russia looked belligerent and obstructive of Western efforts to create peace in Yugoslavia.[21] Initially, however, Russia wanted to play a role in the resolution of conflict as a member of the UN and as a supporter of CSCE efforts at mediation. In 1992, Moscow supported the deployment of UNPROFOR (the UN peacekeeping force) in Croatia and its later extension into Bosnia, the imposition of sanctions against Serbia and Montenegro, and signed accords on the exchange of diplomatic missions with Slovenia and Croatia. Kozyrev's policies generated substantial domestic criticism, most significantly from Yevgenii Ambartsumov, the Chair of the Russian parliament's Committee on International Affairs. Following Ambartsumov's lead, the parliament, which contained many factions disposed to supporting Serbia in the name of pan-Slavic unity, voted for a moratorium on sanctions in June 1992. These criticisms could not be ignored because of the confrontation that was developing between the Russian parliament and Yeltsin. The slowing down of economic reform meant that Yeltsin had to ensure his position in the autumn of 1992 by neutralizing opposition towards his government where possible. Correspondingly, Russian policy towards Yugoslavia underwent a subtle shift. Russia did not break with the West, but tried to find alternative solutions to the conflict on its own as well as working in tandem with the West. To this end, the Russian government supported President Dobrica Ćosić and Prime Minister Milan Panić, the leaders of what remained of the Yugoslav state, in the hope that strengthening pro-Yugoslavia, but anti-Milošević, forces would lead to a political solution to the conflict. At the same time, Russia supported the efforts of Cyrus Vance and David Owen, the co-chairs of the International Conference on Former Yugoslavia, to implement their peace plan. Russian policy was thus still in line with Western priorities but neutralized domestic opposition by being more proactive in seeking a solution to the conflict.

Russian strategy failed. The support given to Panić by Russia was not enough to overcome Milošević and he lost the power struggle in Yugoslavia in December 1992; Russian hopes for a strong political alternative in Milošević with which it could co-operate thus disappeared. Russia continued to support the Vance–Owen plan, but the US line towards Milošević and the Serbs hardened in 1993. After the Bosnian Serbs rejected the Vance–Owen plan in a referendum in May 1993 Moscow proposed that it be implemented 'progressively' by armed forces in areas under Croat and Bosnian control. This would have effectively ended the conflict in Bosnia to the satisfaction of most of the international community. Kozyrev offered the service of Russian troops as a part of the implementation force. The USA, however, rejected Russian proposals. American opposition to the implementation of the Vance–Owen plan left Russian diplomatic efforts without an achievable, constructive goal and confirmed Russia's weakness as a great power. On its own, it did not have the power to force the adoption of the Vance–Owen plan and could not build a European consensus for it in the absence of US support. Russian diplomatic efforts in the rest of 1993 tried to maintain the conditions that would support a political solution to the conflict in Bosnia, supporting the Geneva talks between the three sides in the Bosnian conflict and building support for the partition of Bosnia as a solution amongst Western powers. However, this effort was largely a matter of marking time. The December 1993 elections to a new Russian parliament, the Duma, and in particular the success of the pro-Serb Vladimir Zhirinovsky, created pressure on the government to take a more pro-Serb line and a desire across the Russian political spectrum to appear more active in the defence of Russian national interests. One of the new Duma's first acts in January 1994 was to pass a resolution opposing NATO air strikes and calling for sanctions against Serbia to be lifted.

The failure of the Vance–Owen plan and the increasing Western emphasis on using NATO to pressure the Serbs demonstrated to the Russians both that co-operation was not effective and that it was politically out of step with what seemed to be current Russian electoral opinion. Consequently, Russian policy moved to a new stage, characterized by rhetorical belligerence and strong resistance to efforts by Western powers to control Serbian actions in Bosnia through the use of NATO air power. In February 1994, Yeltsin insisted to John Major, the then British Prime Minister, that there would be no resolution of the conflict in Bosnia without Russian involvement. Russia had decided that it might not have the strength or the influence to secure the peace it wanted, but it could make sure that any peace process recognized it as a significant player. This position was in line with the stance that had begun to emerge in 1993 as the replacement for Atlanticism in the 1993 Foreign Policy Concept, and which would later be called 'multipolarism' by Yevgeny Primakov (Kozyrev's successor as foreign minister in 1996 and briefly Prime Minister in 1998–1999). Unlike Atlanticism, multipolarism proposed to promote Russia as a global power by developing links with other states according to mutual advantage, rather than through the development of links with international institutions, and rested on the principle that it was necessary to resist the dominance of the world by the USA. It was thus a variant of statism; it proposed that Russia would co-operate with the West, but that at the same time it would resist its use of military power and promote its own interests.[22] In Yugoslavia, this meant that Russia continued diplomatic action through the Contact Group, the international body set up to try to negotiate a solution to the Bosnian conflict, but at the same time Russian representatives to the Balkans, most notably Deputy Foreign Minister Vitaly Churkin, worked to stop NATO bombardments of Serb forces, and Russia protested Western actions in strong, often confrontational language. Russia also demonstrated that it no longer considered that it was bound to support Western actions, or think of solutions coming through multi-lateral action from international institutions, by vetoing the extension of sanctions against the Bosnian Serbs at the UN Security Council.

In many ways, multipolarism was just another name for pragmatism: Russia was recognizing that it could not submerge itself in the international system and draw strength from it, but had to deal with the problems that confronted it within the constraints of that system and draw what benefit it could from its policies. This had been reflected in the 1993 Foreign Policy Concept that had defined Russia's immediate area of interest as the former Soviet space and the protection of its hegemony in the area. In relation to the West, it meant rhetorical opposition to Western policies and attempts to force the West to recognize that it had interests that had to be accommodated in some way. In the case of policy towards Yugoslavia, Russia could not force NATO to abandon aerial strikes as a policy, but rhetorical belligerence led to public attempts to mollify Russia by Western leaders that reaffirmed Russia's great power status (at least rhetorically). Russia thus forced Western leaders to deal with it so as to secure the conditions for a settlement of the Bosnian conflict. For example, Yeltsin condemned NATO bombing of Bosnian Serb forces in September 1995 and warned that 'if such actions continue, it could come to something hotter'. Following this threat, President Clinton reassured Yeltsin that Russia's views would be respected when they met for a summit in October 1995. Consequently, Russia agreed to participate in peacekeeping operations in Bosnia but not under direct NATO command; Russia would be there by right as a 'great power'. This agreement to take a part in peace-keeping operations was an important part of building an international coali-tion that could support the Dayton Accords, which were to end the conflict in Bosnia. But in the end, it was not Russia that took the lead in resolving the conflict in Bosnia by pressurizing the Bosnian Serbs to come to an agreement, or acting as the main guarantor of the implementation of the Dayton Accords, it was the USA. A similar process unfolded in 1999 during the crisis in Kosovo. Again, Russia did not have the strength to stop NATO from taking action against Serbia over the persecution of Kosovar Albanians, but once that action started, Russia became an intermediary between NATO and Milošević and its agreement to take part in peacekeeping forces in Kosovo helped to broker a deal. Russia could not secure for itself a com-pletely independent role in Kosovo when the Western powers refused to sanction the idea that Russia should be responsible for a zone of territory within Kosovo independent of the areas occupied by NATO forces. Russia thus saved some face by its involvement in the Kosovo crisis, but did not dominate proceedings.

The other main area where Russia confronted the West was over NATO expansion into Eastern Europe. NATO expansion was rejected by the West in favour of looser co-operation through the Partnership for Peace programme at a NATO summit in January 1994. However, domestic pressure in the USA and pressure from East European states wore away at this position. In July 1997, NATO voted to begin the process of admitting Hungary, Poland and the Czech Republic, and observed that other East European states would be considered for membership at a later date. Between January 1994 and 1997, Russia had kept up a barrage of diplomatic pressure over NATO expansion, arguing that its expansion and elevation as the main body guaranteeing European security was as an explicit rejection of Russia's efforts to manage European security through bodies like the OSCE, perpetuated the life of an organization that no longer had any reasons for existence since the Soviet Union had collapsed, and was drawing a new Iron Curtain across Europe, excluding Russia from influence and from decision-making circles.[23] These protests, as with the NATO actions in Yugoslavia, did not stop the West from going ahead with expansion once it had decided that this was the policy that it wished to pursue. They did, however, lead to efforts to placate Russia. In May 1997, Russia signed the Founding Act on Mutual Relations, Co-operation and Security between NATO and the Russian Federation. This treaty promised that Russia would have a unique consultative role with NATO through a new body, the NATO–Russia Permanent Joint Council (PJC), which would not only serve as a discussion forum, but also on occasions where there was agreement make decisions for joint action, and that NATO had no intention of deploying nuclear weapons on the territory of new member states, or of revising its policies on nuclear weapons.[24] This was a small concession from the West, but it enabled the Russian government to argue that Russian security had not been compromised to too great an extent.[25]

The adaptation of Russian foreign policy from high hopes for co-operation to divergence from Western priorities was more or less complete by 1997 and did not change in the last years of Yeltsin's rule. Russia was able to force recognition of its importance, but was not able to become a proper part of the alliance of states under US leadership that dominate decision making in the international system. The signing of the NATO–Russia founding Act in 1997 did not change relations between Russia and the West and they continued to fluctuate between complaint and compromise. The decision to expand NATO as the chief guarantor of collective security, rather than to work with Russia through the OSCE to develop new sources of common defence, showed that Western powers had become suspicious of Russia's ability to reform and of its future foreign policy. Russian distrust of the West that had developed with the failure of the co-operative strategy of Atlanticism thus found a mirror in the West. The discussion that began in US political circles after the August 1998 economic crisis on 'who had lost Russia' was tacit admission that Russia was perceived to be outside of what Russian politicians had earlier described as the 'community of civilized states' and would remain outside. This view was particularly prominent amongst conservative Western politicians and policy advisers such as made up the foreign policy community of the President George W. Bush. This view of Russia as a lost cause to be managed, rather than as a partner to be worked with, limited the role that could be played by bodies like the PJC. It has not developed a substantial role, did not create consensus over the Kosovo conflict, and played no part in the development of NATO's new strategic doctrine announced at its fiftieth summit in 1999.[26] Russia's involvement in other international bodies such as the G-7 (the meeting of leaders of the seven largest capitalist economies to discuss economic and political co-operation) shows a similar pattern. Yeltsin began to attend G-7 summits in part in 1994; in 1998, the summit was described as a meeting of the G-8 to indicate that Russia was now a full member of the elite group of states. However, the original 'group of 7' met for a day of discussions before Yeltsin arrived at the 1998 summit. Russia was thus at once symbolically recognized by the other major powers as powerful by the appellation 'G-8', but at the same time they emphasized their distance from it.

After 'empire': Russia and the Commonwealth of Independent States

Adapting to the loss of great power status meant that the Russian state had to come to terms with its former enemies and work out how it was going to conceive its national interests in international forums and decide what possible actions it could take to achieve those interests. Adapting to the loss of territory and population that had been a part of the Tsarist empire and the Soviet state involved more basic problems of statehood: the definition of borders, the division of intertwined economies and military forces, citizenship and identity.[27]

For some analysts, these problems are post-imperial problems and are therefore particularly dangerous and likely to lead to conflict. The former core of an empire has more power than its former subjects and so can force solutions to problems rather than negotiate them, has ethnic brethren in these states to protect, and with an imperial tradition to draw upon and is likely to think that its preferences should prevail no matter what the opinion of other states.[28] Russia's strength in comparison to its smaller neighbours has been a problem, but relations with the states that Russians sometime refer to as the 'near abroad' have been shaped by more than post-imperial angst. The USSR differed from other empires in that it mixed imperialism with a type of federalism so that it was neither classically imperial as the Tsarist empire was, nor effectively federal, like the USA or Germany. The strange combination of 'empire' and 'federation' in the USSR shaped its break-up and the management of relations between the newly independent states (NIS) of the former Soviet Union. The Soviet Union broke up partly as a collapsing federation and partly as a disintegrating empire. These two processes occurred in different combinations in each of its republics.[29] The collapse of 'empire' was most marked in the Baltic republics, which moved to break away from the USSR completely and developed bilateral relations with Russia and other Soviet successor states. At the other end of the spectrum, in the Central Asian republics of Kazakhstan, Uzbekistan, Tajikistan,

Turkmenistan and Kyrgyzstan, there was little effective popular, political mobilization. These republics had no national independence tradition to fall back on since they had not been states before their incorporation into the Tsarist empire in the nineteenth century, were highly diverse ethnically and shared ethnic populations with one another and with neighbouring states like China and Afghanistan. Unlike the Baltic nationalists, the political goal of the leaders of these republics (like Kazakhstan's Nursultan Nazarbaev) was not full independence from the USSR, but a more advantageous position within the Union for themselves and their administrations: they wished to expand their powers within the Soviet federal system.

The other republics of the USSR (Russia, Ukraine, Belarus, Moldova, Georgia, Azerbaijan, Armenia) fell between these two poles. These republics had popular democratic independence movements, but they were either not well established (like the Popular Front of Belarus), were not truly national in influence (like Rukh, which was strong in western Ukraine, but weak in the more Russified south and east), or were propelled to prominence by events so that they did not develop social support, organization or political programmes. The governments that came to power in these republics after the elections of 1990 could not always press for independence with full popular support as in the Baltic republics and so developed their powers within the federation as a step towards independence. This worked out differently across these republics. Georgia, for example, was split by independence calls and soon lapsed into civil war. Other governments, which were dominated by members of the old communist elite (for example, Belarus and Ukraine), only drifted towards nationalist politics as the Soviet Union crumbled and their members needed to secure their place in the post-Soviet order.

The dual collapse of the USSR as federation and 'empire' made Russian relations with the other Soviet successor states contradictory at independence: the demands made of Russia by the other successor states and its methods of dealing with them were confused. Some NIS, most notably those where there was only no major struggle for national liberation from the 'empire' wanted to restore some kind of organizational arrangement with Russia that would replace the Soviet federation. Others demanded to be treated as sovereign powers independently of Russia's dealings with other NIS. This demand was made most successfully by the Baltic states. Most of the NIS, however, were caught between needing some political link with Russia so that they could continue to extract themselves from federation, whilst desiring to be treated as fully independent entities. Russia was in a similar position: Atlanticism supposed that Russia would work through international institutions and would not have a special relationship with its new neighbours, but it was at the same time tied to them by the need to sort out the Soviet legacies of interlinked economies, peoples and military forces.

Russia was never able to reconcile all of these contradictions, especially as the first solution to them, the creation of the CIS, was not the result of careful planning, but a hurried response by Yeltsin and the leader of Belarus,

Stanislav Shushkevich, to Ukraine's unilateral movement to complete independence under the leadership of President Leonid Kravchuk in December 1991. This would have left Belarus isolated, complicated Yeltsin's domestic position because of Russian concerns about ethnic Russians in Ukraine and Russian nationalist hostility to Ukrainian independence, and left no institutional mechanisms to solve common problems. In particular, the Russians were keen to manage the economic aspects of independence to support the Gaidar reforms due to begin on 2 January 1992. On 8 December 1991, Yeltsin, Kravchuk and Shushkevich met at Belovezha in Belarus. Yeltsin and Shushkevich sought an agreement on a new structure to replace the USSR and enable the management of common problems. Kravchuk, wearing his new nationalist colours (he had previously been a leader of the communist party organization in Ukraine), sought recognition of Ukrainian independence and did not want this compromised by a successor organization to the USSR.

Both sides got what they wanted: an accommodation of their different concerns. The three leaders signed an agreement that declared the USSR dead so as to ensure independence, and established the Commonwealth of Independent States as a forum to resolve common problems. The agreement on the CIS and the declarations on its formation and economic policy were all very vague.[30] Most of the positive content of the agreements concerned the fate of the USSR and promised things such as respect for international agreements signed by the USSR. The only other practical issue solved by the Belovezha documents was that the signatories recognized existing republican borders as the borders of the new states. Only one supranational CIS institution was established by the agreement on the CIS, a united military command to replace the Soviet high command, although a mechanism for 'implementing inter-republican economic agreements' was promised in a declaration on economic policy, and other institutions were obviously intended since it was announced that the CIS headquarters would be based in Minsk, the capital of Belarus. The working procedures for the CIS were left vague: Article 9 of the CIS agreement stated that 'disputes over the interpretation and application of the norms of this agreement are to be resolved through negotiations between appropriate bodies and, when necessary at the level of heads of government and state', but did not define what these appropriate bodies were to be. Article 10 allowed the signatories to quit the CIS, or opt out of any of its provisions after giving a year's notice, and decreed that the agreement could only be changed by common consent. The bulk of the Belovezha documents were made up of abstract promises to co-ordinate activities between the signatories, to develop programmes on uncontentious issues such as securing living standards.

However, the CIS's development did not rest on a simple agreement between Russia, Ukraine and Belarus. The leaders of the Central Asian successor states met in Ashkhabad on 13 December 1991 and demanded that they be considered co-founders of the new organization and that it take into account the 'historic and socio-economic realities of Central Asia'. The Central Asian leaders were worried about the viability of their economies and states if Russia concentrated on its relations with Western Europe and the USA, as the Atlanticist Russian foreign minister Kozyrev desired, and with Ukraine and Belarus from among the former Soviet republics. They also feared that if Russia turned away from the area, outside powers like Iran and China would be drawn into the strategic vacuum, or that instability would be imported from Afghanistan (this was to occur in Tajikistan). The Central Asians therefore pressed for membership of the CIS and on 21 December they, Moldova, Armenia and Azerbaijan were admitted to the new organization at a meeting at Alma Ata in Kazakhstan. Georgia, which was divided by civil war and ruled by a radical nationalist, refused to join.

The rapid enlargement of the CIS complicated the new organization's identity. All of its member states had very different reasons for being a part of it. The Central Asians and Belarus, as we have noted, feared being cut off from Russia. The Central Asians in particular had concerns about their security, a classic source of federalism.[31] Ukraine, on the other hand, wanted to manage its separation from Russia. Moldova, Armenia and Azerbaijan were all concerned about the economic consequences of the Soviet collapse, but were also keen to have the conflicts within them (Moldova) and between them (the Azeri-Armenian conflict over Nagorno-Karabakh) managed. Russia needed a means of influencing the other Soviet successor states so that it could manage its own economic transition and provide some protection for the Russian diaspora in the NIS. The different concerns of the member states meant that there was no common CIS interest and hence no intellectual foundation, underpinning the organization. Moreover, because the political systems of all of the CIS states were weak it was difficult for them to implement policies that were decided on through the CIS. In the first three years of its existence, over 400 documents were adopted at CIS meetings, but under half of them were ratified by national parliaments.[32] The effectiveness of the CIS was thus hampered by the weakness of its member states. Moldova and Azerbaijan did not become members of the CIS properly until after 1993, when Georgia was also forced to join by Russia in return for Russia's aid in stopping the collapse of the Georgian state totally through internal civil war. This, of course, meant that Georgia was effectively drawn into the CIS against its will and that like many of the other CIS members did not have any interest in seeing the organization develop.

The ineffectiveness of the CIS caused by lack of common interests and state weakness was compounded by the fact that there was little institutional development of the organization. The enlarged CIS agreed to establish two bodies at the end of December 1991, a Council of Heads of State (CHS) and a Council of Heads of Government (CHG). The CHS was to meet at least twice a year, the CHG at least once every three months; the Councils' chair was to rotate among the member states. Each state was to have one vote in each of the Councils and decisions would be made by common consent. However,

states could declare that they had no interest in any issue and CIS decisions would therefore not apply to them. This get out clause reflected the desires of some states such as Ukraine to use the CIS as a vehicle for divorce from Russia and to be treated as sovereign states, and Russia's willingness to accommodate them in the latter at least. Furthermore, the CHS and CHG were both intergovernmental, rather than supranational, bodies. Most of the institutional development of the CIS in its first year of existence (and since) was through intergovernmental commissions and committees, such as the CIS Committee on Nuclear Policy. These bodies differ little from any other meeting of diplomats in committee anywhere else in the world except that they have a 'CIS' prefix attached to them. The record for reaching agreements though these committees is varied and they have no real independent institutional position or power of the sort developed by the Commission of the European Union.

The lack of institutionalization in the CIS, the opt-out of CIS agreements afforded to member states, the weakness of member states and lack of a common idea had serious implications for the development of the organization in its first year. This time was crucial because it overlapped with the period when the CIS states needed to embark on reform. Collective, multilateral action to solve mutual problems might have eased the initial stages of reform and lessened the political costs of change. The CIS also had many things in common that might have supported dealing with their problems collectively: a shared language in Russian, the main language of administration in the USSR; economic ties between enterprises in what had been a single economic space; a common currency, the rouble; near identical structures in areas such as social services, local government; shared standards in such things as educational provision, legal rules etc. Moreover, Russia and the other NIS needed one another. For example, most of the few Soviet successor states depended on Russia for energy supplies or processing facilities; just after independence, Belarus and Moldova received 100 per cent of their gas from Russia, whilst Ukraine received 56 per cent and Georgia 27 per cent of their gas supplies. Ukraine took 89 per cent of its oil from Russia, Belarus 91 per cent, Georgia 82 per cent, and Uzbekistan 55 per cent.[33] Common problems and structures did not, however, overcome the different perceptions of what the CIS should do.

The basic pattern of action of late 1991 was followed by the CIS in 1992. Agreement could be reached on issues to do with the end of the USSR, such as the division of responsibility for the USSR's debt between the CIS states in March 1992, but not on the construction of new practical and co-operative links. The most obvious sign of this was uneven participation in the CIS as states opted out of important agreements negotiated through the CIS. An attempt to increase the effectiveness of the CIS's monitoring of domestic policies and harmonization of legislation, the Inter-Parliamentary Assembly (IPA), was set up in March 1992. Ukraine, Turkmenistan, Moldova, Azerbaijan would not or could not agree to participate. Yeltsin and the

Russian government were also been reluctant to take the IPA seriously since they were in conflict with the Russian parliament at the time the IPA was founded. A CIS peacekeeping agreement was drawn up to provide CIS troops to intervene in conflict in the post-Soviet space at the same time the IPA was created, but Ukraine, Turkmenistan, Azerbaijan and Belarus did not sign it.

Despite the poor start made at institutionalization in 1992 with the CHG, CHS and IPA, further attempts were made at consolidating the CIS through extending the basic agreements signed at Belovezha. However, this process did not fundamentally change the design and operation of the CIS institutions. A Charter of the CIS was worked on throughout 1992 and agreed in principle in 1993. Like the original CIS documents, the Charter was full of grand promises: there was to be (amongst other things) co-ordination and co-operation in economic and military policy, joint efforts to resolve conflict and protect the environment, standardization of laws on copyright and investment, joint programmes in education, science and technology, sport, culture and health care. The Charter incorporated the main points of the agreement establishing the CHG and CHS, and established and gave legal format to a range of new bodies: a Council of Foreign Ministers, a Co-ordinating and Consultative Committee, a Council of Defence Ministers, a Joint Armed Forces High Command, an Economic Court, a Council of Commanders of Border Troops, and a Commission on Human Rights. As their names imply, most of these bodies were, once again, intergovernmental and concerned with a specific function, for example the guarding of borders, and their composition was fixed; foreign ministers to the Council of Foreign Ministers, defence ministers to the Council of Defence Ministers etc.

Some provision was made for the development of supranational institutions: the Co-ordinating and Consultative Committee and the Commission on Human Rights, which were to be made up of permanent representatives from each of the CIS member states, and the Economic Court. The Co-ordinating and Consultative Committee was also to have a Secretariat, an administrative arm. Its job was to prepare documents and proposals for discussion at the CHG and CHS on further co-operation and the development of economic links, and was to 'promote' the 'implementation of accords in specific areas of economic mutual relations', which implied some sort of monitoring function for the new body. The Commission on Human Rights was to monitor the observance of human rights and the Economic Court was to settle economic disputes between member states and interpret CIS agreements on economic issues.[34] However, none of these bodies produced any institutional force behind integration among the CIS states. As usual, not all of the CIS states ratified or signed the Charter. Although the Charter was agreed at the start of 1993, Turkmenistan, Belarus, Moldova and Azerbaijan did not ratify it until 1994, and Ukraine and Tajikistan have still to do so. The Co-ordinating and Consultative Committee did not become a permanent body, but has been a forum for CIS deputy prime ministers, in other words another intergovern-

mental body. Supplementary agreements between the CIS states developed the Economic Court, but its influence has been small. Members of the Economic Court, for example, complained about their limited jurisdiction in August 1995, and have seen other bodies established and agreements signed which overlap their competence. Even the bodies established in the Charter more narrowly as intergovernmental have not always been effective because of poor attendance. The March 1994 meeting of the Council of Foreign Ministers, for example, was not attended by the foreign ministers of Ukraine, Belarus, Moldova, Turkmenistan, Uzbekistan, and Armenia, but by officials from those countries. This substitution of ministers by officials has been a regular occurrence across all CIS meetings. Sometimes, as at the January 1997 Council of Defence Ministers meeting when there were no representatives from Turkmenistan and Moldova, not even officials have turned up.

Finally, its various problems, and the failings of its members, meant that the CIS did not even function properly as an intergovernmental body even at its apex, in the meetings of the CHS. Although supposed to meet at least twice a year, meetings of the CHS have been delayed and postponed almost from the start. The illnesses of Yeltsin also played havoc with the CHS's schedule. The January 1998 meeting was put back to March and then April so that Yeltsin could attend. Nor were the rules of the organization of the CHS observed. The Council's chair was supposed to rotate among the leaders of the member states, but Yeltsin served almost continuously as the CHS chair.

Even if there had been a concerted effort to develop CIS institutions, it is debatable that they could have produced collective action because CIS member states actively pursued their own interests almost from the start. Russia was not always to blame when this happened, but its size and power enabled it to take decisions without thinking of their knock-on effects in the other CIS states and to use the dependence of other CIS states on it to force them to comply with its wishes. As a result, its power began to have a negative effect on the CIS as an institution. Other member states had little incentive either to respect the CIS, or to support moves for collective action because Russia's size would have meant that it dominated them through collective organizations and eroded their newly won sovereignty. The most significant results of self-interested action were the collapse of the common currency inherited from the USSR, the rouble, and the slow progress made on economic integration, and the collapse of military co-operation. Across all these areas, bilateral agreements and unilateral action by Russia replaced co-operation.

The rouble's fate was determined by one of the factors that had brought about the creation of the CIS, the desire of the Russian leadership to control the Russian economy and to reform the economy using the rapid marketization and anti-inflationary policies of 'shock therapy'. Russia embarked on 'shock therapy' independently of the other CIS states and without regard to their ability to cope with economic reform. The other CIS states soon found themselves in dire straits. Price rises and price liberalization in Russia turned the terms of trade heavily in Russia's favour and sucked money out of the other Soviet successor states and into Russia. The CIS states responded by extending unsecured loans to enterprises on their territories, which fuelled inflation in Russia. The lack of co-operation and pursuit of self-interest between the CIS states therefore soon came to have a negative affect on all parties. Agreements reached on managing trade and currency policy, such as the February 1992 agreement on trade regulation and economic co-opera-tion, did little to solve matters. Economic regulation of inter-state trade and currency flows and the liberalized economic environment that the Russian reformists under Yegor Gaidar were trying to create sat uneasily with one another. The Central Bank of Russia and the parliament supported tradi-tional policies that funded the economies of the successor states through the transfer of huge credits to them. In 1992, the International Monetary Fund estimated that the Russian Central Bank financed 91 per cent of Tajikistan's GDP, between 49 to 70 per cent of the GDPs of Uzbekistan, Turkmenistan, Georgia, and Armenia, 20 to 25 per cent of the GDP of Azerbaijan, Ukraine, Kazakhstan and Kyrgyzstan, and 10 per cent of the GDP of Moldova and Belarus.[35] This was ruinous of the Russian reformers' efforts at stringent fiscal management. Efforts were made to co-ordinate CIS fiscal policies, such as the creation of an Interbank Co-ordinating Council on Mutual Settlements in October 1992, but these fell short of the creation of a true CIS Interstate Bank, Russia's favoured solution. Ukraine did not want to participate in such an institution because Russia's size would have ensured that it controlled national central banks (voting in the CIS bank would have been by each member state's capitalization so Russia would have dominated it).

In the absence of collective economic action, CIS member states began to sign bilateral agreements with one another to ensure that trading relation-ships from the Soviet era were maintained. These foreshadowed later agree-ments on customs and tariffs between limited numbers of CIS states. The rouble staggered on as a common currency for the first six months of 1993 until Russia recalled all pre-1993 roubles from circulation in July 1993 and refused to issue more credits to CIS states. The aim was to force the CIS states that had not already introduced their own currency to agree to co-ordinate their monetary policy with Russia and threatened them with inflation if they did not reach agreement with Russia. Belarus, Kazakhstan, Armenia, Uzbekistan and Tajikistan reached an agreement with Russia in September 1993 on a new rouble zone with co-ordinated monetary, customs and banking policies. However, the demands made by the Russians before they would issue new roubles were too much for most of the states and forced the accelerated adoption of national currencies. After 1994 only Tajikistan, which had col-lapsed into civil war and anarchy and was a 'Russian-sponsored garrison state' stabilized by the presence of Russian troops, still remained in the rouble zone.[36] Belarus reached a bilateral agreement with Russia, the Treaty on Belarus–Russian Monetary Union, in 1994 which in theory gave the

Russian Central Bank control over currency in Belarus (in practice Russia has been unwilling to take responsibility for the economy of Belarus).[37]

Economic integration stalled for the CIS as a whole because of fears of Russia's dominance after the rouble zone collapsed. The Co-ordinating and Consultative Committee produced a Treaty on Economic Union very quickly after its formation in 1993. As with the initial formation of the CIS, this was led by an agreement between Ukraine, Russia and Belarus on economic integration that then pulled other states into talks. But although it had been a party to the initial agreement on integration in July, Ukraine did not join the Economic Union as a full member (Turkmenistan did not join either). Ukraine's President Kravchuk insisted on associate member status for his country. Kravchuk lost the 1994 presidential election in Ukraine to Leonid Kuchma, who was initially seen as more amenable to improving relations with the CIS and with Russia. However, Kuchma did not agree to any measures that would dilute Ukrainian sovereignty, or allow Russia to dominate its economy any more than it already did. This weakened the Economic Union considerably since it could not develop institutionally. An Interstate Economic Council (IEC) was established to co-ordinate economic policy in December 1993. However, like the IPA, its parallel political body, it was not effective. A year after the Economic Union was set up, an attempt was made to develop the IEC and create a body that would be more than just a discussion forum. The reformed IEC would, like the CIS Bank before it, have been dominated by Russia since voting would have been by each member state's capitalization of the organization. Russia would provide 50 per cent of the funding and thus have had 50 per cent of the vote. Mechanisms to reassure the nervous were put in place: decisions on trade and financial matters would require a majority of 75 per cent, strategic questions like monetary union would be by consensus so that states could opt out. Despite this, Ukraine and several other states added an amendment to the IEC document stating that it could not overrule national legislation. Not surprisingly, the IEC did not develop into a motor for integration; it had no executive powers and no means of ensuring the adoption of common policies. Integration has remained an aspiration for the CIS as a whole, something to which state leaders have periodically paid rhetorical lip service through the adoption of documents like the January 1997 'Concept for Integrated Economic Development' approved by eight of twelve CIS states, but practically economic integration has not advanced at all.

Bilateralism in military affairs developed even more quickly than in economics and took two forms: the development of national military forces and the use of CIS peacekeeping by Russia as a cover for its essentially unilateral actions in CIS states. Although they had agreed to a unified military structure in the Belovezha agreement in December 1991, the successor states rapidly ordered the construction of national armed forces. The process started in January 1992 when Ukraine's President Kravchuk decreed control over all Soviet armed forces on Ukrainian territory and declared the Black Sea Fleet to be Ukrainian. Russia followed the other states and set up its own ministry of defence and armed forces in May 1992. In the same month, Russia, Armenia, and four of the strategically vulnerable Central Asian states (Uzbekistan, Kazakhstan, Kyrgyzstan and Tajikistan) were the only states to sign the CIS Treaty on Collective Security. Azerbaijan and Moldova could not sign and Ukraine had no intention of being bound in a security agreement with Russia. By mid-1993 the idea of a common defence policy or unified control of armed forces had little meaning left for the CIS as a whole, although there was broad agreement in 1995 on air defence between all of the CIS states bar Tajikistan and Azerbaijan. No outside force or institution significantly influenced the discussions over the Black Sea Fleet, the fate of which was ultimately settled on a bilateral basis in summit meetings between Yeltsin and Kravchuk. Russia has signed other military agreements on a bilateral basis with many of the other CIS states, most notably with Belarus, which has granted Russia the use of military bases and the right to station troops in Belarus in a series of agreements in 1993 and 1995. Russia's ability to influence the security arrangements of the CIS has also been eroded to a degree by NATO expansion. CIS states are not likely to be candidates for NATO membership any time soon, but they have participated in Partnership for Peace programmes and this has emphasized their distance from Russia.

The demise of joint CIS military units and command structures has meant that peacekeeping activities undertaken nominally by the CIS have in fact been little more than unilateral Russian military action. Although the other CIS states formed their own armed forces, Russia alone had the capability, will, need and desire to intervene in the conflicts that sprang up as the USSR crumbled: Russia felt compelled to protect ethnic Russians in the former Soviet space and wanted to keep other states (like China, Iran and Turkey) from developing their influence in its 'backyard'. It has therefore been the Russian army more than 'CIS' forces that have been involved in the Transdnestrian conflict in Moldova (a conflict provoked in part by the old Soviet security apparatus including the army), the border clashes and political chaos in Tajikistan and the regional wars in Georgia.[38] The onesidedness of 'peacekeeping' operations has led to the CIS being labelled a front for Russian security interests. This accusation was not assuaged by developments in Russian thinking on foreign and security policy and Russia has been accused of provoking and supporting some of the conflicts, for example in Georgia in Abkhazia and Ossetia, which it has later been involved in as a peacekeeper. The Foreign Policy Concept developed over 1992 and published in 1993 made it clear that Russia saw itself as having a unique role in the CIS as a peacekeeper and peacemaker for historical and cultural reasons. Peacekeeping operations by organizations other than the CIS, such as the United Nations and the OSCE, would be welcome only as long as they did not involve the stationing of foreign troops on the territory of the CIS.[39] To help ensure that no foreign troops are stationed in the CIS, Russia has pressed the United Nations to recognize its unique role as a peacekeeper in the former Soviet Union and pressed for more use of regional institutions like the CIS in peacekeeping. Peacekeeping was also used to force Georgia into the organization in 1993. Russia only agreed to stop the war in Georgia and save the Georgian government from collapse when it agreed to join the CIS. Attempts to internationalize peacekeeping in the CIS, such as the appeal by Georgian President Eduard Shevardnadze in January 1998 for an international effort to enforce peace in Abkhazia, have been rejected by Russia.

The development of bilateral agreements and arrangements on economic and security matters showed that the CIS had not been a particularly effective mechanism for managing Russia's relations with the NIS. Russia dominated the CIS thanks to its size and the fact that it has an interest in dealing with all of the NIS, but it had little success in getting other states to agree to its proposals through the CIS, or of having any agreements enforced by it. The poor performance of the CIS's eighty bodies was recognized by the CIS leaders at their summit in March 1997 when they declared a moratorium on the establishment of any new CIS bodies. Even integration became a matter of bilateral negotiations. In April 1996 and April 1997, Russia and Belarus signed agreements on creating a new 'Community of Sovereign States' and a new 'union', and in 1999, they agreed a treaty on the formation of a new 'Union state'. Although these agreements created a great deal of enthusiasm amongst Russian nationalists, who saw the possible integration of Belarus with Russia as a counter to NATO expansion and a first step towards creating a new Slavic homeland that might include Ukraine and parts of northern Kazakhstan where there is a Russian majority, practically they have had little more effect than the CIS in creating new political structures.

Conclusion

Russia's adaptation to the new international relations of the post-Cold War world has been not unlike its efforts at democratic consolidation and economic transformation. Initial high hopes and faith that the norms of consolidated democracies and advanced capitalist economies could be transferred to Russia found their mirror in foreign policy in the belief that the international community would open up to it and adjust to its interests just as it was trying to adjust to the interests of the most powerful members of that community. Domestically, the results of these beliefs in the absence of a state that could guarantee reform were a hybrid economy and deformed democracy. Internationally, the result has been broadly similar: Russia has been granted the symbolic status of a great power because of its objections to such things as NATO expansion and potential to obstruct Western policy initiatives, but it does not have the capacity of a great power to shape events, or proffer solutions to problems that it can implement unilaterally or with the help of allies; it dominates the other Soviet successor states, but is not able to treat them as either partners in a project of integration, or as states that it is fully separated from. Consequently, Russia has not resolved for itself or of its neighbours what kind of state it is: is it going to be at the centre of a larger political unit or not, and what kind of larger political unit would it be, a democratic federation, an empire or a new Soviet Union? Since this is the case, Russia's foreign policy looks threatening to states beyond the former USSR not just because it is obstructionist in international affairs. Whilst Russia cannot put the past fully behind it in its relations with the 'near abroad' or structure them in a fashion that allays the fears of states like Ukraine, the question of its expansion through aggressions rather than through negotiation is inevitably raised and casts doubts on Russia's relations across the globe. This in turn decreases the likelihood that Russia will be treated as a partner in the management of global affairs and that international relations can have a positive affect on Russia's internal development through the growth of trust between Russia and the West helping to promote respect for democratic values in Russia.

Notes

1 J. Berryman (2000) 'Russian foreign policy: an overview', in M. Bowker and C. Ross (eds) *Russia after the Cold War*, Harlow: Longman, p. 336; R. Sakwa (1996) *Russian politics and society*, second edition, London: Routledge, p. 345; *Ekonomika i zhizn'*, 1996, (16): p. 1.
2 C. Tilly (1985) 'War making and state making as organized crime', in P. Evans, D. Rueschemeyer and T. Skocpol (eds) *Bringing the state back in*, Cambridge: Cambridge University Press.
3 Zhirinovsky's foreign policy views have been summarized in English in V. Kartsev with T. Bludeau (1995) *!Zhirinovsky!*, New York: Columbia University Press; G. Frazer and G. Lancelle (1994) *Zhirinovsky: the little black book: making sense of the senseless*, London: Penguin.
4 Analysis of the CPRF's foreign policy position can be found in the general texts on the party. See J.B. Urban and V.D. Solovei (1997) *Russia's communists at the cross-roads*, Boulder: Westview; R. Sakwa (1998) 'Left or right? The CPRF and the problems of democratic consolidation in Russia', in J. Löwenhardt (ed.) *Party politics in post-communist Russia*, London: Cass. The views of its leader, Gennady Zyuganov, can be found in G. Zyuganov (1997) *My Russia: the political autobiography of Gennady Zyuganov*, Armonk, NY: M.E. Sharpe, and are analysed in V. Vujacic (1996) 'Gennady Zyuganov and the "Third Road"', *Post-Soviet Affairs*, 12(2): pp. 118–54.
5 Data from VTsIOM and New Russian Barometer polls, January and August 2000 reported at www.russiavotes.org.
6 For a review of this in the early 1990s, see W. Zimmerman (1994) 'Markets, democracy and Russian foreign policy', *Post-Soviet Affairs*, 10: pp. 103–26.
7 What follows is a general overview of Russian relations with the West. Studies of relations with individual states and sub-sections of the 'West' can be found in P. Shearman (ed.) (1995) *Russian foreign policy since 1990*, Boulder: Westview; M. Mandelbaum (ed.) *The new Russian foreign policy*, New York: Council on Foreign Relations Press; M. Bowker and C. Ross (eds) (2000) *Russia after the Cold War*; V. Baranovsky (ed.) (1997) *Russia and Europe. The emerging security agenda*, Oxford: Oxford University Press; R. Allison and C. Bluth (eds) (1998) *Security dilemmas in Russia and Eurasia*, London: Royal Institute of International Affairs.

8 More detailed analyses of Soviet foreign policy thinking before Gorbachev can be found in M. Light (1987) *The Soviet theory of international politics*, Brighton: Wheatsheaf; A. Lynch (1987) *The Soviet study of international relations*, Cambridge: Cambridge University Press. Overviews of Soviet foreign policy more generally pre-Gorbachev can be found in R. Edmonds (1983) *Soviet foreign policy: the Brezhnev years*, Oxford: Oxford University Press; J. Nogee and R. Donaldson (1987) *Soviet foreign policy since World War II*, New York: Pergamon; N. Petro and A. Rubinstein (1997) *Russian foreign policy*, New York: Longman, part 1.

9 M. Webber (1996) *The international politics of Russia and the successor states*, Manchester: Manchester University Press, p. 23.

10 For an analysis of how such struggles fuelled the Cold War see F. Halliday (1986) *The making of the second Cold War*, second edition, London: Verso.

11 R. Jones (1989) *The Soviet theory of 'limited sovereignty' from Lenin to Gorbachev. The Brezhnev doctrine*, Basingstoke: Macmillan

12 S. Woodby (1989) *Gorbachev and the decline of ideology in Soviet foreign policy*, Boulder: Westview; P. Shearman (1993) 'New Political Thinking reassessed', *Review of International Studies*, 19(2): pp. 139–58.

13 H. Adomeit (1995) 'Russia as a "great power" in world affairs: images and reality', *International Affairs*, 71(1): p. 42.

14 For more detailed analysis of the initial development of Russian foreign policy see L. Aron (1994) 'The emergent priorities of Russian foreign policy', in L. Aron and K. Jensen (eds) *The emergence of Russian foreign policy*, Washington: United States Institute of Peace Press; L. Buszynski (1996) *Russian foreign policy after the Cold War*, Westport, Conn: Praeger Publishers.

15 C. Blacker (1998) 'Russia and the West', in Mandelbaum (ed.) *The new Russian foreign policy*, pp. 170–71; H. Timmerman (1992) 'Russian foreign policy under Yeltsin: priority for integration into the "Community of Civilized States"', *Journal of Communist Studies*, 8(4): pp. 163–85.

16 Adomeit, 'Russia as a "great power"...', pp. 43–44.

17 The schools of foreign policy are described in detail in Petro and Rubinstein, *Russian foreign policy*; C. Wallander (ed.) (1996) *The sources of Russian foreign policy after the Cold War*, Boulder: Westview; N. Malcolm, A. Pravda, R. Allison and M. Light (1996) *Internal factors in Russian foreign policy*, Oxford: Oxford University Press; A. Tsygankov (1997) 'From international institutionalism to revolutionary expansionism: the foreign policy discourse of contemporary Russia', *Mershon International Studies Review*, 41(2): pp. 247–68.

18 S. Goncharov and A. Kuchins (1993) 'Domestic sources of Russian foreign policy', in T. Hasegawa, J. Haslam and A. Kuchins (eds) *Russia and Japan: an unresolved dilemma between distant neighbours*, Berkeley: International Studies Research Series number 87, University of California, p. 373.

19 On Russia's relations with the IMF see P. Rutland (1999) 'Mission impossible? The IMF and market transition in Russia', *Review of International Studies*, 25 (special issue): pp. 183–200.

20 S. White (2000) *Russia's new politics. The management of a postcommunist society*, Cambridge: Cambridge University Press, p. 235.

21 For an alternative periodization, see P. Goble (1996) 'Dangerous liaisons: Moscow, the former Yugoslavia and the West', in R.H. Ullman (ed.) *The World and Yugoslavia's Wars*, New York: Council for Foreign Relations Press. A fuller discussion of Russian and international policy towards Yugoslavia can be found in J. Gow (1997) *Triumph of the lack of will: international diplomacy and the Yugoslav War*, London: Hurst.

22 P. Shearman and M. Sussex (2000) 'Foreign policy-making and institutions', in N. Robinson (ed.) *Institutions and political change in Russia*, Basingstoke: Macmillan, p.

160; L. Aron (1998) 'The foreign policy doctrine of postcommunist Russia and its domestic context', in Mandelbaum, *The new Russian foreign policy*, p. 30.

23　For Russian objections to NATO expansion and arguments on the sensibility of expansion see C. Ball (1998) 'Nattering NATO negativism? Reasons why expansion may be a good thing', *Review of International Studies*, 24(1): pp. 43–67; P. Shearman (2000) 'Russia and NATO enlargement: the case against', in Bowker and Ross, *Russia after the Cold War*.

24　Shearman, 'Russia and NATO enlargement ...', p. 307.

25　White, *Russia's new politics...*, p. 238.

26　V. Baranovsky (2000) 'Russia: part of Europe or apart from Europe?', *International Affairs*, 76(3): p. 452.

27　Parts of this section draw on N. Robinson (1999) 'The CIS as an international institution', in P. Heenan and M. Lamontagne (eds) *The CIS handbook*, Chicago: Fitzroy Dearborn Publishers. Overviews of Russia's relations with the CIS states include W. Russell (1995) 'Russian relations with the "Near Abroad"', in Shearman, *Russian foreign policy since 1990*; W.E. Odom and R. Dujarric (1995) *Commonwealth or empire? Russia, Central Asia and the Transcaucasus*, Indianapolis: Hudson Institute; R. Sakwa and M. Webber (1999) 'The Commonwealth of Independent States, 1991–1998: stagnation and survival', *Europe-Asia Studies*, 51 (3): pp. 379–415; M. Webber (2000) 'Russian policy towards the Soviet successor states', in Bowker and Ross, *Russia after the Cold War*.

28　For a discussion along these lines see A.J. Motyl (1998) 'After empire: competing discourses and inter-state conflict in post-imperial Eastern Europe' in B. Rubin and J. Snyder (eds) *Post-Soviet political order. Conflict and state building*, London: Routledge.

29　For discussion of how Soviet power collapsed in the republics, see I. Bremmer and R. Taras (eds) (1997) *New states, new politics. Building the post-Soviet nations*, Cambridge: Cambridge University Press.

30　Copies of these and other documents on the CIS can be found in Z. Brzezinski and P. Sullivan (eds) (1997) *Russia and the Commonwealth of Independent States. Documents, data and analysis*, Armonk, NY: M.E. Sharpe.

31　The classic treatment of this is W. Riker (1964) *Federalism: origin, operation, significance*, Boston: Little, Brown.

32　Brzezinski and Sullivan, *Russia and the Commonwealth of Independent States*, p. 718.

33　Dawisha and Parrott, *Russia and the new states of Eurasia ...*, p. 175.

34　Brzezinski and Sullivan, *Russia and the Commonwealth of Independent States*, pp. 508–09.

35　A. Åslund (1995) *How Russia became a market economy*, Washington, DC: Brookings Institute Press, p. 123.

36　B. Rubin (1998) 'Russian hegemony and state breakdown in the periphery: causes and consequences of the civil war in Tajikistan', in Rubin and Snyder, *Post-Soviet political order ...*, p. 156.

37　Webber, *The international politics of Russia ...*, p. 29.

38　A. Kreikemeyer and A.V. Zagorski (1996) 'The Commonwealth of Independent States', in L. Johnson and C. Archer (eds) *Peacekeeping and the role of Russia in Eurasia*, Boulder: Westview; A. Arbatov, A. Chayes, A. Handler Chayes and L. Olson (eds) (1997) *Managing conflict in the former Soviet Union. Russian and American perspectives*, Cambridge, MA: The MIT Press.

39　Aron, 'The emergent priorities ...', p. 29.

6 Conclusion

A state of uncertainty – Russia between the past and the future

As the Yeltsin period drew to a close, the role of the Russian state came increasingly under scrutiny both in Russia and in the West.[1] In his presidential state of the nation address in 1997, Yeltsin noted that although a new political system had been formed in Russia it had not been 'equipped with new tools of government' and that legislation and state bodies too often served particular interests.[2] He called for the creation of a more efficient state with the capacity to implement policy, one free of corruption and capable of autonomous action by virtue of serving the general interest. Yeltsin did not manage to create 'new tools of government' in his last two years as President. The 1998 economic crisis was blamed by some Russians on 'crony capitalism' and the close connections between powerful interests and politicians that prevented the state from taking measures necessary to escape incipient crisis.[3] Finally, the prospect of the end of the Yeltsin era turned attention to the likelihood of his successor's being able to break free of the alliances and ties – particular interests again – that Yeltsin had built up over the course of his presidency and that had impacted on the introduction and implementation of public policy. This was reinforced when Vladimir Putin, Yeltsin's successor, emphasized the need for the state to play a larger role in reconstruction at the time of his accession as acting President.[4] Western politicians have also highlighted the central role that state building must play in the reconstruction of Russia.[5]

The fact that so much attention was paid to the state in the last years of Yeltsin's rule was a sign that although Russia has undergone a painful transformation since 1991 continuity in Russian political and economic life has at least balanced change and helped produce deformations in the Russian political and economic system that require state action and reform to amend them. The changes that occurred in Russia as communism collapsed were limited. Although many analysts hailed the collapse of communism in Russia as a revolution, the demise of the CPSU and the Soviet political system was not a revolution in the same sense as the events of 1917 and after. The direction given to social mobilization by the Bolsheviks broke the power of the Tsarist aristocracy and Russian capitalists so that by the end of the civil war the Bolsheviks ruled Russia exclusively. Although the Bolsheviks compromised on their social programme for a few years in the 1920s, Stalin mobilized society through the Communist Party once more in the early 1930s to complete the social transformation of Russia through the collectivization of agriculture and rapid, forced industrialization. The result was a qualitatively different social and economic system and a different form of absolutist rule in Russia to what had gone before.

There was no such concerted social mobilization during the late 1980s and as a result, no clean break with the past in 1991. There was an upsurge in independent political organization during *perestroika*, but participation in the *neformaly* (informal) political groups that sprang up in the 1980s was episodic and limited, and the new political groups in Russia were divided and lacked organizational resources to mobilize the people.[6] Limited popular mobilization against the CPSU and the Soviet state meant that change came through officially licensed channels, especially through the competitive elections that Gorbachev established to pressure the CPSU into following his reformist policies. People supported opposition leaders like Yeltsin in the elections so that they could use the opportunities and institutional reforms introduced by Gorbachev to expand their power and begin to unravel the Soviet political system from within.

This meant that change took place within a narrow band. Soviet party-state power was countered and blocked in the 'war of laws' between the centre and the republics, and weakened through the Russian parliament and a few key city councils such as Moscow and Leningrad. This only weakened the apex of Soviet political leadership. The ability of members of the *nomenklatura* to control economic activity and use economic resources went largely unchallenged. Indeed, the processes of spontaneous privatization that took place at the start of the 1990s increased the ability of the elite to manipulate the economy to their own personal advantage. Even the displacement of the top Soviet political elite was only partial before August 1991. Russia and the other republics were able to resist conservative pressure to roll back reform in the winter and spring of 1990–1991 when Gorbachev 'drifted to the right', and forced Gorbachev to compromise with them in the negotiations over a new Union Treaty, but they were still a long way from destroying the power of the Soviet party-state by August 1991. The final destruction of the party-state was achieved by the incompetence of the State Committee for the State of Emergency, the collection of conservative leaders who launched a coup attempt on the eve of the signing of a new Union Treaty. Their inability to unify the security forces behind their coup and failure to appreciate that they did not have active popular support removed the last hurdle to the full achievement of independence for Russia and the other republican governments for them. Russia extricated itself from what was left of the USSR between August and December 1991 as the Russian government took over responsibility for economic management, banned the CPSU and reorganized regional government. In December 1991 the agreement on the formation of the CIS formally made Russia an independent state in the international system.

The new Russian state was weak. It had few resources in comparison to those of former members of the *nomenklatura* and the question of how government in Russia was to be conducted was unresolved at the time of Soviet collapse. The Russian government did not and could not mobilize the people in support of change. Popular anger was directed at some institutions and symbols of the Soviet order as the August coup collapsed, but this was far from a revolutionary sweeping away of the old regime. There was no vehicle for mobilizing the people against the old elite such as the Bolshevik party, or the Soviets and factory committees of 1917. Moreover, the Russian government had come to power in the name of democracy and order, which were antithetical to the disorder that a revolution would have created. Change had come through constitutional, democratic channels, through elections and through the policies made by elected governments, and these were the only mechanisms available to the Russian government to further the transformation of Russia after the fall of the Soviet state. Yeltsin chose to rely on policy, rather than on the electoral mobilization of the people to build up state power. For some analysts, this was Yeltsin's first and greatest mistake and it has been argued that elections at the end of 1991, or at the start of 1992 would have created more legitimate representative power, countered the strong presence of former communists in the Russian parliament and created a better base on which to enact policy.[7] However, Yeltsin did not see the need for fresh elections. As the newly elected president of Russia, he saw himself as the embodiment of reform and the guarantor of the destruction of what remained of the communist order. It was more important to him to secure his powers and force reform policies through than it was to delay reform whilst elections were organized. His personal popularity and authority after the defeat of the August coup attempt were such that he managed to increase his powers over government when parliament granted him the right to rule by decree for a year and organize the government without consulting it. He thus appeared to have created the basis of a reformist administration without the need of a fresh electoral mandate.

Yeltsin's choice of policy rather than elections to build-up the Russian state did not, however, lead to the creation of a governmental system that could guarantee the implementation of reformist policies. If anything it did the opposite. The strengthening of the presidency in the last months of 1991 was a temporary solution to the fragile division of responsibility for legislation between the executive and the parliament that had been created with the hurried formation of the presidency earlier that year. Constitutional conflict over whether Russia was to be a presidential or a parliamentary democracy was bound to emerge. The gathering of power to the presidency to ensure economic reform meant that reform would become a prisoner of constitutional struggles and the deals made to patch up Yeltsin's constitutional position. The association of the presidency with economic reform also meant that such constitutional struggles were likely to emerge sooner rather than later. As economic reform began to threaten the interests of the *nomenklatura*, they were motivated to support Yeltsin's political opponents and were a powerful social constituency for any politician seeking to increase their influence. The organized opposition from industrial elites to reform linked with political opposition from the parliament for a time in 1992, but Yeltsin was victorious in the struggle over the Russian Constitution because he was able to use his position to accommodate, or divert the criticism, of economic groups. He did this by compromising on the composition of government in 1992 and because parts of the reform programme, most notably privatization, were adapted to satisfy industrial interests. At the same time that this process of accommodation developed, Yeltsin maintained his command over the government by creating a coalition within the executive – in the government and the Presidential Administration – between competing elite groups and lobbies. Economic reform duly became a prisoner of the battle over constitutional order and was diminished by the compromises made to secure victory by Yeltsin in that battle. We should remember also that the plans for reform were perhaps too ambitious. As we saw in Chapter 4, the legacies of the Soviet economic system and a lack of institutions such as commercial banks to support reform also influenced the failure of radical marketization plans.

Yeltsin's victory over the parliaments through compromise secured a forced constitutional settlement in December 1993 that created a new legislature and delineated strong powers for the presidency. There were strong doubts at the end of 1993 about the durability of this constitutional settlement, but it has managed to last. This was an achievement given the rifts in Russian political society. However, the relative stability of the 1993 constitutional settlement did not mean that Russian democracy has been consolidated. The 1993 Constitution provided a structure for legislative activity and governance, but the content of that structure was generally not in keeping with the spirit of liberal democratic principles.

Elections to the new Duma in 1993 and 1995 had only a limited effect on the composition of government and the development of government policy. Changes in government personnel that occurred in the wake of elections were made as Yeltsin sought to rid himself of people he thought were a political liability. Hence, the market reformers of 1992–1993 left office after the Duma election of 1993 as Yeltsin no longer thought that their presence in government served his best interests. Likewise, Chubais and Andrei Kozyrev, the liberal foreign minister, left government after the 1995 Duma election as Yeltsin distanced himself from them before the 1996 presidential elections. The chief electoral effect on government composition was thus highly personal; popular opinion as expressed in the Duma elections did not create governments except that it influenced how Yeltsin thought about his political future and best interests. This meant that there was always great potential for dispute between the presidency and the Duma over policy. Outright conflict that might have lead to a breakdown of the constitutional order was avoided, but this was not necessarily because workable compromises over policy were achieved. There was some co-operation over policy matters, but in many instances conflict was avoided because of a balance of fear.[8] Neither side, parliamentary or presidential, was certain that conflict would benefit it. This led to backtracking from crisis. For example, in 1995, the Duma voted no confidence in the government over its handling of the Chechen conflict. The government then forced another vote of confidence, which failed by a significant margin since the Duma did not want to run the risk of dissolution. The Duma elected in 1995 had a large CPRF faction that was close to a simple majority and that could have upset the legislative process and used moments of crisis to force a breakdown of the constitutional order. However, as was noted in Chapter 3, the CPRF also gained organizational resources as a party from its large Duma faction and power in the Duma administration, and could not be sure that constitutional crisis would not lead Yeltsin to dispense with parliament altogether. It therefore had an interest in backing down from giving him reasons to dissolve the parliament so that it might continue to develop as a party from within parliament. When relations between the executive and the legislature approached crisis point, as they did when Kiriyenko's nomination as Prime Minister went to a third vote in 1998, the CPRF backed down so that Yeltsin could not dissolve the Duma.

The relative political peace between legislature and executive after 1993 enabled Yeltsin to carry on ruling through incorporating elite groups in government and arbitrating between them to keep open as many political options as possible. This gave Yeltsin an ability to duck responsibility for policies and to change political course according to the demands of circumstance. It also made the style of administration patrimonial. Yeltsin, as he had in 1992–1993, created new executive institutions with overlapping competencies, what following Eugene Huskey we referred to in Chapter 3 as 'institutional redundancy'. The poor delineation of executive roles and competition between executive groupings meant that officials and their organizations had to have a link to Yeltsin, or to a powerful member of his entourage, or group, if they were to influence policy. Increasingly this meant that central policy-making was influenced by what has been called Yeltsin's 'Family'. This included members of Yeltsin's biological family (his daughter Tatyana Dyachenko was made a presidential adviser in a presidential decree in July 1997) and close political associates and powerbrokers such as Boris Berezovsky. Yeltsin never managed to extricate himself from relying on patronage for political support or to give himself options in times of crisis. The weaknesses of the Russian state meant that there was always a crisis in the making or that the political future was so uncertain that a crisis could not be ruled out. Indeed, crisis was useful to Yeltsin since it allowed him to make himself indispensable. As Lilia Shevtsova, one of Russia's best political commentators has pointed out, Yeltsin was a 'Leader-Arbiter' of a regime that 'was impossible to consolidate, because doing so would deprive the Leader-Arbiter of the manoeuvring room that is essential for the regime's survival.'[9]

Similar developments took place in Russia's regions. Where they could, local political leaders built up their powers and created presidential-style powers for themselves that mirrored Yeltsin's. They were aided in this by the weakness of political parties in the provinces, their close links to economic elites, and Yeltsin's willingness to compromise with them so that they supported, or at least did not actively dispute, his rule.[10] The development of powerful regional leaders was detrimental to constitutionalism generally and weakened the development of bureaucratic impersonalism nationally since policy was implemented unevenly and local courts were used to subvert the development of a uniform legal order across Russia.

Patrimonialism and institutional redundancy were not only allowed to thrive within the structure of the 1993 Constitution because of Yeltsin's personal political interests. Economic weakness and reform failures also played a part. The compromising of economic reform in 1992 meant that continuity with the Soviet system was most marked in the economy. The failure of commercialization and monetary stabilization and the compromise over privatization meant that there was not a great deal of turnover in industrial management. Barter and particularistic exchange continued to be used to ensure the operation of factories and help to preserve *nomenklatura* control of industry. Financing the state under these conditions was difficult because the economy was demonetized and 'virtual'. The government response was to work with commercial banks and deficit finance through the sale of state bonds and the 'shares for loans' scheme, as was described in Chapter 4. This relationship was instrumental in creating the impression that Russia's bankers had a special relationship with the state and could dictate policy to it. The power of the bankers was perhaps exaggerated, although two of them, Vladimir Potanin and Boris Berezovsky did briefly attain government office. Impressions, however, are important and often contain an element of truth. The fact that there was a relationship between the state and the banks and that Yeltsin and his (biological) family had financial links to Berezovsky created the idea that private interests had captured the state. Moreover, Berezovsky and other bankers continued to interfere in politics even after 1997 and the crash of 1998, not least because of their media holdings. The state's economic weaknesses thus compromised its autonomy after 1993 even though there was an attempt to make the banks and the industries that they controlled pay taxes after 1996.

Finally, Russia's relations with the outside world did not pressure it or help it to move more directly towards the consolidation of democracy. As we saw in Chapter 5, Russia has been unable to stabilize its relations either with other Soviet successor states, or with the advanced capitalist states of the West. This meant that it could not deal with the problems of the collapse of the Soviet Union effectively and through multilateral political development and that there was a limited transfer of democratic and capitalist practices from the West to Russia. Both of these failures helped to sustain extremist political sentiment in Russia as the West was seen as a competitor and unsympathetic to Russian problems and because Russian interests in the states of the 'near abroad' have been dealt with piecemeal. Moreover, the states of the West were not always consistent in their support for democracy and democratic practice in Russia. Although relations with the Yeltsin regime were often troubled, the West supported Yeltsin out of fear that the alternative might be a resurgence of communist power and a new Cold War. Although there was some criticism of things such as human rights abuses in Chechnya, the Yeltsin government was not consistently put under pressure on such things as constitutional development. For example, Western criticisms of Yeltsin's actions in 1993 when the parliament was destroyed were subdued. When Russia has been criticized from abroad the lead has very often not come from governments, but from international organizations such as the United Nations Human Rights Commission. Russian leaders have felt able to resist or ignore such criticisms because they know that Western governments are more concerned with moderating Russian behaviour in places like former Yugoslavia than with supporting criticisms from human rights bodies. It also knows that Western governments will not take up such criticisms and act on them in any significant fashion for fear of disturbing the political balance in Russia. Together, the uneven pressure from the West for democratization and Russia's variable relations with the outside world meant that its domestic political development has been left to settle into constitutional-patrimonialism undisturbed by significant international pressure.

Yeltsin's legacy to his successor was thus a state formation that is a long way from the constitutional-bureaucratic state that exists in consolidated democracies. Such state formations, as was argued in Chapter 1, have the facility to reproduce themselves because they possess infrastructural power. This enables them to deal with changing social management tasks and international relations because it helps them to gather resources from society easily and to make and honour the agreements that they conclude with one another. States with infrastructural power have high capacity because bureaucratic impersonalism creates organizational integrity, and because social resources can be drawn upon to ensure policy implementation and the regulation of the bureaucracy. The relatively effective operation of a constitutional division of powers between representative legislatures and governments facilitates a particular form of embedded state autonomy. Political decisions are seen as the product of neutral processes of decision making that all society has an equal influence over, and autonomy is embedded because the state is not distanced from the society that it represents internationally and in whose name it undertakes domestic governance.

In Russia, on the other hand, the state remains distant from the people as a constitutional-patrimonial state formation.[11] As can be seen in Table 6.1, despite Putin's personal popularity and after some months of his rule, Russian political institutions enjoy very low levels of popular trust at all levels of administration, from the central executive and parliament down to local administration. Currently as many, if not more, Russian citizens have a

Table 6.1 Trust in the institutions of Russian government, 1993–2000 (per cent)

	1993 Trust	1996 Trust	1998 Trust	2000 Positive towards/trust	2000 Negative attitude towards/distrust
President	28	10	11	21	22
Parliament	9	5	7		
Of which:					
State Duma				6	33
Council of Federation				5	18
Government of the Russian Federation	18	6	8	11	21
Regional authorities	10	11	17	13	20
City and village authorities	13	8	18	6	16

Sources: figures for 1993–1998 from S. White (2000) *Russia's new politics. The management of a postcommunist society*, Cambridge: Cambridge University Press; figures from 2000 are from a Public Opinion Foundation survey in October 2000, reported at www.fom.ru.

negative attitude towards, and distrust, the institutions of government as have a positive attitude towards it. The sceptical attitude of Russians towards political institutions means that there is little possibility of popular participation immediately or quickly revitalizing the constitutional structure of the Russian state or pressuring its leaders to take actions to create an effective and impersonal system of public administration. Whilst the connections between the mass of people and politicians remain weak, elites and their interests dictate political life and competition between elites is unconstrained except by considerations of what contesting elites will tolerate. The chances of infrastructural power developing in such a system are slight. The Constitution and the fact that power is ultimately accessed through electoral channels place some constraint on executive power and despotic tendencies. However, the Constitution's influence is itself limited because the power of the executive, particularly of the President, is based on patronage. This means that the Russian state has little organizational integrity and only a small ability to gather resources from society. Consequently, it has only a limited ability to manage society peacefully, to redistribute wealth to the needy and provide them with social security, and to provide society with public goods such as law and order that might increase their respect for the state. One sign of this is the lawlessness of Russian society and the rise of organized crime, which replaces the state's regulation of economic activity with that of private coercion.[12]

Escaping from constitutional-patrimonialism and developing a state that is constitutional-bureaucratic in form is difficult. Where power is derived as much from being able to manipulate the state and patronage as from the

Constitution and command of an effective state bureaucracy given by elected office, reform of the state and its bureaucracy are the subject of political calculation. A reform-minded politician has to assess whether reforms will inhibit his ability to shore up personal power and stay in office by distributing favours and manipulating institutional competencies.[13] Reform may narrow political options if constitutionalism and bureaucratic impersonalism replace patronage and might not benefit its initiator since it might increase support for his rivals, or give them powers of patronage. Against this, a possible reformer has to consider the possible advantages of state reform, namely that a strengthened state might be able to deal with political and economic shocks more effectively and protect them against wavering elite interests and support. A constitutional-patrimonial state is inherently unstable. It does not have a bureaucracy that is capable of responding to problems efficiently because it has little organizational integrity or autonomy to override particular, powerful social interests to act in the public good. It also does not have well-developed infrastructural power and so is not assured of a regular, routinized flow of resources from society that it can deploy to either head off crises, or to ameliorate them when they occur.

Russia's new President, Vladimir Putin, has to decide between and balance the merits and demerits of reform over the next few years. Essentially, Putin has two choices. He can rule Russia in the same fashion as Yeltsin, offer himself to Russia's elites as the best protector of their interests, and seek to use his office and the limited powers of the Russian state to arbitrate between elite groups. The simple benefit that Putin would gain from this is that it would generate support for him amongst Russia's business and regional elites at the next presidential election. The downside to this for Putin – as opposed to Russia as a whole, which would continue to have a weakened economy and democracy – would be that, first, Putin would be a hostage to fortune, and second, that he would run the risk of being challenged in his second presidential term. By ruling like Yeltsin, Putin faces the prospect that the Russian state will not be able to act to avert, or cope with, an economic or other type of crisis and that he will be weakened. The sinking of the nuclear submarine *Kursk* in August 2000 illustrated the sorts of problems that might arise if Putin continues to rule like Yeltsin. The sinking of the *Kursk* was an accident that was waiting to happen because of the chronic condition of the Russian military, its technological backwardness and the strain of maintaining a nuclear deterrent with limited resources. The Russian state was unable to respond as public opinion thought it should to the *Kursk* disaster and Putin, as President and head of the state and its armed forces, was exposed to public censure. In the end, the *Kursk* disaster did not damage Putin too greatly because the tragedy, although a national embarrassment, only directly affected a few people, and because people distinguished between his general performance and his handling of this first national crisis. However, it showed how problems could emerge that are beyond Putin's control because of state weakness. A larger crisis than the *Kursk*, such as an economic reversal like that of

August 1998, could lead to his power being more effectively challenged if his competence is more widely questioned. Challenges might also be expected in Putin's second term as President because other politicians will try to put themselves in a position where they can succeed him, or try to build up their strength so that they can influence the presidential succession. Yeltsin managed to control these succession struggles by using his powers to appoint governments that were dependent upon him. Putin could do the same, but there are no guarantees that he would be as successful as Yeltsin.

Alternatively, Putin can embark on reform and try to build up the powers of the state and create more effective public administration. Potentially, this would benefit Russia since it would lay the political basis of a market economy that might eventually deliver economic growth and provide the state with the resources necessary to fund welfare programmes and to supply public goods such as law and order. The danger for Putin here is that reform involves the same collective action problems today that it did at the end of the communist period. Although most people will gain from reform, they have little incentive to bear the costs of ensuring that reform works. On the other hand, reform would negatively affect the privileges of elite groups since it would curtail their ability to influence policy and to take rent from the state. Elites thus have incentives to subvert reform and to oppose Putin in his efforts to secure a second presidential term if he takes a reformist course. A key calculation to be made before reform is embarked upon is can it deliver enough benefits to the population at large before the next presidential election to compensate for a loss of elite support?

Which of these two basic choices Putin will finally make is not yet clear. On taking office Putin enjoyed two advantages that gave him freedom of manoeuvre against Russia's elites. First, he had an uncompromised personal mandate from his election as President. As can be seen in Table 6.2, Putin was elected to the presidency with 52.9 per cent of the vote. He therefore managed to avoid a second round vote and could claim that he was mandated by a majority of the Russian people to act in their name for change. Even more importantly, Putin had not had to make any deals with either Russia's oligarchs, who control the mass media, or with Russia's regional leaders, who can manipulate voting in the provinces. His government's actions had been broadly popular before the election and he had secured strong personal approval ratings because of popular confidence in him and support for his actions against Chechnya. Putin thus came to power without any significant debts to powerful elite groups. They had supported him in the election because it was obvious that he was going to win; his personal popularity and approval for the government guaranteed his victory and meant that there was no credible alternative to him once Yeltsin resigned in his favour on 31 December 1999.

Second, Putin's popularity meant that he has some Duma support. As Putin's popularity grew in the autumn of 1999, the political movement most associated with him, Medved-Unity, managed to overtake rivals such

Table 6.2 The Putin election

Candidate (party)	Total vote
Vladimir Putin	52.9
Gennady Zyuganov (CPRF)	29.2
Grigory Yavlinsky (Yabloko)	5.8
Aman-Geldy Tuleev	3.0
Vladimir Zhirinovsky (LDPR)	2.7
Konstantin Titov	1.5
Ella Pamfilova (Citizen's Worth)	1.0
Stanislav Govorukhin	0.4
Yuri Skuratov	0.4
Aleksei Podberezkin (Spiritual Heritage)	0.1
Umar Dzhabrailov	0.1
Against all	1.9
Invalid votes	0.6
Turnout	68.6

Source: www.russiavotes.org/President.htm

as the Fatherland-All Russia movement and gained 23 per cent of the PR vote in the December 1999 elections (only 1 per cent less than the CPRF) and nine seats in the single-mandate constituency elections (Table 3.4).[14] This made Unity the second largest faction in the Duma with 73 seats after the election (Table 6.3), and it soon gained more members when the Duma convened as independent deputies and deputies from minor parties joined it. Moreover, Putin could also rely on some support from the Union of Right Forces faction and from the deputy factions such as Russia's Regions that were formed after parliament was elected by independent deputies elected in the single-mandate constituency vote. The success of Unity at the polls and in attracting more deputies after the election meant that the CPRF and its parliamentary ally, the Agro-industrial deputy faction (some of the deputies elected on the CPRF ticket joined this faction after the election so that it could register) did not have as much control over the Duma and its committees as they did after the 1995 election. The CPRF compromised with Unity over the allocation of key Duma posts, such as the Chair of the Duma and the heads of committees. This enabled the CPRF to retain influence in the Duma and use it as a base for its political organization, and meant that Putin was able to guarantee a more pliable Duma in the first months of his administration.

Putin used these two advantages and the freedom of manoeuvre that they gave him to consolidate his power by attacking the power of the 'oligarchs' and regional leaders. The attack on the oligarchs focussed on their control over the media and their control over companies gained under the 'shares for loans' scheme. Taking action against the oligarchs fulfilled one of the few promises that Putin made during his low-key election campaign. In May 2000, the tax police raided the offices of Media-Most (a TV, radio and

Table 6.3 Parties and deputies' factions in the Duma elected in December 1999

Deputy group	At election	October 2000	Change
CPRF	114	86	−28
Unity	73	83	+10
Fatherland-All Russia	66	46	−20
Union of Right Forces	29	32	+3
Yabloko	20	19	−1
LDPR	17	16	−1
Our Home is Russia	8		−8
People's Deputy[a]		62	+62
Russian Regions (Union of Independent Deputies)[a]		44	+44
Agro-industrial[a]		42	+42
Independents/minor parties/unregistered	114	15	−90

Note

a Formed in Duma after the election.

Sources: www.russiavotes.org/Duma_align.htm and the party faction lists reported at www. duma.ru/deputats/fraction.htm, October 2000.

press consortium owned by Vladimir Gusinsky's Most Bank), and in June, Gusinsky was arrested in connection with an investigation in to the fraudulent privatization of a St Petersburg television station. Gusinsky was later released and allowed to leave Russia, but his control over NTV, Russia's most independent television station, was threatened. Media-Most's debts to Gazprom (in which the state has a 38 per cent share) were called in and it tried to take over Gusinksy's stock in Media-Most in lieu of repayment. Other oligarchs were soon also targeted. Vladimir Potanin's control over Norilsk Nickel was challenged by a lawsuit from the Moscow Procurator's office, which alleged that the firm's privatization had been conducted illegally. The case against Potanin was not legally very sound according to a Moscow court, but in July Potanin was threatened with investigation by the General Prosecutor's office unless he surrendered US$140 million that it was alleged he had underpaid for his stake in Norilsk Nickel. The Tax Police began investigations into tax evasion by the Lukoil group and Avtovaz (the group connected to Boris Berezovsky), and police looking for evidence of illegal share dealings raided the offices of the Tyumen Oil Company. The Duma's Audit Chamber recommended an investigation against UES, the electricity supply monopoly headed by Anatoly Chubais, and the Deputy Minister of Finance recommended investigations into tax evasion by the Sibneft oil company. Berezovsky's control over the ORT television station was soon compromised and he attempted to deflect government moves to reduce his control over the station by setting up a new firm, Teletrust, to manage his stake in the station.[15] The oligarchs protested their fear of government action against them in a meeting with Putin at the end of July 2000. Putin reassured them that there would be no reversal of privatization of industry, but did not promise an amnesty for illegal actions during privatization, or for tax evasion.[16]

Putin's moves to curtail the independence of regional leaders also began in May 2000. He issued decrees establishing seven new federal districts and reforming the institution of Presidential Representatives to the regions, and presented a set of bills to the Duma on reform of the upper house of parliament, the Federation Council, and on giving him the power as President to remove regional leaders. As with the oligarchs, the move against regional independence was helped by the fact that Putin had not had to rely on regional leaders' support in the presidential elections to the same extent that Yeltsin had. It was also possible because of his support in the Duma. Putin's intention in initiating reform of centre-regional relations was, he explained, to strengthen the 'presidential vertical' that Yeltsin had established in 1991 to ensure the implementation of government policy, but which had fallen foul of the compromises over reform in 1992 (see Chapter 3).[17]

The creation of seven new Federal Districts inserts an additional layer of administration between Russia's 89 regions and republics and the central government. Central to this new layer of administration is the reformed institution of Presidential Representatives. Putin's decree raised the status of Presidential Representatives by reducing them in number from 89 to seven, one for each new Federal District. The objective of this was to ensure that Presidential Representatives did not become dependent on regional authorities as they had under Yeltsin. Being responsible for several provinces would mean that the Presidential Representatives would not be likely to compromise with any one regional leader. The status of the new Presidential Representatives was further raised because they are to be directly responsible to Putin and are members of the Security Council, which is part of the Presidential Administration and has a broad remit to discuss domestic and international policy. Putin further ensured the loyalty of the new Presidential Representatives to him by appointing people with backgrounds in the security services, where he had spent his earlier career, instead of appointing people with connections to the regions that they are responsible for as Yeltsin had.

At the same time as the status of Presidential Representatives, and hence central state authority in the regions, was raised, Putin sought to diminish the status of regional leaders and their autonomy. First, Putin proposed that the Federation Council no longer be made up *ex officio* of regional executive and legislative heads; in the future regional executives and legislatures will each send a representative to work in the Federation Council on a full-time basis. Regional leaders would thus lose their ability to directly intervene in the passage of federal legislation and no longer enjoy parliamentary immunity from legal prosecution. Not surprisingly, the existing Federation Council received the proposed reform unfavourably. However, Duma support for the changes meant that it was passed with only minor changes: Putin had originally proposed that all Federation Council members be replaced by their representatives by April 2001; the final law passed by the Federation Council and signed by Putin replaces existing members of the Federation Council as their regional terms of office expire so that they will not all be replaced until January 2002. Second, the centre's ability to intervene in the regions was increased by changes to an existing law 'On the General Principles of the Organisation of Legislative (Representative) and Executive Organs of State Power in the Subjects of the Russian Federation'. Putin proposed that this law be changed to permit the President to take action against regional chief executives (their governors or presidents) and legislatures for violating the Constitution. Putin proposed that the President be entitled to issue warnings against both regional legislatures and executives in the event of a court finding that they had passed laws or issued instructions that contradicted the Constitution. After the issuing of a presidential warning, Putin proposed, a second contravention of the Constitution would entitle the President to submit a federal law to the Duma on the dissolution of the regional legislature, or to dismiss a regional chief executive and appoint a temporary replacement. Again, the Federation Council did not receive these proposals with enthusiasm. Putin's Duma support, however, overcame the Federation Council's veto of the reformed law with a few amendments. The most significant of these is that the region legislatures, rather than the President, appoint a temporary replacement for a suspended executive head. This was an important concession, but it does not stop Putin from suspending regional chief executives. Finally, the Federation Council passed a new tax code that gives the centre more control over tax collection and the redistribution of tax revenue, and requires regional authorities to hand over an increased amount of the tax revenue that they raise to the federal government. This potentially limits the financial autonomy of the regions.

Putin's use of his freedom of manoeuvre to take action against the oligarchs and to curtail some of the independence of regional authorities seems to indicate that he does not intend to rule as Yeltsin did. Moreover, his actions are consistent with his public pronouncements on the future of the state. The state has been a major theme of Putin's writings and speeches and he has explicitly and directly argued for a 'strong state' and described this in terms that would be comparable to what we have called a constitutional-bureaucratic state formation. In an article published on the internet in December 1999, just as he became acting President, Putin argued that creating a strong state in Russia meant ridding it of corruption, creating a more effective bureaucracy, increasing the role of the courts in regulating public administration and 'creating conditions that will help to develop a full-blooded civil society to balance and monitor authorities'. After the election, in his first presidential state of the nation address to the Duma in July 2000, Putin declared that only 'a strong state, an effective – and if anyone does not like the word "strong" we'll say effective – an effective and democratic state can protect civil, political and economic freedoms and create conditions for people to live prosperously and for our homeland to thrive.' Again, this was linked to the creation of civil society as a 'fully fledged partner of the state' and Putin also pointed out the need for political parties to develop to 'ensure constant communication between the people and the authorities'.[18]

These are worthy sentiments, but they also recognize a fundamental dilemma before Russia. Without social support for change and channels for society to influence politics and fix change in place, any action that is taken to strengthen the state is ambiguous and can be reversed or compromised if it turns out to be a threat to the leader's political future. Freedom to manoeuvre in the name of reform can equally be freedom to manoeuvre for personal advantage. Without social pressure to fix state reform in place, building a good state depends too much on the goodwill of a good leader. Administrative reforms and measures to constrain powerful elite interests do not of and by themselves infuse Russia's constitutional structure with a democratic character even if they do increase the efficiency of the state and ensure some measure of bureaucratic impersonalism in the short-run. If the will of the leader changes, so too can the character of reform that is too dependent on one person to carry it through.

For this reason, Putin's actions can be read two ways. His moves against the oligarchs can be taken as a move towards creating state autonomy and increasing its organizational integrity by detaching it from powerful economic interests and weakening their ability to corrupt policy making in their favour. But they can also be seen as a warning from Putin to the oligarchs that the balance of power has changed and that they have to establish a new *modus vivendi* with the executive if they are to be left in peace. In short, actions to control the oligarchs can be taken both as a necessary step towards creating a stronger state and as step towards making the oligarchs, and in particular their media outlets, submissive to the will of the President, who might be more interested in his own survival than in constraining the rich for the public good. Putin's actions against the oligarchs have shown that the Russian state is not totally helpless, that it retains some despotic capabilities, and that the power of the presidency can be built up if the President decides to use those despotic capabilities. However, a powerful President is not the same thing as a strong state, and the use of despotic state power generally only has a limited influence on the development of state capacity. For the more positive reading of Putin's actions to be confirmed, the power of the oligarchs not only needs to be curtailed in favour of presidential well-being. More far-reaching economic reforms need to be introduced that stabilize the Russian state's finances and create alternative centres of economic power to the commercial banks and financial-industrial groups. The government has plans for reform that promise 5 per cent economic growth a year and has tried to simplify tax collection through the new tax code and by creating a flat rate income tax of 13 per cent so as to ensure a more regular flow of tax income to its coffers. However, although growth has occurred because the rouble is weak and oil prices are high, finding new sources of economic growth and sustaining it remain elusive and converting growth into social support will take time. Putin's government under Prime Minister Kasyanov hopes to develop a more activist industrial policy and support industrial transformation financially to create new centres of economic growth. However, that requires the state either to take on an investment burden that it may not be able to sustain, or to turn to business and create more financial-industrial groups that it will then have to control.

Likewise, Putin's actions against regional elites can be taken as a necessary step to control them, to create adherence to the Constitution across all of Russia's provinces and to increase the effective monitoring of policy implementation. However, many regional governors and republican presidents have tight control over their territories and may not fear presidential censure or removal from office. Their power, even if Putin suspends them, is such that they can be sure of re-election; credible alternative leaders to them often do not exist. An increase in the powers of the central executive over regional authorities is thus not the same as a democratic check on their power from below. Without further development of mechanisms to assert constitutional rule in the regions and ensure that Presidential Representatives can effectively monitor regional government, Putin's decrees and legal changes look more like a move to keep regional leaders in line and in support of the President than a step towards creating more effective policy implementation.

Russia's state of uncertainty will thus not be escaped quickly, if at all. Putin's initial moves to shore up the power of the state and to establish a new form of state power and state-society relations will in all probability suffer reverses and compromises. To what extent such compromises will occur cannot be foreseen. If Putin is true to his pronouncements, he may not compromise with elite interests during a time of crisis. He may even be able to persuade the Russian people that a refusal to compromise shows that he has their best interests at heart so that they continue to support him at the ballot box. This would be a significant accomplishment and the best hope for progress in Russia. It would demonstrate that the ability of elites to influence Russia's rulers can be overcome and that they cannot use crisis to force their interests higher on the political agenda than those of society as a whole. Still, even this would not be the same as the consolidation of democracy in a constitutional-bureaucratic state: would a politically courageous Putin be followed by equally brave successors until such time that political heroics can be replaced by a politics of compromise between parties and their leaders, rather than between rulers and elites? It is more likely that both Putin and his successors to the Russian presidency will alternate reform with compromise as they worry about their ability to stay in office and make concessions to shore up their power. Russia, probably more than any other country in the world, deserves brave politicians, but is no more likely than any other country to get them.

A gradual evolution away from constitutional-patrimonialism is in all likelihood the best hope for Russia. Reform will be initiated and then compromised, and then initiated again as Putin and his yet unknown successors try to consolidate state power, compromise and try again to create a state that can deal more effectively with the demands that are made of it and them. And whilst such an evolutionary process develops, the unfortunate possibility will remain that a Russian President may reach a point where the gradual development of a constitutional-bureaucratic state and the compromises that such an evolution entails no longer suits their interests. If such a point is reached because of economic crisis, social breakdown, conflict with the regions or a constitutional crisis that cannot be patched over, creating an absolutist regime, concentrating all decision-making powers on the presidency or in some state council and relying on despotic power to rule, may be more attractive. With the lessons of Russia's past in mind, a Russian President may realize that removing political opposition to his rule may not be a long-term solution to Russia's problems. However, a new Russian autocrat would not be the first world leader to argue that the strength of despotic state power is necessary in the short-term to cut through barriers to reform of the economy and provide the basis for a more secure democratic, capitalist future.

Notes

1 See, for example, E. Hoffman (1998) 'The dynamics of state-society relations in post-Soviet Russia', in H. Eckstein, F.J. Fleron, E. Hoffman and W. Reisinger with R. Ahl, R. Bova and P. Roeder, *Can democracy take root in post-Soviet Russia? Explorations in state-society relations*, Lanham: Rowan & Littlefield Publishers; C. Roberts and T. Sherlock (1999) 'Bringing the Russian state back in', *Comparative Politics*, 31(4): pp. 477–98; G. Smith (1999) 'State-building in the new Russia. Assessing the Yeltsin record', and R. Bova (1999) 'Democratization and the crisis of the Russian state', both in G. Smith (ed.) *State-building in Russia. The Yeltsin legacy and the challenge of the future*, Armonk, NY: M.E. Sharpe; T. Gustafson (1999) *Capitalism Russian-style*, Cambridge: Cambridge University Press, pp. 192–215; S-Y. Ma (2000) 'Comparing the Russian state and the Chinese state', *Problems of Post-Communism*, 47(2): pp. 3–12.
2 *Rossiiskie vesti*, 11 March 1997.
3 See, for example, the article by Boris Nemtsov on oligarchy in *Nezavisimaya gazeta*, 17 March 1998.
4 V. Putin (1999) 'Rossiya na rubezhe tysyachiletii', http://www.pravitelstvo. gov.ru/minister/article-vvp1.html. An English version can be found as an appendix to V. Putin (2000) *First person*, London: Hutchinson.
5 See the article by Laurent Fabius and Hubert Vitrine, the French finance and foreign affairs ministers, in *Financial Times*, 25 April 2000. Fabius and Vitrine lay out a set of guidelines for EU co-operation with Russia and put 'greater emphasis ... on Russia's building and strengthening effective state structures' at the top of the list.
6 M.S. Fish (1995) *Democracy from scratch. Opposition and regime in the new Russian revolution*, Princeton: Princeton University Press.
7 See, for example, M. McFaul (1993) *Post-Communist Politics. Democratic Politics in Russia and Eastern Europe*, Washington: Center for Strategic and International

Studies, 1993, p. 89; M.E. Urban with V. Igrunov and S. Mitrokhin (1999) *The rebirth of politics in Russia*, Cambridge: Cambridge University Press.

 8 T.F. Remington (2000) 'The evolution of executive-legislative relations in Russia since 1993', *Slavic Review*, 59(3): pp. 499–520.

 9 L. Shevtsova (2000) 'Can electoral autocracy survive?', *Journal of Democracy*, 11 (3): p. 37.

10 V. Gel'man (2000) 'Subnational institutions', in N. Robinson (ed.) *Institutions and political change in Russia*, Basingstoke: Macmillan.

11 For variations on the idea of constitutional-patrimonialism see R. Sakwa (1997) 'The regime system in Russia', *Contemporary Politics*, 3(1): pp. 7–25 and (2000) 'State and society in post-communist Russia', in Robinson (ed.), *Institutions...*, L. Shevtsova and I. Klyamkin (1999) *Vnesystemnii rezhim Borisa II: nekotorie osobennosti politicheskogo razvitiya postsovetskoi Rossii*, Moscow: Carnegie Center.

12 There are many accounts of Russian organized crime. For overviews of its rise and influence see S. Handelman (1995) *Comrade criminal. Russia's new mafiya*, New Haven: Yale University Press; F. Varese (1994) 'Is Sicily the future of Russia? Private protection and the rise of the Russian mafia', *Archives Europeennes de Sociologie*, 35(2): pp. 224–58 and (1997) 'The transition to the market and corruption in post-socialist Russia', *Political Studies*, 45(3): pp. 579–96.

13 For a fuller explanation of this problem see B. Geddes (1994) *Politician's dilemma. Building state capacity in Latin America*, Berkeley: University of California Press.

14 For analysis of the December 1999 Duma election and the 2000 presidential election see S. White (2000) 'Russia, elections, democracy', *Government and Opposition*, 35(3): pp. 302–24; R. Sakwa (2000) 'Russia's "permanent" (uninterrupted) elections of 1999–2000', *Journal of Communist Studies and Transitional Politics*, 16(3): pp. 85–112.

15 *RFE/RL Newsline*, 17 October 2000.

16 Details of Putin's move against the oligarchs can be found in *Russia Watch*, 2000, (2), www.ksg.harvard.edu/bcsia/sdi.

17 For details of Putin's plans for the regions see M. Hyde (2000) 'Putin's federal reforms and their implications for presidential power in Russia', *Essex Papers in Politics and Government*, Colchester: University of Essex, no. 154.

18 See Putin 'Rossiya na rubezhe ...', *First person*. An analysis of the December internet article and its treatment of the state can be found in T.F. Remington (2000) 'Russia and the "strong state" ideal', *East European Constitutional Review*, 9 (1/2): pp. 65–9. The text of Putin's state of the nation address in *Rossiiskaya gazeta*, 11 July 2000.

Select bibliography

Acton, E., V. Cherniaev and W.G. Rosenberg (eds) (1997) *Critical companion to the Russian revolution, 1914–1921*, London: Edward Arnold.

Andrle, V. (1994) *A social history of twentieth-century Russia*, London: Edward Arnold.

Aron, L. (2000) *Boris Yeltsin. A revolutionary life*, London: Harper Collins.

Aron, L. and K. Jensen (eds) (1994) *The emergence of Russian foreign policy*, Washington: United States Institute of Peace Press.

Åslund, A. (1995) *How Russia became a market economy*, Washington, DC: Brookings Institute Press.

Baranovsky, V. (ed.) (1997) *Russia and Europe. The emerging security agenda*, Oxford: Oxford University Press.

Bowker, M. and C. Ross (eds) *Russia after the Cold War*, Harlow: Longman.

Brown, A. (1996) *The Gorbachev factor*, Oxford: Oxford University Press.

Easter, G.M. (2000) *Reconstructing the state. Personal networks and elite identity in Soviet Russia*, Cambridge: Cambridge University Press.

Fainsod, M. (1963) *How Russia is ruled*, London: Oxford University Press.

Figes, O. (1997) *A people's tragedy. The Russian revolution 1891–1924*, London: Pimlico.

Fitzpatrick, S. (1982) *The Russian revolution, 1917–1932*, Oxford: Oxford University Press.

Fitzpatrick, S. (1999) *Everyday Stalinism. Ordinary life in extraordinary times: Soviet Russia in the 1930s*. New York: Oxford University Press.

Gaddy, C. and B. Ickes (1998) 'Russia's virtual economy', *Foreign Affairs*, 77(5), pp. 53–67.

Gaidar, Ye. (1999) *Days of defeat and victory*, Seattle: University of Washington Press.

Gatrell, P. (1986) *The Tsarist economy 1850–1917*, London: Batsford.

Gill, G. (1990) *The origins of the Stalinist political system*, Cambridge: Cambridge University Press.

Gill, G. (1994) *The collapse of a single-party system. The disintegration of the Communist Party of the Soviet Union*, Cambridge: Cambridge University Press.

Gorbachev, M. (1987) *Perestroika. New thinking for our country and the world*, London: Collins.

Gorbachev, M. (1996) *Memoirs*, London: Doubleday.

Gustafson, T. (1999) *Capitalism Russian-style*, Cambridge: Cambridge University Press.

Henderson, K. and N. Robinson (1997) *Post-communist politics*, London: Prentice Hall.

Hewitt, E. (1988) *Reforming the Soviet economy. Equality versus efficiency*, Washington, DC: Brookings Institution.

Hill, R. and P. Frank (1986) *The Soviet Communist Party*, third edition, London: Allen and Unwin.

Holmes, S. (1996) 'Cultural legacies or state collapse? Probing the postcommunist dilemma', in Michael Mandelbaum (ed.) *Postcommunism: four perspectives*, New York: Council for Foreign Relations.

Hosking, G. (1990) *A history of the Soviet Union*, revised edition, London: Fontana.

Hosking, G. (1998) *Russia. People and empire, 1552–1917*, London: Fontana.

Huskey, E. (1999) *Presidential power in Russia*, Armonk, NY: M.E. Sharpe.

Jowitt, K. (1992) *New world disorder. The Leninist extinction*, Berkeley: University of California Press.

Keep, J. (1995) *Last of the empires. A history of the Soviet Union 1945–1991*, Oxford: Oxford University Press.

Kenez, P. (1999) *A history of the Soviet Union from the beginning to the end*, Cambridge: Cambridge University Press.

Kornai, J. (1992) *The socialist system. The political economy of communism*, Oxford: Clarendon Press.

Löwenhardt, J. (1995) *The Reincarnation of Russia. Struggling with the legacy of communism, 1990–1994*, Harlow: Longman.

Malcolm, N., A. Pravda, R. Allison and M. Light (1996) *Internal factors in Russian foreign policy*, Oxford: Oxford University Press.

Mandelbaum, M. (ed.) *The new Russian foreign policy*, New York: Council on Foreign Relations Press.

Morrison, J. (1991) *Boris Yeltsin. From Bolshevik to democrat*, Harmondsworth: Penguin.

Nove, A. (1982) *An economic history of the USSR*, Harmondsworth: Penguin.

Petro, N. and A. Rubinstein (1997) *Russian foreign policy*, New York: Longman.

Pipes, R. (1977) *Russia under the old regime*, Harmondsworth: Penguin.

Polan, A.J. (1984) *Lenin and the end of politics*, London: Methuen.

Putin, V. *et al.* (2000) *First person: an astonishingly frank self-portrait by Russia's President Vladimir Putin*, London: Hutchinson.

Robinson, N. (1992) 'Gorbachev and the place of the party in Soviet reform, 1985–1991', *Soviet Studies*, 44(3), pp. 423–43.

Robinson, N. (1995) *Ideology and the collapse of the Soviet system. A critical history of Soviet ideological discourse*, Aldershot: Edward Elgar.

Robinson, N. (1999) 'The global economy, reform and crisis in Russia', *Review of International Political Economy*, 6(4), pp. 531–64.

Robinson, N. (ed.) (2000) *Institutions and political change in Russia*, Basingstoke: Macmillan.

Robinson, N. (2000) 'The economy and prospects for anti-democratic development in Russia', *Europe-Asia Studies*, 2000, 52(8): pp. 1391–416.

Rutland, P. (1993) *The politics of economic stagnation in the Soviet Union. The role of local party organs in economic management*, Cambridge: Cambridge University Press.

Sakwa, R. (1990) *Gorbachev and his reforms, 1985–1990*, London: Philip Allen.

Sakwa, R. (1996) *Russian politics and society*, second edition, London: Routledge.

Sakwa, R. (1999) *The rise and fall of the Soviet Union 1917–1991*, London: Routledge.

Sakwa, R. (1999) *Soviet politics in perspective*, London: Routledge.

Service, R. (1997) *A history of twentieth-century Russia*, London: Penguin.

Shearman, P. (ed.) (1995) *Russian foreign policy since 1990*, Boulder: Westview.

Shleifer A. and D. Treisman (2000) *Without a map. Political tactics and economic reform in Russia*, Cambridge, MA: The MIT Press.

Shevtsova, L. (1999) *Yeltsin's Russia. Myths and reality*, Washington, DC: Carnegie Endowment for International Peace.

Skocpol, T. (1979) *States and social revolutions. A comparative analysis of France, Russia and China*, Cambridge: Cambridge University Press.

Solzhenitsyn, A. (1974–76) *The Gulag archipelago*, London: Fontana.

Suny, R.G. (1998) *The Soviet experiment. Russia, the USSR and the successor states*, New York: Oxford University Press.

Tikhomirov, V. (2000) *The political economy of post-Soviet Russia*, Basingstoke: Macmillan.

Urban, M.E. (1985) 'Conceptualizing political power in the USSR: patterns of binding and bonding', *Studies in Comparative Communism*, 18(4): pp. 207–26.

Urban, M.E. (1990) *More power to the Soviets. The democratic revolution in the USSR*, Aldershot: Edward Elgar.

Urban, M.E. with V. Igrunov and S. Mitrokhin (1997) *The rebirth of politics in Russia*, Cambridge: Cambridge University Press.

Wallander, C. (ed.) (1996) *The sources of Russian foreign policy after the Cold War*, Boulder: Westview.

Webber, M. (1996) *The international politics of Russia and the successor states*, Manchester: Manchester University Press.

Weiss, L. and J.M. Hobson (1995) *States and economic development. A comparative historical analysis*, Cambridge: Polity Press.

White, S. (1993) *After Gorbachev*, Cambridge: Cambridge University Press.

White, S. (2000) *Russia's new politics. The management of a postcommunist society*, Cambridge: Cambridge University Press.

White, S., Z. Gitelman and A. Pravda (eds) (1997) *Developments in Russian politics 4*, Basingstoke: Macmillan.

White, S., R. Rose and I. McAllister (1997) *How Russia votes*, Chatham, NJ: Chatham House Publishers.

Wolosky, L. (2000) 'Putin's plutocrat problem', *Foreign Affairs*, 79(2): pp. 18–31.

Woodward, D. (1999) *Money unmade. Barter and the fate of Russian capitalism*, Ithaca, NY: Cornell University Press.

Yeltsin, B. (1990) *Against the grain. An autobiography*, London: Jonathan Cape.

Yeltsin, B. (1994) *The view from the Kremlin*, London: Harper Collins.

Index